MW00778589

WISDOM FROM ST. AUGUSTINE

Books by V. J. Bourke

Augustine's Quest of Wisdom (Milwaukee: Bruce, 1945). Pp. xi, 323.

St. Augustine, *Confessions*, trans. VJB (New York: FOC, 1953). Pp. xxxii, 481.

St. Augustine, *The City of God*. Abridged edition by VJB (New York: Image Books, 1958). Pp. 551.

Augustine's View of Reality (Villanova: Univ. Press, 1964). Pp. xi, 152.

The Essential Augustine (New York: Mentor Books, 1964). Pp. 268.

Joy in Augustine's Ethics (Villanova: Univ. Press, 1979). Pp. 122.

Wisdom from St. Augustine

VERNON J. BOURKE

CENTER FOR THOMISTIC STUDIES
University of St. Thomas
Houston, Texas 77006

Copyright © 1984 by
The Center for Thomistic Studies

NIHIL OBSTAT:
Reverend Terence P. Brinkman, S.T.D.
Censor Deputatus

IMPRIMATUR:
Most Reverend John L. Morkovsky, S.T.D.

Bishop of Galveston-Houston
December 28, 1983

All rights reserved. No part of this book may be used or reproduced in any manner whatsoever without written permission, except in the case of brief quotations embodied in critical articles or reviews. For information, write to The Center for Thomistic Studies, 3812 Montrose Blvd., Houston, Texas 77006.

Library of Congress Cataloging in Publication Data

Bourke, Vernon Joseph, 1907-
    Wisdom from St. Augustine.

    Includes index.
    1. Augustine, Saint, Bishop of Hippo—Addresses, essays, lectures.   I. University of St. Thomas. Center for Thomistic Studies.   II. Title.   III. Title: Wisdom from Saint Augustine.
BR1720.A9B645   1984   230'.14'0924   83-73622
ISBN 0-268-01934-7
ISBN O-268-01935-5 (pbk.)

Manufactured in the United States of America

Contents

Acknowledgments

Chapter 1 is written especially for this volume. Chapter 2 is revised from "Perler's Contribution to Augustine Biography," *Augustinian Studies* vol. 2 (1971) pp. 219-229. Chapter 3 is from my "Introduction" to Eugene Portalié, *A Guide to the Thought of St. Augustine*, translated by Ralph J. Bastian, S.J. (Chicago: Regnery, 1960) pp. xxi-xxxvii. Chapter 4 is from "Wisdom in the Gnoseology of St. Augustine," *Augustinus* (Madrid) vol. III (1958) pp. 331-336. Chapter 5 is from "Augustine of Hippo: the Approach of the Soul to God," in *The Spirituality of Western Christendom*, edited by E. Rozanne Elder (Kalamazoo, Mich: The Medieval Institute, Western Michigan University and Cistercian Publications, Inc., 1976) pp. 1-12, 189-191. Chapter 6 is revised from "St. Augustine and the Cosmic Soul," *Giornale de Metafisica* vol. IX (1954) pp. 431-440. Chapter 7 is from "Augustine and the Roots of Moral Values," (the J. H. Taylor, S.J. Annual Lecture at Gonzaga University, Spokane) printed in *Augustinian Studies* vol. 6 (1975) pp. 65-74. Chapter 8 is from "Light of Love: Augustine on Moral Illumination," *Mediaevalia* vol. 4 (1978) pp. 13-31. Chapter 9 is from "St. Augustine and Situationism," *Augustinus* (Madrid) vol. XII (1967) pp. 117-123. Chapter 10 is from "The Political Philosophy of St. Augustine," *Proceedings of the American Catholic Philosophical Association* vol. VII (1932) pp. 45-55. Chapter 12 is from "Socio-Religious Issues in Augustine's Day," *Augustinian Studies* vol. 4 (1973) pp. 205-212; and "Lamirande on Augustine and Tolerance," *Augustinian Studies* vol. 9 (1978) pp. 103-108. Chapter 13 is from "The City of God and the Christian View of History,"

vii

in *Mélanges à la Mémoire de Charles De Koninck* (Québec: Les Presses de l'Université Laval, 1968) pp. 69-80. Chapter 14 is from "An Augustine Revival?" *Thought* (Fordham University) vol. XXIV (1949) pp. 203-210.

I
The Man and His Works

CHAPTER 1

The Genius of St. Augustine

In the ancient Greek world seven (or more) sages were recognized as possessors of what was then regarded as wisdom. Their skills were very largely practical: the ability to foretell the weather, predict good harvests, organize town politics, and that sort of thing. Probably the man who came nearest to meriting the name "philosopher" among these sages was Thales. He is credited with some thinking about water as the basic ingredient of all material things. Indeed the word "philosopher" is derived from the fact that later Greek teachers came to be known as *philosophoi* (lovers of wisdom).

About a thousand years after Thales' time there lived in North Africa a man named Augustinus[1] who developed into one of the wisest men in early Christendom. His wisdom was not simply practical (in the sense of the ability to get along in earthly affairs); it was spiritual and other-worldly. Yet Augustine of Hippo has left a heritage of sage thought that has influenced every subsequent century down to the present day. Born in A.D. 354 in the town of Tagaste (today's Souk Ahras in modern Algeria near the border of Tunisia) Augustine was the son of a pagan father, Patricius, and a Christian mother, Monica.[2]

The first nine books of his *Confessions* tell much of the story of Augustine's early life. He was not baptized as an infant but was enrolled by his mother as a catechumen in the Catholic Church. Elementary schooling at Tagaste and nearby Madaura stressed grammar and Latin literature. At the age of sixteen he began the study of rhetoric in the famous city of Carthage. His father died in this year (A.D.

3

370) and Augustine's expenses at Carthage were paid by a rich businessman of Tagaste, Romanianus. Within his first years at Carthage Augustine became interested in philosophy from reading Cicero's *Hortensius*. This was a dialogue in praise of the pursuit of wisdom. In the same period Augustine met a young woman at a church service, began to live with her, and fathered a son named Adeodatus (God's Gift). By 373 he had joined the Manichean religion as an auditor. He remained a novice in this strange cult which taught that there are two supreme gods, one good and one evil, and similarly two competing souls within the human person. The central theme of Manicheism was the eternal struggle of the forces of good and evil. Augustine was to maintain his interest in this cult for about nine years.

After teaching grammar in Carthage for a year Augustine decided to seek a career in the heart of the Roman Empire. In Rome he lodged with a fellow Manichee. Under the influence of the skeptical philosophy of the later Platonic Academy he gradually came to doubt the validity of the religion of Mani.

In 384 he went to Milan, then the residence of the Imperial Court of the empire, and began to teach there as public rhetorician. Within two years Augustine had come under the influence of the local bishop, Ambrose, and an elderly and wise priest named Simplicianus. In a touching scene in a garden at Milan (described in the eighth book of the *Confessions*) he underwent a striking conversion to Christianity and decided to give up his teaching position.

A fellow teacher, Verecundus, offered Augustine and more than a dozen friends and relatives the use of a country estate some distance to the north of Milan. There at Cassiciacum Augustine meditated on his future, discussed philosophical problems with his associates (including his mother, brother Navigius, and son), and prepared himself for baptism, which sacrament he received at the hands of Ambrose just before Easter of 387.

Augustine and his group decided to return to North Africa but their sea trip was delayed for more than a year, probably by bad weather and a sea war. While waiting at the port of Ostia Monica and her son shared a remarkable spiritual experience, the ecstatic vision at Ostia. Monica died in 387 and was buried at the seaport. It was toward the end of 388 that Augustine finally reached Tagaste, where with his son and friends such as Evodius and Alypius he established a sort of monastery on his family land. Adeodatus died within a year, at the age of sixteen.

In 391 on a visit to the seaside town of Hippo, Augustine was chosen by popular acclamation to become a priest and he was ordained by Bishop Valerius. Although preaching in that period was reserved to bishops, Valerius was Greek speaking and he lacked facility in Latin and so he permitted Augustine to preach almost from the beginning of his priesthood. One of his early sermons (on the Creed) was delivered in Carthage to a General Council of African Bishops in the year 393. By 395 Augustine had been consecrated as auxiliary bishop to Valerius who died in 396 leaving Augustine in full charge of the diocese. He was to serve as bishop of Hippo for thirty-five years.[3]

The philosophical discussions at Cassiciacum were written up as dialogues on topics such as the good life, the futility of skepticism and the problem of evil. They form an important part of Augustine's early literary production. Soon after his ordination he turned to religious polemics, writing many critiques of Manicheism, Donatism, and later of Pelagianism and Arianism.[4] By the year 400 Augustine was finishing his autobiographical *Confessions* and beginning the fifteen books of his famous doctrinal treatise, *The Trinity*. His sermons and commentaries on the Bible show how his earlier secular and philosophic wisdom was gradually acquiring new spiritual dimensions from Scripture and the early Fathers of the Church. In the course of his many writings seven explanations of the opening verses of Genesis are found but his major work in this category of Scripture exposition is the *Literal Commentary on Genesis* whose twelve books were completed in 414.[5]

Throughout the years of his episcopacy Augustine preached almost daily. Even on his frequent land travels[6] he was accustomed to speak at stops on the wayside and at shrines, wherever a crowd would gather. Hundreds of these sermons have been preserved, as have an extensive set of sermons and meditation notes on the Psalms which were named *Enarrationes in Psalmos* by the famous Renaissance editor, Desiderius Erasmus. These *Enarrations* constitute the longest of Augustine's writings and are a rich source of information on his personal thinking. Also during his long adult career he wrote many letters, of which about two hundred and fifty have been preserved, together with a few responses from his correspondents. Many letters are actually small treatises on a variety of topics.[7] For readers approaching Augustine for the first time the *Letters* are a good starting-point.

In the year 410 Alaric led an army of Goths across southern Europe and ravaged the City of Rome. Charges were made that Christianity had weakened the warlike spirit of the Romans and caused them to capitulate. By 413 Augustine had started to reply to this charge in one of his greatest works, *The City of God*. In its twenty-two books he endeavored to show the true relation between Christianity and the state. He contrasts God's City with the terrestrial State in a magnificent but frequently misunderstood philosophy of history and political life.[8]

Toward the end of his life, in 426, Augustine undertook to review and complete his many writings, some of which had been lost or left unfinished in his earlier years. The result was a chronological listing and personal evaluation of practically all his treatises, under the title *Retractationes*. This does not mean retractions but retreatments (from *re-* and *tractare*). The *Retractations* do not cover the *Letters* or the *Sermons* but almost all the other writings are carefully appraised. The result is that there are few problems of authenticity (except for the *Sermons*) or chronology in connection with Augustine's writings.

The invading Vandals swept over North Africa in 430. Augustine fell ill in the spring of that year, while the Goths held Hippo under siege for several months. Unlike some other bishops who fled before the invaders, Augustine stayed in his diocese. He died on August 28, A.D. 430.

Augustine's thought was sapiential, not scientific. He was interested, of course, in the world of natural things, its wonders and beauties, but he did not think that a science of creatures was comparable in importance to the appreciation of eternal truths and values. Mathematical axioms and principles fascinated him: he frequently used the equation, seven plus three equals ten, to illustrate the character of truths that are immutable and everlasting. Religious and moral virtues he regarded as similarly unchanging and eternal. But his wisdom went beyond mere cognitive experience to encompass the love of self, of neighbor, and of God.[9] For him, Wisdom is not only the virtue of knowing what is right, it is also the virtue of doing what is right. Thus wisdom culminates in a spiritual peace and joy which he called *fruitio*.[10] Speaking of the gift of Wisdom, St. James (3:17) had written: "the wisdom that comes down from above is essentially something pure; it also makes for peace, and is kindly and considerate; it is full of compassion and shows itself by doing good; nor is there any trace of partiality or hypocrisy in it." Certainly Augustine's wisdom fully manifested these qualities.[11]

When he looked over his writings in preparation for his review in the *Retractations*, Augustine was astounded to find that he had produced more than a thousand "books." These are roughly the equivalent of chapters in a modern work. His *Opera Omnia* are about the size of an encyclopedia. The following listing of the English and Latin titles, with the years of their writing, may be of assistance to readers.

AUGUSTINE'S WRITINGS: CHRONOLOGICAL LIST

A.D.

380	On the Beautiful and Fitting (*De pulchro et apto*) [not extant]
386/430	Letters (Epistulae) [for details see the edition by A. Goldbacher in *Corpus Scriptorum Ecclesiasticorum Latinorum*, Vienna 1895-1904, vols. 34, 44, 57, 58.
386	Against the Skeptics (*Contra Academicos*)
386	The Happy Life (*De beata vita*)
386	On Order (*De ordine*)
386/7	Soliloquies (*Soliloquia*)
387	The Immortality of the Soul (*De immortalitate animae*)
387	Six Books on the Liberal Arts (*Disciplinarum sex libri*) [except for the next item, never completed]
387/390	On Prosody (*De musica*)
387/388	The Magnitude of the Soul (*De quantitate animae*)
387/389	The Customs of Catholics and Manichees (*De moribus ecclesiae catholicae et manichaeorum*)
388/389	On Genesis against the Manichees (*De Genesi contra manichaeos*)
388/395	On Free Choice (*De libero arbitrio*)
389	The Teacher (*De magistro*)
391/430	Sermons (*Sermones*) [for chronology and types consult P. Verbraken, *Etudes critiques sur les sermons authentiques de s. Augustin*, Bruges/The Hague: Nijhoff, 1976]
391	On True Religion (*De vera religione*)
388/395	Eighty-three Different Questions (*De diversis quaestionibus 83*)
392	The Advantage of Believing (*De utilitate credendi*)
392/393	On Dual Souls against the Manichees (*De duabus animabus contra manichaeos*)
392	Proceedings against Fortunatus the Manichee (*Acta contra Fortunatum manichaeum*)
392/426	Enarrations on the Psalms (*Enarrationes in Psalmos*)
393	Sermon on Faith and the Creed (*De fide et symbolo*)
393	Incomplete Book on the Literal Meaning of Genesis (*De Genesi ad litteram, liber imperfectus*)

NOTES

1. In later histories Augustine is frequently given the added name "Aurelius" but I know of no evidence from his own writings or contemporaries that he was called Aurelius.

2. For factual information the most helpful recent biography is: Peter Brown, *Augustine of Hippo* (Berkeley and Los Angeles: University of California Press, 1967).

3. On Augustine's episcopal career see: F. Van der Meer, *Augustine the Bishop*, trans. by B. Battershaw (London: Sheed & Ward, 1961).

4. Gerald Bonner, *St. Augustine of Hippo. Life and Controversies* (Philadelphia: Westminster Press, 1963) is a balanced survey of these religious polemics.

5. Not yet available in English, *De Genesi ad litteram* is promised for early publication in a version by the late John H. Taylor, S.J., in the Ancient Christian Writers Series.

6. On Augustine's travels the best study is: Othmar Perler, *Les voyages de saint Augustin* (Paris: Etudes Augustiniennes, 1969).

7. In the list of writings at the end of this chapter the more important epistolary treatises are included under separate titles.

8. Of the abundant literature on the *City of God*, John O'Meara's *Charter of Christendom: The Significance of the City of God* (New York: Macmillan, 1961) is brief and informative. For other items consult: Terry L. Miethe, *Augustinian Bibliography, 1970-1980* (Westport, CT: Greenwood Press, 1982).

9. Oliver O'Donovan, *The Problem of Self-Love in St. Augustine* (New Haven and London: Yale University Press, 1980) stresses these three objects of Augustinian love.

10. This theme is developed in my book, *Joy in Augustine's Ethics* (Villanova University Press, 1979).

11. The version of James 3:17 is from the *Jerusalem Bible* (New York: Doubleday, 1968) *The New Testament*, p. 297.

CHAPTER 2

Augustine's Travels and Friends

With the publication of Othmar Perler's study of St. Augustine's travels the investigation of the life of the bishop of Hippo reached a new peak of scholarship.[1] This meticulously conducted piece of research makes improved use of some source materials that scholars have had for centuries and it also exploits new sources that have become available only recently. Thinking back to the time of publication of my biography of Augustine,[2] I am keenly aware of the improved techniques of recent Augustinian studies and the newfound riches of source materials.

For one thing, the texts of Augustine's writings are now in much better shape than they were earlier in this century. We had the *Opera Omnia* in the old Maurist edition (reprinted with added errors in *Migne's Patrologia Latina*) and about half the works were critically edited in the *Vienna Corpus* (CSEL). With the centenary celebrations in 1931 many new editions and studies made an appearance. The *Sermons* edited by Dom G. Morin in 1931 (*Miscellanea Agostiniana* I) marked a real advance. With the exception of a few volumes, the *Bibliothèque Augustinienne* printing of the works (1939 ff.) in Latin and French did not improve the text but it provided a cheaper printing of the vulgarized text with some useful notes. Then the launching of the *Corpus Christianorum* (Turnhout, 1954 ff.) inaugurated a wholly new critical edition of the *Opera Omnia*. In the fifty volumes of patristic writings that CC has published up to 1970, there are eleven (or twelve, if the two fascicles of the *De Trinitate* in tome 50 are considered distinct) devoted to St. Augustine's works.[3] It may be useful to some readers to know that

the following writings of Augustine are now published in the
Corpus Christianorum:

vol. 32 De doctrina Christiana, De vera religione
    33 Quaestiones et Locutiones in Heptateuchum
    35 De sermone Domini in monte
    36 Tractatus in Iohannis Evangelium
    38, 39, 40 Enarrationes in Psalmos
    41 Sermones de Vetere Testamento
    47, 48 De civitate Dei (cura B. Dombart et A. Kalb)
    50, 50A De Trinitate (cura W. J. Mountain et F. Glorie)
    46 De fide rerum, Enchiridion, etc., 1969

Of these volumes three are especially noteworthy. First
of all, the *Sermons* edited by C. Lambot in volume 41 are
quite important. Second, since the Dombart and Kalb edition of the *City of God* (which is the best Latin text) has
become difficult to obtain in the original printing (Leipzig
1928), it is good to have it reprinted with emendations in
CC. Finally, the beautiful new edition of *The Trinity* by
Father Mountain (with F. Glorie as assistant editor) shows
that American scholarship in this textual area has finally
come of age.[4]

Othmar Perler makes good use of all these new texts.
After the *Confessions*, the *Sermons* and *Letters* are the most
fruitful biographical sources. I must confess some amaze-
ment at finding Perler citing the *Confessions* in the edition by
Pius Knöll (CSEL 33). This is not the best edition: it is generally admitted that the best text is the revision by Martin
Skutella (Teubner Series, 1934) which is also available in the
Bibliothèque Augustinienne. Scholars do become accustomed to
certain favorite printings, of course. Gerald Bonner uses
Pierre de Labriolle's text, for instance, and Spanish scholars
seem to prefer the unusual edition of the *Confessions* made by
A. C. Vega in the *Biblioteca de Autores Cristianos*. There is
some justification for a decision to cite all the editions that

are available in the *Vienna Corpus* and that is probably what motivated Perler in regard to the Knöll *Confessiones*.

A second major source of information on Augustine's life and work consists of the archaelogical remains of the culture of North Africa and Italy in the fourth and fifth Christian centuries. Whatever we may think of the other effects of German, French, Italian and British colonialism in the lands along the southern shores of the Mediterranean, we must admit that European investigators have done a great deal in the twentieth century to uncover the evidences of early North African civilization. The French did a particularly good job in Algeria and Tunisia. Augustine lived close to the borderline between these two modern nations. Perler has been able to profit from the publications in this field by people such as Charles-Picard and Marec.[5] Oddly, Perler makes no reference to Van der Meer's biography of Augustine which was a successful popularization of information from these archaeological sources.[6]

Also prominent among Perler's sources are some new studies of the regions in Italy with which Augustine had some contact. Thus the port of Ostia has been investigated by Meiggs.[7] However, what would seem to many the most interesting recent discovery in the ruins at Ostia, the unearthing in 1945 of a stone bearing part of the epitaph of St. Monica who died there, is passed over with but brief mention in one of Perler's footnotes. (See p. 146, note 2.) It must be admitted that Meiggs (p. 400) also pays little attention to this artifact, for the reason that the inscription was already known. To my mind, the existence of this Ostia stone strongly confirms the historicity of the *Confessions*.

What is really distinctive of this part of Perler's study is his assembly of pictures of more than seventy artifacts and archaeological remains illustrating the places, means and modes of travel in Augustine's world. Since these show the kinds of ships available, the carts and vehicles pulled by horses and oxen, the clothes worn by travellers, and the stopping places along the public roads, we have here a marvellous gathering of data on the conditions that Augustine faced on his extensive trips. Travel was not easy in those days.

As far as Perler can determine, Augustine's only sea trips were his voyage across the Mediterranean to Rome, in 383, and his return from Rome to Carthage in 388. We all know that the Bishop of Hippo spent a great deal of time in Carthage and that he must have gone from Hippo to Carthage in almost every year of his episcopate. It was easy to assume that, since Hippo-Regius and Carthage were almost adjacent seaports, at least some of these journeys would be by water. However, on the basis of *Letter* 122 to Paulinus of Nola (A.D. 410), Perler concludes that Augustine never used a ship after A.D. 388.[8] There is some evidence from later sermons and letters that, after A.D. 410, Augustine's health would hardly have permitted sea travel. Indeed, it is quite apparent that an extended trip in the small boats of this period was quite an ordeal. Moreover, from mid-November to mid-March the bad winter weather made sea voyages on the Mediterranean practically impossible.[9] On the other hand, land travel was comparatively safe and the resting facilities along the more frequented routes in North Africa were arranged so that travellers could stop overnight after riding for thirty or more miles per day.

Fascinating as these details may be, we must ask the basic question about Perler's work: is travel as an organizing principle a good approach to the study of Augustine's life? One may admit immediately that this device has enabled Perler to uncover biographical materials that are new to this field. Still it is difficult to see how travel is really central to the story of this man who wrote: "noli foras ire, in teipsum redi; in interiore homine habitat veritas."[10] This is the man who elsewhere contrasted the riches of inner mental experiences with the observation of geographical sights:

> Yet men go to admire the mountain's peaks, giant waves in the sea, the broad courses of rivers, the vast

> sweep of the ocean, and the circuits of the stars — and
> they leave themselves behind. They feel no wonder that
> I did not see with my eyes all these things when I was
> talking about them. Yet I could not have talked of them
> unless I could see within, in my memory, in their vast
> expanses, as if I were seeing them externally, the
> mountains, waves, rivers and stars which I have seen,
> and the ocean which I take on faith.[11]

There is something ambivalent about Augustine's attitude toward the externals of life on earth. As Hugh Pope showed in a remarkable chapter on "Augustine and the World of Nature,"[12] this great introspective saint was also fascinated, at times at least, with the minutiae and marvels of the world of sense experience. Augustine fought against such preoccupations but felt that his sensory interests were redeemed by his awareness of the presence of God throughout nature.

So, although the approach to Augustine's personality through the travel theme is, on the surface, an unlikely one, it is not unfruitful. Rather obviously, Perler intends to write a full-scale biography of Augustine, eventually. This sort of preliminary study certainly brings some balance to the many "psychographs" that have been devoted to St. Augustine.

The plan of *Les Voyages de saint Augustin* is relatively simple. An opening section of about a hundred pages reviews the general conditions of land and sea travel in the fourth- and fifth-century Roman Empire. This is followed by a chapter on the trips prior to Augustine's episcopate, among which the sea voyage to Italy (A.D. 383-388) is extensively discussed. Two more chapters treat the thirty-five, or so, land journeys to various points in North Africa made by Augustine the Bishop. In all of these chapters chronology is very important and such data are gathered in very complete tables: "Chronologie et topologie Augustiniennes," (pp. 427-477) which connect the dates of the travels with the places, key events, writings, sermons and sources of information for each trip. This compilation by Jean Louis Maier constitutes a valuable instrument for further research on the career of St. Augustine.

Besides its multiple *Indexes*, this book also includes five *excursus* on a variety of problems. One is the still unsettled question of the location in north Italy of the villa called Cassiciacum. Most scholars agree that it was either at Casciago or at Cassago. The first is about fifty-five kilometers northwest of Milan, while Cassago is but half that distance to the north of Milan. Perler favors Cassago as the site of Augustine's country interlude. To other arguments he adds the suggestion that Casciago is too far away from Milan to permit the apparent one-day trips made by Navigius and, possibly, Alypius. Rather recent archaeological studies of the Cassago area suggest that the villa of Verecundus may have been situated there.

In four other appendices Perler studies the date of the death of Maximus the Usurper, the anti-pagan proceedings in Carthage in 399, Augustine's sermons on the Sack of Rome, and the Christian church buildings of Carthage that have some connection with Augustine. On several of these problems Perler has already published noteworthy journal articles.

Of course there are other problems that one could have hoped to see treated by Perler. To mention these is not to criticize his accomplishment: there are always other things that might have been done in an important piece of scholarship. However, I might point to two themes that are related to the travels of St. Augustine and which are not developed by Perler. These are the question of Augustine's ethnic background and the matter of his association with the imperial *agentes in rebus*.

Obviously connected with matters of geography, cultural mobility and adaptation, is the problem of Augustine's racial origins. It is firmly established that he was a native of a little town that was near the border between the present Tunisia and Algeria. His mother seems to have come from the same area. Some older biographies contain the suggestion that his father may have descended from Roman soldier-stock that had emigrated to Numidia. I have never seen any real evidence of this claim. We must take it that both of Augustine's parents were North Africans.

In these days of interest in black studies and emergent African nationalism, it would be interesting to know more about Augustine's descent. Quite possibly he was the most famous and influential African writer and thinker that has ever lived. He may have been black. In 1945, a small book made this claim but its arguments were more emotional than scholarly.[13] Much more evidence on this point could be assembled.

The famous Lateran fresco of Augustine (reproduced in Perler's plates 1 and 2a) is dated as early as A.D. 600. This is thought by many to be as close as we can come to a real portrait of an ancient Christian saint. The picture shows a small elderly man seated in a high-backed armchair, reading from a large book. Thin-faced, he has a prominent nose and, apparently, a dark complexion. Perler agrees that this is a portrait of Augustine but he thinks the clothing may not be authentic for the period.[14] Not too much can be concluded from this portrait as to Augustine's racial origins. After all, the Lateran fresco must have been painted in Rome by a man who lived at least a century after Augustine and who could never have seen his subject in the flesh. The best that one can say is that the fresco does not preclude the possibility that Augustine was a black man.

Arguments from language are difficult to handle but could be important. In various places Augustine gives the impression that he knew a non-Latin language which he called "Punic." Thus there is an early *Letter*[15] in which he points out to a pagan critic that the "Punic" names of some Christian Africans are no more laughable in form and meaning than many names associated with Roman polytheism. Some twenty years later, preaching on the text of St. Paul (Ephes. 5:15) that speaks of "redeeming the time," Augustine said:

There's a well-known Punic proverb that I'll put into Latin for you, because not all of you know it in Punic. Indeed, the Punic proverb is an old one: 'Pestilence asks a penny: give him two and he will go away.' Now doesn't this proverb seem to spring from the Gospel?[16]

He goes on to tie in the Punic saying with the notion of redeeming the time. For our present purposes, the importance of the text lies in its implication that Augustine, as well as some of his audience, knew some language called Punic. He suggests that he could have repeated the proverb in this native language but refrains from doing so, out of consideration for others of his listeners. It is, then, incorrect to suggest that Augustine could speak only Latin.[17] In point of fact, we know that both Augustine and his mother had nurses who influenced their speech habits — and these domestics were no doubt country people who spoke a little Latin but were accustomed to use some native dialect.

During Augustine's episcopate there were people in his immediate vicinity who did not know Latin. Thus in a letter concerning Donatism and the practice of second baptism, he suggests that both he and his opponents should clearly state their cases and then have them translated into "Punic," so that the residents of Mappalia (a rural estate near Hippo) could understand them.[18] In a later letter (A.D. 423) Augustine makes quite a point of the fact that he has secured for the Catholics of Fussala (a town originally in the diocese of Hippo) an episcopal candidate who speaks Punic.[19]

There is some question as to what language Augustine's "Punic" really was. Some authorities think that the native language of these country people in the vicinity of Tagaste and Hippo was Libyan, an African language from which the Berber dialect was derived.[20] Libyan inscriptions found in the region of Augustine's origin show some influence from Latin but practically none from the ancient Phoenician. Since this Libyan tongue is the "direct ancestor of the modern Berber,"[21] it seems clear that Augustine was

linguistically related to the ancestors of the Berber people. In
fact, in at least one place he identified the "Punic" language
with what he called the *Afram*.[22]

However, other scholars have argued that Augustine
used the name "Punic" for any of the non-Latin dialects of
his part of North Africa.[23] Peter Brown is sure that this
native language was not the tongue of the ancient Phoeni-
cians.[24] But Augustine seems to have thought that it was!
He frequently claims that his "Punic" is closely related to
Hebrew and he uses his knowledge of this native language
to explain the meaning of Hebrew terms. Thus, he takes a
Hebraicism (God "stretching out his hand") and says that
this is a very familiar Punic expression. Then he adds that
there are many verbal similarities between Hebrew and
Punic.[25] This claim is frequently made in Augustine's writings on Scripture. Now some modern scholars ridicule Augustine's knowledge of Hebrew and his fanciful etymologies.
The fact of the matter is that Augustine was right many
times about the root meanings of biblical terms—and yet he
had never studied Hebrew or the other languages of the
Bible. For instance, he explains the word "Baal" as meaning
"lord," for, he suggests, that is what the Punic ba'al means.[26]
Again, in a sermon, he is discussing the phrase "mammon
of iniquity" (Luke 16:9) and he explains that *mammona* means
"wealth" in Punic.[27] In another work Augustine indicates
that *Christus* and *Messia* both mean the anointed—and he
bases this on the similarity between Hebrew and Punic.[28]

All of this only adds to the mystery of Augustine's an-
cestry. In spite of his acquired Latin culture, he sprang from
a people whose language did have some connection with
Hebrew. This native language was probably the forerunner
of the Berber language. It is quite probable that Augustine
stemmed from Berber stock.

Linguistic considerations would not establish Augustine as a black, in any case, for there were "Libyans" in ancient times who were white.[29] However, I am inclined to

think that Augustine was a dark-faced man who identified himself as an African (*Afer*) and who never tried to pretend that he was a Roman in anything other than the political sense. This conclusion is supported by his comment to his mother on his Latin accent:

> Of course, if I should say that you would easily acquire a mode of expression that would be free from defect of pronunciation and diction, I would indeed misrepresent the truth. Even I, for whom a thorough study of these matters has been a dire necessity, am nevertheless censured by the Italians for my pronunciation of many words; they, in turn, are taken to task by me with regard to pronunciation itself. The assurance that comes from theory is one thing; that gained by nativeness is quite different. And it is likely that any learned man, giving careful attention, would discover so-called solecisms in my speech.[30]

This is a rather revealing admission from a speech teacher: Augustine must have felt quite alien to some of his associates in Milan and Rome. He never forgot that he was an African.

A more thorough investigation of this problem by someone with Othmar Perler's scholarly qualifications might bring us nearer to certainty on this matter of Augustine's ethnic origins.

Another problem in Augustine's biography involves his relations with a number of Roman officials known as *agentes in rebus*. I am not satisfied that we know the whole story of these travelling agents. In connection with Evodius, the best known of these functionaries to Augustine, Perler simply says that an *agens in rebus* was an *"inspecteur de l'administration."*[31] Actually these government agents seem to have combined the roles of men of the F.B.I., the C.I.A., and other such agencies. In view of the fact that Augustine's parents, and he himself as a youth, saw his studies in rhetoric as an avenue to some sort of government job, one may conjecture

that Augustine had more than a passing interest in the life
of an imperial agent.

There were several such *agentes in rebus* who played
some part in Augustine's career. Apart from Evodius (whose
story has been adequately studied, perhaps) we know of the
nameless young man who asked Augustine to come to Hippo
in 391 to counsel him in regard to entering the religious life.
Possidius is the source of our information that this man was
an *agens in rebus*.[32] While nothing more is known to me concerning this man, it is obvious that he, unwittingly perhaps,
occasioned the selection of Augustine for ordination as a
priest in Hippo.[33]

Whether Augustine ever met the two former *agentes in
rebus* who gave up their secular careers and entered a
monastery near the Imperial city of Trèves, we do not know.
Certainly Augustine was impressed by Ponticianus' account
of their conversion and by their reception of spiritual inspiration from the *Life of St. Anthony*. It is likely that Ponticianus was himself an *agens in rebus*, for Augustine mentions
his distinguished service at court.[34] Obviously, Ponticianus
was a close associate of the two imperial agents who embraced the religious life at Trèves.

Another Roman official, the Dulcitius who played a
key role in the affair of the Donatist Bishop Gaudentius (he
threatened to burn himself in his church to prove his sincerity) was quite possibly a former *agens in rebus*. Dulcitius is
called a "tribune and notary" in both Augustine's *Retractations*
and Gaudentius' *Letter to Dulcitius*.[35] Augustine mentions another tribune, Eleusinus, who was stationed at Timgad at
about this time.[36] This may be the same Eleusinus who
owned some property at Hippo.[37] Whether service as an
agens in rebus usually led to higher appointments in the imperial service is not clear.

Clearly, the precise role and reputation of these *agentes
in rebus*, in the early fifth-century, should be further studied.
Descriptions of these agents in standard reference works
have remained verbally the same for centuries. They were

officials directly under control of the Roman Emperor. They carried his orders to officials in the provinces, reported on the conduct of provincial governors, inspected the public post, oversaw the collecting of taxes, and generally snooped into the public and private affairs of provincial citizens.[38] The early laws concerning these imperial agents stress the requirements of good character and devotion to duty.[39] However, like most secret police forces, the *agentes in rebus* eventually acquired an unfavorable popular image. To put it bluntly, "their avarice and corruption were notorious."[40]

Yet St. Augustine writes of several of these agents with evident respect and even admiration. Evodius became a noteworthy figure in the African episcopacy. One gets the impression that Augustine cultivated the friendship of several of these government officials while he was teaching in Milan and then continued these friendly relations with others that he encountered as a bishop in Africa. An investigator of Perler's resources could doubtless discover much more concerning these associates of Augustine.

On the whole, *Les Voyages de saint Augustin* makes no direct contribution to the study of Augustine's thought. But, in a larger sense, the book provides many of the tools that we have needed to work on the personality and career of this great African Bishop. Augustinian scholarship is much richer as a result of the efforts of Othmar Perler and his associate, Jean Louis Maier.

NOTES

1. *Les Voyages de saint Augustin* (Paris: Etudes Augustiniennes 1969. Pp. 564, 4 cartes, 2 plans, 79 planches. 112 francs). Jean Louis Maier assisted Perler, writing up the travels during the episcopate and compiling the extensive *Tables*.

2. *Augustine's Quest of Wisdom* (Milwaukee 1945).

3. See the pamphlet: *1954—1969, Corpus Christianorum 1—50* (Turnhout: Brepols 1970) pp. 23; and also José Oroz, "Los

50 primeros volúmenes del 'Corpus Christianorum," *Augustinus* 15, 58 (1970) 207-212.

4. Also published in 1970: vol. 29 *Contra Academicos*, *De beata vita*, *De libero arbitrio*, *De magistro*, *De ordine*, and vol. 44 *Ad Simplicianum de diversis quaestionibus*, *De diversis quaestionibus 83*.

5. G. Charles-Picard, *La civilisation de l'Afrique romaine* (Paris 1959); *La Carthage de saint Augustin* (Paris 1965); and E. Marec, *Hippone-la-royale: antique Hippo Regius* (2me éd. Alger 1954); *Monuments chrétiens d'Hippone, ville épiscopale de saint Augustin* (Paris 1958).

6. F. Van der Meer, *Augustinus de zielzorger* (Utrecht 1947), translated as *Augustine the Bishop* by Brian Battershaw and G.R. Lamb (London-New York 1961). Perler twice cites (pp. 136 & 211) the *Atlas of the Early Christian World* compiled by Christine Mohrmann and Van der Meer but both times to differ with their data.

7. R. Meiggs, *Roman Ostia* (Oxford 1960).

8. In this letter Augustine mentions the many sea voyages that his ecclesiastical colleagues have been compelled to undergo (*quae saepe sanctos fratres et collegas meos etiam labores marinos et transmarinos compulit sustinere*) and then he notes that his feeble health has excused him from such voyages (*a quibus me semper non indeuotio mentis sed minus idoneo valitudo corporis excusauit*). *Epist.* 122.1 (CSEL 34 II, 742). See Perler's initial discussion of this letter, pp. 15-16.

9. Perler, *op. cit.* pp. 68-74: "La suspension hivernale."

10. *De vera religione* 39.72 (CC 32,234).

11. *Confessiones* X.8.15 (ed. M. Skutella, Bibliothèque Augustinienne 14, pp. 166-8; trans. Bourke, FOC 21.276).

12. *Augustine of Hippo* (Westminster, Md. 1949) pp. 228-253.

13. René Pottier, *Saint Augustin le Berbère* (Paris 1945).

14. "Nous sommes par conséquent favorable à l'identification du portrait du Latran et à son historicité, mais nous ferons des restrictions au sujet du costume." *Les Voyages* p. 19, note 2.

15. *Epist.* 17, ad Maximum (ca. A.D. 390, CSEL 34.39-44).

16. "Proverbium notum est Punicum, quod quidem Latine vobis dicam, quia Punice non omnes nostis. Punicum enim pro-

verbium est antiquum: Nummum quaerit pestilentia, duos illi da, et ducat se. Numquid non hoc proverbium de Evangelio videtur natum?" *Serm.* 167.4 (PL 38.910).

17. Peter Brown, *Augustine of Hippo* (Berkeley and Los Angeles 1967) p. 22: "It is most unlikely that Augustine spoke anything but Latin."

18. *Epist.* 66.2 (CSEL 34.235-236). See *Augustine's Quest of Wisdom*, p. 154.

19. *Epist.* 209.3 (CSEL 57.347-353).

20. W. H. C. Frend, *The Donatist Church: A Movement of Protest in Roman North Africa* (Oxford: 1952) pp. 57-58.

21. Frend, *op. cit.* p. 57; see his earlier study: "A Note on the Berber Background in the Life of Augustine," *Journal of Theological Studies* 43 (1942) 188-191.

22. *In Epistolam Ioannis ad Parthos* 2.3 (PL 35.1991) points out that two languages are used by the Donatists: "Latinam et Punicam, id est Afram."

23. This is the view of M. Simon, "Punique ou Berbère?" *Annuaire de l'Institut de Philologie et d'Historie Orientales et Slaves* 13 (1955) 613-629; reprinted in *Recherches d'Histoire Judéo-Chrétienne* (Paris 1962) pp. 88-100.

24. *Op. cit.* p. 22.

25. *Locutiones in Heptateuchum* I.24 (CC 33.384): "*Et extendit manum suam* . . . locutio est, quam propterea hebraeam puto, quia et punicae linguae familiarissima est, in qua multa inuenimus hebraeis uerbis consonantia."

26. *Quaestiones in Heptateuchum* VII, q. 16 (CC 33.341): "Nam Baal Punici uidentur dicere dominum." Cf. *Webster's Collegiate Dictionary* (1948) p. 76: *Baal* (Hebr. from Phoenician *ba'al* lord).

27. *Serm.* 113.2 (PL 38.648): "Quod Punici dicunt mammon, Latine lucrum vocatur. Quod Hebraei dicunt mammona, Latine divitiae vocantur." (Webster gives *māmōnā* as an Aramaic term.)

28. *Contra litteras Petiliani* II.104.239 (CSEL 52.152): "Nam et ipse Christus a chrismate appellatur, id est ab unctione. Hunc Hebraei dicunt Messiam, quod verbum Punicae linguae consonum est, sicut alia Hebraea permulta et pene omnia." Cf. Webster p. 627: *Messiah* (Aram. *mēshiḥā*, Hebr. *māhsiāh* anointed).

29. See Charles Tissot, *Géographie comparée de la province romaine d'Afrique* 2 vols. (Paris 1884-8) I, 385-444; cf. H. Pope, *op. cit.* p. 16.

30. *De ordine* II.17.45 (CSEL 63.178; trans. R. P. Russell, FOC I.321-322).

31. *Les Voyages* p. 144, citing Pierre Courcelle, *Recherches sur les Confessions de s. Augustin* (Paris 1960) p. 181, n. 6.

32. "Quidam ex eis, quos Agentes in rebus, apud Hipponemregium constitutus, bene Christianus Deumque timens, comperta ejus bona fama atque doctrina, desideret atque optaret eum videre, promittens se posse mundi hujus omnes contemnere." Possidii, *Vita Augustini* cap. 3 (in *Vita di S. Agostino*, testo critico a cura di M. Pellegrino, Roma 1955, pp. 48-50). Cf. G. Bonner, *St. Augustine of Hippo* (Philadelphia 1963) p. 111, who speaks of this man as a member of the "secret police."

33. *Serm.* 355.2 (PL 39.1570); see the English in *Selected Sermons of St. Augustine* translated and edited by Quincy Howe, Jr. (New York 1966) pp. 205-213. Cf. *Epist.* 21, ad Valerium (CSEL 34.49-54) and *Epist.* 126.7 (CSEL 44.12).

34. Thus he speaks of Ponticianus as "praeclare in palatio militans." *Conf.* VIII.6.14 (Bibl. Aug. 14.36).

35. "Per idem tempus Dulcitius, tribunus et notarius, hic erat in Africa executor imperialium iussionum contra Donatistas datarum." *Retract.* II.85.58 (CSEL 36.198). CF. *Contra Gaudentium* 1.2 (CSEL 53.202-3) where Augustine quotes long passages from Gaudentius' *Letter* which begins: "Honorabili, ac nimium nobis, si sic volueris, desiderando Dulcitio tribuno et notario, Gaudentius episcopus."

36. *Epist.* 204.9, ad Dulcitium (CSEL 57.322).

37. See *S. Aurelii Augustini Vita*, opera et studio Monachorum Ordinis S. Benedicti, lib. VIII.1.3.

38. See "Secret Service, Government Agents (*agentes in rebus*)" in the *Glossary* (p.594) to *The Theodosian Code*, trans. Clyde Pharr (Princeton 1952). This entry is practically a translation from A. Forcellini, *Totius Latinitatis Lexicon* (Prati 1858-9) I.166. Cf. H. M. Gwatkin in *Cambridge Medieval History* (1936) I.36-37.

39. See *Codex Theod.* 6.27.1-23.

40. Pharr, "Glossary" in *op. cit.* p. 594.

CHAPTER 3

A Guide to Reading Augustine

It is a remarkable thing to find a scholarly work written more than fifty years ago which is still among the best in its field. There is little doubt that this is true of Eugène Portalié's study of St. Augustine of Hippo.[1] Etienne Gilson, himself the author of an excellent general work on Augustine, has called Portalié's the indispensable introduction.[2] Similar encomia are found in other Augustinian studies of our day.[3] Such universal esteem is all the more unusual when the study in question is a relatively inaccessible article in an encyclopedic dictionary. Clearly, the publication in book form of an English translation of this work is well advised.

Eugène Portalié lived and worked quietly; he was not too well known, even by his fellow Jesuits. Born on January 3, 1852, at Mende, France, he entered the Jesuit Novitiate for the Toulouse Province, in December, 1867. His scholarship was completely the product of his training in the Society of Jesus, and of his own efforts. Distinguishing himself in the regular course in theology, he spent at least two years in advanced studies. Portalié held a "Grand Act" (a rare type of disputation reserved for a few brilliant Jesuit scholars) at Uclès. The Papal Nuncio of Madrid presided, attended by his secretary, the future Pope Benedict XV.

In his theological teaching at several Jesuit centers of study, Father Portalié was a successful and highly personal professor. His knowledge of the history of his subject made his lectures informative and interesting. Central in his scholarly interests were the problems of faith and grace. Most of his writing was done for the Jesuit periodical,

Etudes. Though some of these articles have been separately published, notably a collection concerned with the Diana Vaughan affair,[4] the magistral article on St. Augustine remains as his only publication of major size.[5] In 1899 he was called to the chair of positive theology at the Institut Catholique, Toulouse, where he was an associate of Msgr. Pierre Battifol, another enthusiastic student of St. Augustine. From 1899 to 1902, Portalié wrote six articles for the newly projected *Dictionnaire de théologie catholique*; of these the one on Augustine has been the most influential.

In his later years, Father Portalié became much concerned with the Modernist movement in French Catholicism. He engaged in energetic polemic against Loisy and his colleagues. This activity is thought to have sapped his energies and contributed to his death, April 20, 1909.[6]

Interest in St. Augustine has not dwindled since Father Portalié's time. Hundreds of valuable works have been written in the ensuing fifty years. Augustine's original writings have been partly re-edited and translated into modern languages. Archaeological discoveries have brought precious information about Augustine's world. His religious and philosophical teachings have been studied by an ever-increasing number of interpreters. New journals and publication series are devoted in whole or in part to the study of his writings. While it is not possible to cover all this material adequately, a brief survey of some of the main trends and publications of the last fifty years may serve to supplement this already excellent work.

I. BIOGRAPHY

Dozens of biographies of St. Augustine have been published in this century. Some very popular lives have been written by prominent literary figures (Louis Bertrand, Rebecca West, Giovanni Papini) but these have added little that is new. One of the best scholarly biographies is that by

Canon Bardy.[7] This book describes very fully the later life of Augustine—a period often passed over briefly because it is not covered in the autobiographical section of the *Confessions*. Much material can be gathered on Augustine's mature work as a bishop from his letters and sermons, and from the contemporary *Life* by Possidius.[8]

Several remarkable archaeological discoveries, related to Augustine studies, have been made in North Africa; extensive investigations have been made of the ruins of the old cities. Père Delattre and others have verified Augustine's description of the waterfront and topography of ancient Carthage.[9] At Hippo, the ruins of two cathedrals (apparently Augustine's and the Donatist church) have been uncovered.[10] The mosaic floor, partially preserved in Augustine's cathedral, shows that the building was large (162 x 65 feet). A baptismal font, episcopal throne, and several tombs have been found in this church. Meanwhile, in Italy, striking evidence of the historicity of the account of St. Monica's death and burial at Ostia (*Conf.*, 9, II, 28) came to light about ten years ago. A stone bearing a partial text of what seems to be an epitaph for Augustine's mother was found in the yard of the church of St. Aurea at Ostia.[11]

Concerning the personal life of Augustine, one of the most significant controversies had started before Father Portalié wrote and has continued to the present day. This is the dispute about the details of his conversion. Briefly, certain writers[12] claim that, at the time of his baptism, Augustine was a devotee of Greek philosophy rather than a convinced Christian. Implied in this interpretation is the non-historicity of certain parts of the *Confessions*. Opposition to the early versions of this thesis is found in Portalié, of course, and elsewhere.[13] The outstanding later rebuttal to Alfaric, and this whole position, was written by Father Charles Boyer.[14] He strongly supports the historicity of the *Confessions*, and maintains the sincerity of Augustine's religious conversion. More recent works have stressed the complexity of the problem.[15] The present tendency among Catholic scholars is to grant the intellectual impact of Plotinus, Porphyry, even of Stoicism, on Augustine's mental development—but also to maintain his acceptance of the essentials of Christianity at the time of his baptism.[16]

It is impossible to review here the many new studies of detailed points in the biography of Augustine—of his illnesses (Legewie), the location of Cassiciacum (Morin, Meda, Rota), his ethnic background (Poittier), his association with Carthage (Lapeyre), his priestly development (Pincherle), and his preaching (De Bruyne, Pope).[17] A great deal of such patient research remains to be done.

II. WRITINGS

No complete, critical edition of the Latin works of St. Augustine has been published. Many scholars still use the Migne reprint of the famous Renaissance edition by the Benedictines of St-Maur.[18] Critical texts of about one third of Augustine's writings are to be found in the *Corpus Scriptorum Ecclesiasticorum Latinorum* (Vienna, 1864-   ). Augustine volumes in CSEL are not grouped in one numerical sequence; hence it is necessary to use a table (such as Portalié gives) to locate his works therein.[19] Inexpensive and useful for the small library is the Latin-French printing of the works of Augustine, now in progress.[20] Publication of a new critical edition of the Fathers has started in Holland; Augustine's writings are to be in volumes XXVII to LIX.[21] There is also an edition of the Latin works under way in Spain.[22]

We also lack a complete English version of St. Augustine. For the older collected translations in English, and for some versions of individual treatises up to 1937, Father Pope's table may be consulted.[23] Two translation series are in progress in the U.S.A. *Ancient Christian Writers* now contains many of the shorter works, well annotated.[24] *The Fathers of the Church* series[25] includes some of the short works and also certain major treatises have been printed.[26] A practical two-volume collection of shorter works plus most of the *Confessions* and *City of God* has been assembled from available versions by Protestant scholars.[27]

For up-to-date information on the authenticity and chronology of these writings, with bibliographical references in this field, Bardy's annotated edition and translation of the *Retractationes* is recommended.[28] There is an earlier general study of the chronology of all the works.[29] Several important articles on major writings (De Bruyne, Kunzelmann, Wilmart) are printed in the second volume of *Miscellanea Agostiniana* (Roma, 1931). Many points connected with the literary and philological study of St. Augustine were discussed by outstanding scholars (Marrou, Courcelle, Mohrmann, Henry, etc.) at the International Augustinian Congress of Paris, 1954. The first and third volumes of these proceedings contain much information in this area.[30] Hundreds of special studies of various works of Augustine have been printed since Father Portalié worked. Many volumes of the *Patristic Studies* (Catholic U. of America) fall in this category. New work has been done on the editing of the *Sermons*.[31] Several critical editions of the *Confessions* have appeared; it is generally agreed that Skutella's text is the best.[32] In the first volume of the *City of God* (FOC translation, 1950), Etienne Gilson has provided a brilliant *Foreword* of almost one hundred pages. On the historicity of the early dialogues, and their relation to the *Confessions*, there is now an abundant literature.[33] Goldbacher's edition of the *Epistulae* (CSEL, vols. 34,44,57, and 58) is well annotated and conveniently indexed.

Because of Augustine's care in reviewing most of his literary production, in the *Retractationes*, there has never been great difficulty about matters of authenticity and chronology. Portalié's information on such questions is still sound. It might be noted that *De octo quaestionibus ex veteri Testamento*, formerly suspect, is now considered quite authentic.[34] But the *Speculum 'Quis ignorat'* seems to be spurious.[35]

III. THOUGHT

Introductions

Of the many introductions to the thought of St. Augustine, some stress the interests of the philosopher.[36] However, it is admittedly difficult to maintain a distinction between philosophic and religious thought in Augustine. He is a theocentric thinker; some introductory works emphasize this.[37] Augustine scholarship is by no means exclusively Catholic; it would seem that Protestant interest is now increasing in America.[38] There is also an impressive three-volume study of patristic thought, by a noted Jewish scholar, which stresses the contributions of Augustine.[39] Despite the title, the problems explored in this large work are primarily theological.

Sources

There is an abundant literature on the backgrounds of Augustine's thought. One of the most useful bibliographies of this material is found in Courcelle's *Recherches sur les Confessions* (pp. 259-278). This work emphasizes the importance of Plotinus and Neo-Platonism as influences on Augustine.[40] Some reaction to this emphasis, with the claim that Porphyry is at least as important a source as Plotinus, is found in the works of J. J. O'Meara, already mentioned.[41] The influence of Plato and Cicero has also been studied.[42] It has even been argued that there was considerable Aristotelian influence on St. Augustine.[43] If there was, it was indirect; apart from the *Categories*, he read none of Aristotle's works. Some Stoic themes, however, are apparent in his thought, especially in the *City of God*.[44]

Holy Scripture, of course, was a most important source of information for Augustine. It appears that a general index of his biblical citations is now under way in Europe.[45] An-

other religious influence, largely negative, was Manichaeism. In the past few decades, new texts have been discovered
which indicate that Augustine's reports on this religion were
precise, but also that this sect had much more variety in its
teaching than was realized either by Augustine or the historians of the nineteenth century.[46] A recent tendency is to
stress the special and restricted character of this religion in
North Africa.[47]

Psychology and Theory of Knowledge

There are several works in English on the psychology
of St. Augustine which are consciously omitted here, for
they are not reliable.[48] The outstanding study of the "trinitarian" analysis of the human soul has not been translated.[49]
A key part of his psychology is the "active" theory of sensation, in which the mind makes within itself its images of
certain events in the bodily world. This is a quite different
explanation from that of later scholasticism.[50] It is very important to our understanding of the body-soul relations in
St. Augustine.

Twentieth-century explanations of Augustine's theory
of knowledge, and especially of the divine illumination texts,
have continued to follow much the same diverse paths described by Portalié. There are still some exponents of the notion of a rather direct vision of the divine truths.[51] Opposed
to this intuitionist interpretation is the abstractionist view;
this takes Augustine's theory of intellection as an early form
of Thomistic abstraction. The "light" of the mind is thus
identified with the agent intellect.[52] A third (and, to this
writer, better) position lies somewhere between the foregoing interpretations. It would appear that St. Augustine's
divine illumination doctrine is not so much a theory of the
origin of concepts as of the manner in which the human
mind is enabled to make some *judgements* with certitude.
These judgements correspond with those which would be
called first principles of logic, mathematics, morals, and

possibly metaphysics, in later Scholasticism. Father Portalié makes a start on such an interpretation: his view has had other distinguished followers.[53] It should be noted, however, that "illumination" is still a bone of contention among Augustine scholars; some now doubt that the text of Augustine offers an intelligible account of the light metaphor.[54]

On God and His Works

Since Augustine lived long before the teaching of Catholic theology became scientifically organized (twelfth and thirteenth centuries), he can hardly be regarded as a systematic theologian like Thomas Aquinas. However, Augustine is the greatest and most influential religious writer among the Fathers; there are many introductions to his religious doctrine.[55] Especially valuable is the study of trinitarian thinking by Michael Schmaus, already mentioned.[56] Later literature on the theology of St. Augustine is fully cited in the most recent printing of his *De Trinitate.*[57]

St. Augustine's thinking on creation[58] has continued to be the subject of much argument, particularly regarding his possible anticipation of transformistic evolution. His theory of the *rationes seminales* has been taken by some interpreters as a type of evolutionism.[59] Others have vigorously denied that Augustine gives any support to Darwinism.[60] Indeed, Augustine does grant the actual appearance on earth of living members of "new" species; but, in the view of the present writer, he thinks that the *rationes* of such species have always existed in the creative mind of God. Hence, he combines a fixity of species theory (after the first six days of creation, no new *rationes seminales* are made) with a recognition of the fact that the "seeds" of certain species may lie dormant in the texture of matter, for long periods of time, before conditions are right for the actual growth of living members of these species.

Reality, as Augustine sees it, falls on three levels. God and the *rationes aeternae* constitute the top layer, characterized by absolute immutability of being. Human souls (and in a sense angelic spirits) dwell on the middle level: immutable in regard to place but mutable in time. On the lowest level are all bodily things: mutable both in space and time.[61] So situated, the soul of man is able to look upward to God and the eternal truths (this is the *conversio ad Deum*), or downward to mutable creatures (the *perversio animae*). In the upward gaze of the soul, we find the working of the *ratio superior*; in the downward glance, the *ratio inferior*. These are not two faculties of the soul but two dispositions of one and the same mind; there are no "faculties" in the psychology of Augustine. It is on the same basis that two "loves" are distinguished, and so two societies of intellectual creatures, as described in the *City of God*.[62] Similarly, the distinction of time and eternity, a topic dear to the heart of Augustine, depends on the foregoing.[63] The same theme runs through Augustine's esthetics.[64]

Grace and Predestination

Though Augustine's writings on divine grace are of major import in the history of theology, they are difficult to interpret today. One source of difficulty is the very complexity of later thinking (even among Catholics), resulting from the Renaissance controversies on grace. St. Augustine, moreover, did not stress the distinction between the natural and the supernatural, as later writers do.[65] He spoke of the original state of Adam as the "natural"[66] (as did St. Anselm of Canterbury and many Anglican theolgians), and so fallen man is, for Augustine, in a less than "natural" state. On the same basis, the *libertas* which characterizes man's highest freedom is found at its best in this original state, before the Fall. Man is helped by grace to regain something of what was lost by Adam's sin. In opposition to Pelagius, Augustine came in later life to insist more and more on the necessity of grace for good and meritorious human action.[67] A thorough study, in English, of Augustine's whole teaching on grace is much to be desired.

The rôle of divine predestination in Augustinism is well explained by Father Portalié. Augustine's views on divine fore-knowledge and the influence of God's will on man's destiny were distorted by some of the reformation thinkers. Indeed, few authors have exalted the liberty of man as did Augustine; yet few have so strongly affirmed the certainty and extent of God's knowledge of the ways in which man will use and abuse his freedom. That the relation of these two themes involves mystery and obscurity for the imperfect human mind, Augustine readily admits.[68]

Ecclesiology

While Augustine wrote no separate treatise on the Church, his whole later life was devoted to his diocese, to the ecclesiastical problems in North Africa, and indeed to Catholicism in the civilized world of his day. Of course, the Church figures prominently throughout the *City of God.*[69] Important in his ecclesiological thinking were his successive polemics against Manichaeism, Donatism, and Pelagianism.[70]

Much contemporary writing has been done on Augustine's contribution to sacramental theology. While it is clear that the term, *sacramentum*, had not yet achieved its technical usage in Augustine's time, the doctrine of the sacraments was well presented in his writings.[71] Numerous special studies of his teaching on the individual sacraments are now available.[72]

Moral Teaching

The outstanding study of Augustine's moral theory is still that of Joseph Mausbach.[73] Since he did not know the *Nicomachean Ethics* of Aristotle, St. Augustine has a different approach to moral theory from that of the later Scholastics. He makes no distinction between moral theology and ethics, stresses the love of God above all else, regards the eternal law as the immediate rule of man's life on earth.[74] Of course, in the work of a man who has written and preached so much, it is possible to find texts in which Augustine faces nearly all the problems treated in a complete course in moral theology.[75] However, his way of handling these questions (man's end and beatitude, voluntariness, principles and laws, virtues, moral conscience, and so on) is frequently rhetorical and non-technical. There are few significant differences between Augustine's answers to special moral problems and the later tradition of Catholic morality. The Decalogue supplies the foundation for the whole tradition.

Much work has been done on the political and social views of the Bishop of Hippo, particularly by English writers.[76] Gilson's *Foreword* to the *City of God* has been mentioned; it refers to many foreign language studies in this area.[77] Augustine's vision of a Christian state of mind imbued with the love of God was operative in, and distorted by, many of the political efforts of mediaeval rulers.[78]

The problem of the mysticism of St. Augustine has occasioned much controversy. Some historians consider him the most important writer on mysticism in the early Church.[79] Others deny that Augustine was a mystic at all.[80] The latter group uses a much restricted definition of mysticism. Thus the problem reduces not so much to the interpretation of Augustine as to the finding of an accepted definition. Father Boyer sums up the difficulty in these penetrating words: "M. Meyer sets up an opposition between intellectualism and mysticism. I say: if we admit this, then even the intuitive vision in Heaven will not be mystical. In that case, I wonder what mysticism is."[81] It should be understood that some hesitancy regarding the validity of Augustine's mystical experience stems from an almost disconcerting resemblance of certain ecstatic passages in the *Confessions* to texts in Plotinus' *Enneads*.[82]

Eschatology

Regarding the future life of man, Augustine's teaching is basically the same as that of present-day Catholic theology.[83] Heaven and hell are very real sanctions.[84] One editor of the *City of God* (F.W. Bussell, 1903) has tried to get rid of hell by omitting the passages which mention it.

IV. INFLUENCE

Contemporary scholarship continues to rank Augustine among the great minds in western civilization. His authority as a Christian writer is second only to the canonical writings and the official pronouncements of his Church. He is still regarded as the outstanding Father of the Church.[85] It is probably impossible to exaggerate the influence of his life and thought.

Augustine's contribution to the development of monasticism was fundamental. His *Rule* for the religious life has been followed not only by the Order which bears his name, the Augustinians, but has formed the basis for the regulation of many other religious communities.[86] Prominent among such groups is the Order of Preachers, founded by St. Dominic. The fifth Master General, Humbert de Romans, perfected the Dominican rule by means of a famous commentary on the Rule of St. Augustine.[87] As mediaeval philosophy is becoming better known, our appreciation of Augustine's rôle in its development is increasing. From Boethius to Nicholas Cusa, the story of intellectualism in the middle ages is replete with references to his works.[88] In the growth of Christian theology, Augustine is always a key author.[89]

Among modern and contemporary philosophers Augustine is read by people of widely diversified interests. We have seen how many of his works have been printed, both in Latin and in the vernaculars, throughout this century. Existentialists, phenomenologists, philosophers of history, actionists, idealists, introspective psychologists, representatives of a dozen other movements, find or think they find a patron in St. Augustine.[90]

NOTES

1. "Augustin, Saint," *Dictionnaire de théologie catholique* (Paris, Letouzey, 1902; reprinted 1923), tome I, col. 2268-2472.
2. *Introduction à l'étude de s. Augustin* (Paris, 1947), p. 329; see also, *History of Christian Philosophy in the Middle Ages* (New York, 1955), p. 591.
3. See for example the works of Sciacca, Most, Pope, Boyer, and Wolfson, cited later in this *Introduction.*
4. *La fin d'une mystification* (Paris, 1897).
5. For a list of his writings see *Bulletin de littérature écclésiastique* (Paris, 1909).
6. F. Cavallera, "Portalié, Eugène," *DTC*, 12, 2 (1934), col. 2590-2593; see also: *Etudes*, 119 (May 5, 1909) 297-302, for a memorial note.
7. Gustave Bardy, *Saint Augustin, l'homme et l'œuvre*, 6me éd. (Paris, 1946); my book, *Augustine's Quest of Wisdom* (Milwaukee, 1945), is listed by Father Boyer (*Gregorianum*, 36, 1955, 486) as an "un ouvrage semblable de langue anglaise."
8. Now unfortunately out-of-print in the best English version: *S. Augustini vita scripta a Possidio episcopo* (Latin and English), ed. H. T. Weiskotten (Princeton, 1919). There is also an English version in: E. A. Foran, *The Augustinians* (London, 1938).
9. For details, see the report in Pope, *op. cit.*, p. 10; also G. G. Lapeyre, "Saint Augustin et Carthage," *Miscellanea Agostiniana* (Roma, 1931), II, 92-100.
10. Reported by M. Leglay and Erwan Marec in "L'Afrique chrétienne," *Augustinus Magister* (Paris, 1954), I, 1-17.
11. R. Arbesmann, "A Lucky Archaeological Find," *Classical Bulletin*, 28 (1946) 9 ff.; V. Grumel, "Découverte à Ostie d'un inscription relative à sainte Monique," *Revue des études latines*, 24 (1946) 70-71.
12. Older advocates of this thesis are Adolf Harnack, S. Loofs, L. Gourdon, and W. Thimme. The most discussed later

work, in the same category, is: P. Alfaric, *L'Evolution intellectuelle de saint Augustin*, I (Paris, 1918; the second volume was never published).

13. F. Wörter, *Die Geistesentwicklung des hl. Aurelius Augustinus* Paderborn, 1892). A still useful study.

14. *Christianisme et néoplatonisme dans la formation de saint Augustin* (Paris, 1920). Much the same argument in English is found in: Garvey, Sister M. Patricia, *St. Augustine: Christian or Neo-Platonist?* (Milwaukee, 1939).

15. In *Recherches sur les Confessions de s. Augustin* (Paris, 1950), P. Courcelle argues that Milan was an important center of Neo-Platonism, during Augustine's residence, and that even St. Ambrose was well read in this philosophy. J. J. O'Meara, *The Young Augustine: The Growth of St. Augustine's Mind up to his Conversion* (London, 1954), criticizes some of Courcelle's findings but admits the strong influence of Porphyry.

16. Cf. J.-M. Le Blond, *Les conversions de saint Augustin* (Paris, 1950); M. Sciacca, *S. Agostino* (Brescia, 1954).

17. Many such studies appear in the centenary publications listed at the head of the Bibliography. The *Bibliographia Augustiniana* (Rome, 1928) by C. M. F. Nebreda is not well done; of greater help are: Gonzalez, R., "Bibliografia Augustiniana del Centenario," *Religion y Cultura*, XV (1931) 461-509; F. Van Steenberghen, "La philosophie de s. Augustin d'après les travaux du Centenaire," *Revue néoscolastique de philosophie*, 34 (1932) 366-387; 35 (1933) 106-126, 230-281. For more recent material, see the bibliographical sections of the *Revue philosophique de Louvain*; the *Revue des études augustiniennes* (Paris); and the new Spanish journal, *Augustinus* (Madrid), which began publication in 1956.

18. *Patrologia Latina*, volumes 32-47.

19. This table forms the appendix of this book. Later listings include some writings added in the twentieth century: Ueberweg-Geyer, *Grundriss der Geschichte der Philosophie*, Bd. II (Berlin, 1928), p. 96; Pope, *op. cit.*, pp. 368-383; Bourke, *op. cit.*, pp. 303-307.

20. *Œuvres de saint Augustin* (Paris, Desclée, 1948-   ). Sixteen volumes now printed; to contain about 85 vols.

21. *Corpus Christianorum*, under the direction of the Abbey of St. Pierre de Steenbrugge (The Hague, Nijhoff, 1953-   ).

22. In the *Biblioteca de Autores Cristianos* (Madrid-Escorial, 1931-   ).

23. *Op. cit.*, pp. 368-389.

24. ACW is edited by J. Quasten and J. C. Plumpe; published by the Newman Press, Westminster, Md.; first Augustine volume, 1946; 17 volumes of Augustine have now appeared.

25. FOC was founded by L. Schopp, is now directed by R. J. Deferrari; first Augustine vol. in 1947; 18 vols. of his works now in print (Fathers of the Church, Inc., 475 Fifth Ave., New York).

26. *City of God*, translated by G. G. Walsh et al., 3 vols. (1950-1954); this version is now available, with some deletions, in a paper-back volume (Doubleday Image Books, New York, 1958); *Confessions*, translated by V. J. Bourke (1953).

27. *Basic Writings of St. Augustine*, ed. W. J. Oates (New York, 1948).

28. *Les révisions*, par G. Bardy, in *Œuvres de s. Augustin*, XII (Paris, 1950).

29. S. M. Zarb, *Chronologia Operum S. Augustini* (Roma, 1934).

30. See *Augustinus Magister* (Paris, Etudes Augustiniennes, 1954), tome I, in toto; III, 27-50.

31. Dom G. Morin has devoted the whole first volume of *Miscellanea Agostiniana* (Roma, 1930) to the texts of previously un-printed *Sermones*, and notes thereon; cf. A. Kunzelmann, "Die Chronologie der Sermones des hl. Augustinus," *ibid.*, II, 417-520.

32. *Confessionum Libri Tredecim*, post P. Knoell, iteratis curis edidit Martinus Skutella (Leipzig, Teubner, 1934).

33. Consult J. J. O'Meara's translation, *Against the Academics*, ACW, 12 (Westminster, Md., 1950), and also his *The Young Augustine*, for further documentation.

34. See De Bruyne in *Miscellanea Agostiniana*, II, 327-340.

35. G. De Plinval, "Une œuvre apocryphe de saint Augustin: Le speculum 'Quis ignorat'," *Augustinus Magister*, I, 187-196.

36. E. Gilson, *Introduction à l'étude de saint Augustin*, 3me éd. (Paris, 1949); the bibliography (pp. 325-351) covers work up to 1943. F. Cayré, *Initiation à la philosophie de saint Augustin* (Paris, 1947).

37. S. J. Grabowski. *The All-Present God. A Study in St. Augustine* (St. Louis, 1954); thoroughly documented. H. Weinand, *Die Gottesidee, der Grundzug der Weltanschauung des hl. Augustinus* (Pader-

born, 1910). For an introductory anthology: E. Przywara, *An Augustine Synthesis*, introd. by C. C. Martindale, S.J., (New York, 1936).

38. For this trend, see: T. W. Battenhouse, *A Companion to the Study of St. Augustine* (New York, 1955).

39. H. A. Wolfson, *The Philosophy of the Church Fathers* (Cambridge, Mass., 1956). Only the first volume has appeared, as yet.

40. On the same theme, there are several French studies by Paul Henry; his "Augustine and Plotinus," *Journal of Theological Studies*, 38 (1937) 1-23, gives a brief summary in English.

41. In the same vein: W. Theiler, *Porphyrios und Augustin* (Halle, 1933).

42. Hans Dyroff, "Ueber Form und Begriffsgehalt der augustinischen Schrift De Ordine," in *Aurelius Augustinus* (Köln, 1930), pp. 16-62; see also his introduction to L. Schopp's translation: *Augustinus Selbstgespräche* (München, 1938).

43. N. Kaufman, "Les éléments aristotéliciens dans la cosmologie et la psychologie de s. Augustin," *Rev. néoscol. de philos.*, II (1904) 140-156.

44. Bushman, Sister Rita Marie, "St. Augustine's Metaphysics and Stoic Doctrine," *New Scholasticism*, 26 (1951) 283-302.

45. Briefly mentioned as the "fichier de de Lagarde" in *Augustinus Magister*, III, 243.

46. P. Alfaric, *Les écritures manichéennes* (Paris, 1918); A. V. W. Jackson, *Researches in Manichaeism* (London, 1931); Schmidt-Polotsky, *Ein Mani-Fund in Aegypten* (Berlin, 1933); H. C. Puech, *Le Manichéisme* (Paris, 1949); still useful is: F. C. Burkitt, *The Religion of the Manichees* (Cambridge, 1925); for further data, see *Catholic Biblical Quarterly*, VII (1945) 206-222, 306-325.

47. L. Tondelli, *Mani: Rapporti con Bardesane, S. Agostino, Dante* (Milano, 1932); L. H. Grondijs, "Manichéisme Numidien au IVme siècle," *Augustinus Magister*, III, 391-410.

48. Though not a formal treatment of the psychology, Pegis' "Mind of St. Augustine," *Mediaeval Studies*, 6 (1944) 1-61, gives the essential information; see also, Gilson, *Introduction*, pp. 31-147.

49. M. Schmaus, *Die psychologische Trinitätslehre des hl. Augustinus* (Münster i. W., 1927).

50. Cf. Gannon, Sister M. Ann Ida, "The Active Theory of Sensation in St. Augustine," *New Scholasticism*, 30 (1956) 154-180.

51. J. Hessen, *Die unmittelbare Erkenntnis nach dem hl. Augustinus* (Paderborn, 1919); *Augustinus Metaphysik der Erkenntnis* (Berlin, 1931). For a survey of recent German interpretations of "Illumination" see: F. Körner, *Das Prinzip der Innerlichkeit in Augustins Erkenntnislehre* (Würzburg, 1952).

52. C. Boyer, *L'idée de vérité dans la philosophie de s. Augustin* (Paris, 1921); "La philosophie augustinienne ignore-t-elle l'abstraction?" *Nouvelle revue théologique* (1930) 1-14; I. Sestili, "Thomae Aquinatis cum Augustino de illuminatione concordia," *Divus Thomas* (Piacenza), 31 (1928) 50-82.

53. B. Kälin, *Die Erkenntnislehre des hl. Augustinus* (Sarnen, 1920); E. Gilson, *Introduction*, pp. 88-170; for an English statement of Gilson's views on the relation of Augustine to Aquinas, see: *A Gilson Reader* (ed. A. C. Pegis [New York, 1957], pp. 68-81). Consult also: L. Keeler (ed.), *S. Augustini Doctrina de Cognitione* (Romae, 1934).

54. Notably R. Allers ("Illumination et vérités éternelles," *Augustinus Magister*, I, 477-498) and Canon F. Van Steenberghen (*Augustinus Magister*, III, 190).

55. Recommended for English readers: S. J. Grabowski, *The Church: An Introduction to the Theology of St. Augustine* (St. Louis, 1957); and his previously cited book: *The All-Present God*. The section by F. Cayré in *Les directions doctrinales de s. Augustin* (Paris, 1948), is an excellent survey. See also: A. Pincherle, *La formazione teologica di S. Agostino* (Roma, 1948); M. Grabmann, *Die Grundgedanken des hl. Augustinus über Seele und Gott* (Köln, 1929); F. Cayré, "The Great Augustinism," *Theology Digest*, II (1954) 169-173.

56. *Supra*, note 49.

57. *Œuvres de saint Augustin,* tome 15: *La Trinité* (Livres I-VII), texte, traduction et notes par M. Mellet et Th. Camelot, introduction par E. Hendriks (Paris, 1955); tome 16: *La Trinité* (Livres VIII-XV), par P. Agaësse et J. Moingt (Paris, 1955).

58. C. J. O'Toole, *The Philosophy of Creation in the Writings of St. Augustine* (Washington, 1944).

59. H. de Dorlodot, *Le darwinisme au point de vue de l'orthodoxie catholique* (Bruxelles-Paris, 1921). In a less extreme sense: L. Pera, *La creazione similtanea e virtuale secondo S. Agostino* (Firenze, 1928).

60. H. Woods, *Augustine and Evolution* (New York, 1924); M. J. McKeough, *The Meaning of the Rationes Seminales in St. Augustine* (Washington, 1926); C. Boyer, "La théorie des raisons

séminales," in *Essais sur la doctrine de s. Augustin* (Paris, 1932), pp. 97-137. For a more qualified view: E. C. Messenger, *Evolution and Theology* (New York, 1931).

61. Cf. B. J. Cooke, The Mutability-Immutability Principle in St. Augustine's Metaphysics," *The Moderm Schoolman*, XXIII (1946) 174-193; XXIV (1946) 37-49. The same theme is developed in my article, "Wisdom in the Gnoseology of St. Augustine," in *Augustinus* (Madrid, 1958).

62. See my introduction to the Image Book edition (New York, 1958) for this socio-political application of the mutability-immutability principle.

63. J. Guitton, *Le temps et l'éternité chez Plotin et saint Augustin* (Paris, 1933); J. F. Callahan, *Four Views of Time in Ancient Philosophy* (Cambridge, Mass., 1948).

64. E. Chapman, *St. Augustine's Philosophy of Beauty* (New York, 1939); K. Svoboda, *L'esthétique de s. Augustin et ses sources* (Paris, 1933).

65. On this point the research of H. de Lubac, *Surnaturel* (Paris, 1946), is fundamental.

66. *Retractationes*, 1, 10, 3: "hoc dictum ad naturam talem referatur, qualis sine vitio primitus condita est: ipsa enim vere ac proprie natura hominis dicitur." Cf. J.-B. Kors, *La Justice primitive et le péché originel d'après s. Thomas* (Le Saulchoir, 1922), p. 11.

67. C. Boyer, "Le système de s. Augustin sur la grâce," in *Essais* (Paris, 1932), pp. 206-236; V. Capanaga, *La teologia agustiniana de la gracia* (Madrid-Escorial, 1933); K. Janssen, *Die Entstehung der Gnadenlehre des hl. Augustinus* (Rostock, 1936); L. Bovy, *Grâce et liberté chez s. Augustin* (Montreal, 1939); P. Platz, *Der Römerbrief in der Gnadenlehre Augustins* (Würzburg, 1937); E. J. Carney, *The Doctrine of St. Augustine on Sanctity* (Washington, 1945).

68. Gilson, *Introduction*, p. 204. On the whole question of predestination in Augustine: J. Saint-Martin, *Le pensée de s. Augustin sur la prédestination* (Paris, 1930); A. M. Jacquin, "La prédestination d'après s. Augustin," *Miscellanea Agostiniana* (Roma, 1931), II, 855-868; A. Polman, *De Predestinatie van Augustinus, Thomas van Aquino, en Calvijn* (Franeker, 1936); T. Deman, "La théologie de la grâce," in *Augustinus Magister*, III, 247-257, cites more recent studies.

69. S. J. Grabowski, "St. Augustine and the Primacy of the Roman Bishops," *Traditio*, 4 (1946) 89-113; his later book, *The*

Church, has been mentioned *supra*, note 55. Father Portalié's colleague, P. Battifol produced a fundamental study: *Le Catholicisme de s. Augustin* (Paris, 1920). See also: F. Hofmann, *Der Kirchenbegriff des hl. Augustinus* (München, 1933); G. Spaneddo, *Il misterio della Chiesa nel pensiero di Sant' Agostino* (Sassari, 1944).

70. G. Bardy, "Manichéisme," *DTC*, IX (1927), col. 1841-1895; P. Monceaux, *Histoire littéraire de l'Afrique chrétienne*, tome VI: Donatisme (Paris, 1923); A. Guzzo, *Agostino contro Pelagio* (Torino, 1934); for criticism of the moral position of these sects, see: J. Mausbach, *Die Ethik des hl. Augustinus* (Freiburg i. B., 1909), volume II. Consult also: W. B. O'Dowd, "Development of Augustine's Opinions on Religious Toleration," *Irish Theol. Quarterly* (1919), pp. 337-348.

71. J. P. Christopher (ed.), St. Augustine, *The First Catechetical Instruction* (Westminster, Md., 1946), pp. 108-109. See also: J. Hymnen, *Die Sakramentlehre Augustinus* (Bonn, 1905); G. Pierse, "The Origin of the Doctrine of the Sacramental Character," *Irish Theol. Quarterly* (1911), pp. 196-211; C. Spallanzani, "La nozione di sacramento in S. Agostino," *Scuola Cattolica*, IX (1927) 175-188, 258-266.

72. A. Gendreau, *S. Augustini Doctrina de Baptismo* (Baltimore, 1939); B. Busch, *De initiatione christiana secundum doctrinam S. Augustini* (Romae, 1939); K. Adam, *Die geheime Kirchenbusse nach dem hl. Augustin* (Kempten, 1931); A. Reuter, *S. Augustini doctrina de bonis matrimonii* (Romae, 1942); B. A. Pereira, *La doctrine du mariage selon s. Augustin* (Paris, 1930).

73. Cited above, note 70. See also: B. Roland-Gosselin, *La morale des s. Augustin* (Paris, 1925); C. Boyer, *Saint Augustin* (*Les moralistes chrétiens*: Paris, 1932); S. J. Grou, *Morality Extracted From the Confessions*, introd. by R. Hudleston (London, 1934); J. F. Harvey, *Moral Theology of the Confessions of Saint Augustine* (Washington, 1951).

74. G. Combès, *La charité d'après s. Augustin* (Paris, 1934); A. Schubert, *Augustins Lex-aeterna-Lehre nach Inhalt und Quellen* (Münster, 1924).

75. Such a systematic collection of Augustine's moral texts has recently been made: G. Armas, *La moral de San Agustin* (Latin and Spanish) (Madrid, 1955), pp. 1, 181.

76. J. N. Figgis, *The Political Aspects of St. Augustine's City of God* (London, 1921); E. G. Sihler, *From Augustus to Augustine* (Lon-

don, 1924); E. Humphries, *Politics and Religion in the Days of Augustine* (New York, 1927).

77. Deserving of special mention: O. Schilling, *Die Staats- und Soziallehre des hl. Augustinus* (Freiburg i. B., 1910); G. Combès, *La doctrine politique de s. Augustin* (Paris, 1927); A. Brucculeri, *Il pensiero sociale di S. Agostino* (Roma, 1932).

78. H. X. Arquillière, *L'augustinisme politique. Essai sur la formation des théories politiques du moyen âge* (Paris, 1934); V. Bourke, "The Political Philosophy of St. Augustine," *Proc. Amer, Cath. Philos. Assoc.*, VII (1931), 45-55.

79. C. Butler, *Western Mysticism* (London, 1927); F. Cayré, *La contemplation augustinienne* (Paris, 1927).

80. E. Hendriks, *Augustins Verhältnis zur Mystik* (Würzburg, 1936); H. Meyer, "War Augustinus Intellektualist oder Mystiker?" *Augustinus Magister*, III, 429-437; see the same volume (pp. 103-168) for a survey of the whole problem, and for bibliography.

81. *Augustinus Magister*, III, 168.

82. Cf. P. Henry, *La vision d'Ostie* (Paris, 1938).

83. D. J. Leahy, *St. Augustine on Eternal Life* (New York, 1939); H. Eger, *Die Eschatologie Augustins* (Paderborn, 1933).

84. A. Lehaut, *L'éternité des peines de l'enfer dans saint Augustin* (Paris, 1912).

85. P. von Sokolowski, *Der hl. Augustin und die christliche Zivilisation* (Halle, 1927); C. Dawson, "St. Augustine and his Age," in *Monument to St. Augustine* (London, 1930), pp. 34-76.

86. E. A. Foran, *The Augustinians* (London, 1938).

87. P. Mandonnet, *Saint Dominique. L'idée, l'homme et l'œuvre* (Paris, 1937), vol. I, 188.

88. E. Gilson, *History of Christian Philosophy in the Middle Ages* (New York, 1955); "Pourquoi saint Thomas a critiqué saint Augustin," *Archives d'histoire doctrinale et littéraire*, I (1926-7) 5-127; M. Grabmann, *Mittelalterliches Geistesleben* (München, 1926), I, 1-62.

89. M. Grabmann, *Geschichte der katholischen Theologie* (Freiburg i. B., 1933); see also the *Patrologies* of Cayré, Quasten, and Altaner.

90. J. Geyser, *Augustin und die phaenomenologische Religionsphilosophie der Gegenwart* (Münster, 1923); E. Przywara, "St. Augustine and the Modern World," *Monument to St. Augustine*, pp. 249-286; M. Blondel, "The Latent Resources of St. Augustine's

Thought," *Ibid.*, pp. 317-353; V. Capanaga, "San Agustin en Nuestro Tiempo," *Augustinus*, II, 6 (1957) 155-175; for further references, see: P. Vignaux, "Influence augustinienne," *Augustinus Magister*, III, 265-273.

II

Reality and Knowledge

CHAPTER 4

Wisdom and Knowledge

One can read St. Augustine for many years and not be aware of the unconscious importation of foreign elements to one's understanding of him. The person who has learned Scholastic philosophy may find it very difficult to avoid coloring what he reads. Faculties of the soul, motion as a transition from potency to act, the four causes, transcendental properties of being, passivity in sense perception — these and a dozen other key attitudes are natural to a Thomist but alien to the mind of Augustine. There are verbally similar things in his writings, of course, but Augustine's outlook on God and man is simply not that of a peripatetic philosopher. Nor is modern philosophy a better training for the reading of Augustine. Today, knowledge and its problems have become a central theme: to know is to philosophize. In the mind of Augustine, knowledge has its place but it is not of transcending importance.

It is the purpose of this brief study to offer some description of the wisdom which Augustine found, and of the rôle which this wisdom plays in his general theory of knowledge. We shall try to see why the sapiential life is more than an epistemology and to suggest certain relations which Augustinian wisdom has with some types of present-day philosophy.

For this purpose, perhaps one of the best points to start with is Augustine's over-all view of reality. He was fully convinced that there are three distinct levels in substantial being. At the top is God, absolutely Immutable. On the second level are created spirits, angels and human souls. These middle beings are immutable in place but mutable in time.

The lowest level is that of bodies, mutable both in place and in time.[1] In this three-layered hierarchy of substances, God is in all ways supreme. God creates and moves creatures, both spiritual and corporeal. The human soul is moved and regulated by God. In turn, the soul of man moves and regulates bodies.[2] Thus situated, the soul is between God and bodies. The gaze of the soul, turned upward to God and divine things, is the *ratio superior*; looking downward to mutable creatures, its aspect is the *ratio inferior*. In this Augustinian sense, ratio has not the Aristotelian connotation of discursive reasoning. It is simply the gaze of the mind; for Augustine, *ratio est aspectus mentis.*[3]

THE CHARACTER OF HUMAN WISDOM

We can now place wisdom (*sapientia*) and knowledge (*scientia*) in terms of this hierarchy of realities. The formal treatment of their relations is given, as is well known, in Books XII to XIV *De Trinitate*. Briefly, human wisdom is there described as that quality of man's soul enabling him to know eternal things; while science qualifies the soul to know temporal things.[4] There are two different tasks (*officia*) which the soul must do during this life: it must keep looking in one direction toward the eternal verities, and in another toward the events of time. Wisdom pertains primarily to the higher function but is applicable to the direction of things which occur in time and place. Moreover, wisdom brings not only knowledge of the immutable, it confers a love of the eternal, the unchanging, the supreme good.[5]

Now it is not easy to say precisely *what* human wisdom is, for St. Augustine.[6] Indeed, one of the great sources of difficulty for the interpreter is Augustine's tendency to multiply the meanings of *sapientia*. It is possible to list dozens of suggested equivalents.[7] One gets the impression, of course, that wisdom is a virtue of the higher part of the soul (the *ratio superior*) but it is neither one of the four principal moral virtues enumerated by the Greek and Latin Philosophers,[8] nor is it a theological virtue. The precise relation of wisdom to charity, for instance, is a matter of obscurity. Augustine knew something of the *habitus* theory (from Cicero and the Stoics) but he does not develop an explanation of wisdom in terms of habit, as St. Thomas Aquinas will do later.[9] It is obvious that human wisdom is some sort of quality of man's soul, of course.[10] But it is more than that. It seems to imply a real and objective relation between man and God. Many of Augustine's statements about wisdom approach the notion of a special commitment, a condition of adherence both cognitive and affective, to God and the eternal truths. In fact, the earliest works (*De beata vita* and *Contra Academicos*) suggest that human wisdom is coextensive with the totality of a happy life.

HOW WISDOM IS ATTAINED

In any case, Augustine clearly teaches that no man may attain wisdom through his own unaided efforts. One must accept and work with the help of God. This point is well brought out in the famous Augustinian definition of virtue, gathered from several of his writings and discussed in the treatise on virtue in most of the mediaeval *Summas* of theology: "virtus est bona qualitas mentis, qua recte vivitur, qua nullus male utitur, quam Deus in nobis sine nobis operatur."[11] That God is the principal agency in the production of wisdom in man, as of any other human virtue, goes without saying. How God does this, is obviously a mystery to Augustine, as it is to all earthly men. Yet the doctrine of divine illumination is obviously intended by Augustine to help us to understand that man needs divine help to attain wisdom. In its simplest form illumination uses this analogy: as the sun sends forth its light to illumine sensible bodies so

that they may be seen through man's corporeal eyes, so does
God send forth His light to illumine the objects of understanding in order that they may be seen through the eye
of the human soul. The history of Augustinian scholarship
to the present day shows what difficulties and variations
of honest opinion beset any further attempt to clarify the illumination theory.[12] Indeed, there is some tendency in recent studies to claim that no coherent exegesis of the texts on
illumination is possible.[13]

There is a passage in *De Genesi ad litteram*[14] in which
Augustine makes a great effort to state how much man can
understand of divine illumination. He is explaining how
God spoke to Adam but he broadens the discussion to God's
enlightenment of any spiritual creature. He reminds us once
more of the three levels of reality and suggests that God
speaks to the spiritual creature from within rather than
through outward signs.[15] Admitting that God's illuminative
action is beyond human description and explanation (*miro et
ineffabili modo*), he sets up this comparison: as God works
upon the created spirit, so does the human soul move its
body. If man could understand precisely how his soul moves
his body in time and space (though the soul is not in space),
then he might rise to the vision of how God moves the soul
in time (though God dwells above both time and space).[16]
Yet Augustine is doubtful of man's ability to understand his
soul's function in regard to bodies, and so he is not at all
hopeful of pursuing the analogy to the level of God's action.
Indeed he says: "if man cannot grasp what goes on within
himself, how much less is his hope of grasping what goes on
above him?"[17]

To me, this means that men (and angels) should be
aware of the fact, that God helps creatures inwardly to become wise and blessed, but the operative mode of this divine
illuminative help simply surpasses creaturely understanding. Indeed, though some Augustinian scholars[18] insist that
natural illumination is clearly distinguished from super-

natural illumination by St. Augustine, I do not find this distinction in the texts. He does not think of the natural order in contrast to the supernatural.[19]

What man himself must do to achieve wisdom is expressed by Augustine in three terms: *studium*, *fides*, and *boni mores*.[20] One must actively co-operate with divine help in the eager search for wisdom. This is the theme which runs through Augustine's whole life.[21] This zealous quest does not spurn the resources of scholarship but it must start with faith in God, and confidence in the attainability of truth, and proceed in the context of a morally ordered life. To become wise is not simply to acquire knowledge but to grow in virtue. The culmination of such a life of faith, continuous searching, and good behavior, lies in the grasping of wisdom itself.

The consequences of man's attainment of wisdom are varied; they are found in the cognitive, the affective, even the metaphysical orders. The wise man knows with greater certainty and clarity; he loves the supreme good with more ardor; he exists and operates on a higher level than the *insipiens*. Let us limit our consideration, however, to the cognitive rôle of wisdom.

There is little question that Augustine associates some sort of *seeing* of the eternal truths (of numbers, morals and right thinking) with the possession of wisdom. This contemplative, or intuitive, function of the wise man is stressed in the early works (*De magistro*, *Soliloquia* and *De libero arbitrio*) and ties in with the three *visiones* teaching of *De Genesi ad litteram*.[22] Some interpreters consider this intuitive function of the soul as the essential point of his illuminative and sapiental teaching. This position is well presented in the works of F. Cayré and J. Hessen.

Another function of the wise soul consists in *judging* the information acquired through lower experience. This directive and judicative action of wisdom is encountered in the theory of the judicial numbers (Book VI, *De musica*) and in the long description of the *ratio superior* and *inferior* in the last

Books of *De Trinitate*. Certain commentators (for example,
E. Gilson and B. Kälin) take this judicative function as the
characteristic mark of the enlightened soul.

Both views are well supported in the text of Augustine
and I think we must take both into account. The wise man
sees the immutable objects of intellectual vision (but not the
essence of God in this life) and he judges the objects of the
ratio inferior in terms of the *regulae* of wisdom. There is both
a contemplative and a practical side to the cognitive function
of Augustinian wisdom. The practical work of wisdom extends to the personal attainment of happiness. The happy
life is imperfectly achieved by the wise person here on earth,
more perfectly in a future life.[23]

CONTEMPORARY RELEVANCE OF
AUGUSTINE'S WISDOM

While Augustine's language and *milieu* are different
from those of contemporary philosophy, his insights are still
pertinent to the problems of our day. In concentrating on
the subjective, the free act of personal commitment, the details of personal experience, contemporary existentialism
seems to have rediscovered the "interiorism" of St. Augustine.[24] Christian existentialists (Kierkegaard, Marcel, Jaspers)
are responding to a demand of modern man: to recover the
human element which was almost lost in the strongly objective emphases of modern science and philosophy. In Augustine, they have an important and sympathetic ally from early
Christian tradition. Even the phenomenological method is
not foreign to the Augustine who examined himself in the
Soliloquies, and the contents of his consciousness in Book X
of the *Confessions*. Perhaps the tortured progress of existentialism is a living demonstration of the need for Augustine's
fides, studium, boni mores. Yet Augustine's "unquiet heart" is
not unsympathetic to the anxieties of the modern mind.

One strong, though not dominant, trend in British and

American moral philosophy is toward ethical intuitionism. Faced with the position of analytical positivism (that all meaningful propositions must be either verifiable in sense experience or tautological), some moral writers are now arguing for a special intuition of the right and the good. While Augustine would deny the dichotomy between empiricism and intuitionism (for inner experience may be as vitally important as that of the senses), he has much to tell us about the higher insights of man's consciousness. Indeed, there is some evidence that Thomism is becoming aware of the importance of intellectual intuition.[25]

Yet St. Augustine's wisdom-theory does not offer an explanation of the origin of empirical concepts. That is not its purpose. One will look in vain in the text of Augustine for a theory of universals; it is not there. Nor do we find potency and act, or Aristotelian matter and form. Attempts to re-cast Augustine's views on wisdom and knowledge in the framework of Thomistic abstraction and epistemology are doomed to failure. Augustinian wisdom lives on a higher plane.[26]

Rather, Augustine's view has more affinity with modern value theory. The notion that man grasps cognitively certain objects of understanding which are neither Aristotelian universals nor the individual objects of sense experience, that such intelligible objects are available for all men to consult and to use as standards for the evaluation of mutable things and human actions — this approaches an objective axiology. Augustinian wisdom is discriminative, judgmental. It enables its possessor to determine what is good and what is bad in human life.

What is lacking in much contemporary philosophy is a conviction about the ultimate. If to be contemporary is to be relativistic, then Augustine is not contemporary. He is fully convinced that God exists as the supreme Good and Truth. He thinks that God gives meaning to all inferior realities. The theocentric character of his teaching is inescapable. Without God. Augustinian wisdom is nothing.

NOTES

1. *De Gen. ad. litt.*, VIII, 19-20: Neque enim est in ejus substantia qua Deus est, quod brevius sit in parte quam in toto, sicut necesse est esse, quae in locis sunt; aut fuit in ejus substantia quod jam non est, vel erit quod nondum est, sicut in naturis quae possunt temporis mutabilitatem pati.

Hic ergo incommutabili aeternitate vivens creavit omnia simul, ex quibus currerent tempora et implerentur loca, temporalibusque et localibus rerum motibus saecula volverentur. In quibus rebus quaedam spiritalia, quaedam corporalia condidit . . . Spiritalem posset, corporalis autem per tempora et loca. Cf. *De div. quaest. ad Simpl.*, I, 2, 18; *De mus.*, VI, 5, 13; *De ver. relig.*, 10, 18; *Confess.*, XI, 4, 6; *De nat. boni*, 1, 1; *De civit. Dei*, VIII, 6.

2. *De mus.*, VI, 5, 13: Oportet enim animam et regi a superiore et regere inferiorem. Superior illa solus Deus est, inferius illa solum corpus, si ad omnem et totam animam intendas.

3. *Soliloq.*, I, 6, 12: Ego autem Ratio ita sum in mentibus sicut in oculis est aspectus. See further texts and explanation in: S. Augustini, *Doctrina de cognitione*, ed. Leo W. Keeler, S.J. (Romae, Gregorianum, 1934), pp. 37-40.

4. *De Trinit.*, XII, 15, 25: ad sapientiam pertinet aeternarum rerum cognitio intellectualis, ad scientiam vero temporalium rerum cognito. Cf. *De div. quaest. ad Simpl.*, II, 2, 3.

5. *Enarr. in Ps.*, 135, 8: non incongruenter intelligimus sapientiam in cognitone et dilectione ejus quod semper est, atque incommutabiliter manet, quod Deus est.

6. Cf. K. Forster, "Metaphysische und heilgeschichtliche Betractungsweise in Augustins Weisheitsbegriff," *Augustinus Magister* (Paris, 1954), III, 382: "Im Werke *De civitate Dei* . . . ist schwerlich eine umfassende Definition zu finden." What Forster says here of wisdom in the *City of God* is generally true of all the writings. See F. Cayré, "La notion de sagesse chez saint Augustin," *Annéc théologique*, IV (1943), 433-456.

7. Thus Cayré, *art. cit.*, p. 433, enumerates thirty-one meanings of *sapientia*, and H. I. Marrou finds at least thirteen usages (*Saint Augustin et la fin de la culture antique*, Paris, 1938, pp. 564-569).

8. Though the name is used by St. Ambrose, Augustine never seems to speak of the virtues as *cardinal*. See O. Lottin, "Les vertus cardinales et leurs ramifications," *Psychologie et morale* (Louvain-Gembloux, 1949), III, 2, pp. 153-194.

9. The only place, that I know, in which he relates habit to wisdom is very brief. *De div. quaest* LXXXIII, q. 73, 2: *Sed illum habitum, qui est in perceptione sapientiae et disciplinae, Graeci vocant. . .*

10. Cf. Forster, *art. cit.*, p. 383.

11. Cf. S. Thomae Aq., *Summa theologiae*, I-II, 55, 4, *videtur quod.* The definition is gathered chiefly from *De lib. arb.*, II, 19. On the history of the definition, see Lottin, "Les premières définitions et classfications des vertus au moyen âge," *Revue des sciences philos. et théol.* (1929), p. 371.

12. "La doctrine de l'illumination reste une des plus difficiles et des plus discutées dans l'oeuvre d'Augustin." G. Bardy, "Notes complémentaires," in *Oeuvres de s. Augustin*, tome X (Paris, 1952), p. 733. For a recent survey of various interpretations of illumination in St. Augustine, see F. Koerner, *Das Prinzip der Innerlichkeit in Augustins Erkenntnislehre*, Wurzburg (Univ. Dissert.), 1952.

13. See Rudolf Allers, Communication to the Congrès International Augustinien (Paris, 1954) in *Augustinus Magister*, I, 477 ff. Canon F. Van Steenberghen agrees with Allers, *ibid.*, III, 190.

14. VIII, 20-26.

15. Intus ei quippe loquitur Deus miro et ineffabili modo, neque per scripturam corporalibus instrumentis affixam, neque per voces corporalibus auris insonantes, neque per corporum similitudines . . . (Ibid., 25, 47).

16. *Ibid.*, 20, 40.

17. Si enim quod in seipso agitur capere nondum potest, quanto minus illud quod supra est? Ibid.

18. Thus. E. Portalié, "Augustin, saint," *DTC*, I, 2236-2237; and E. Gilson, *Introduction à l'étude de s. Augustin* (Paris, 1949), pp. 111, 125.

19. See Keeler, *op. cit.*, p. 55, a: Neque solet [Augustinus] distinguere illuminationem naturalem quae ad quamlibet intellectionem requiritur, ab illuminatione fidei et gratiae.

20. *Contra Faust. manich.*, XXII, 53: Concupisti sapientiam . . . in his qui flagrant ingenti amore perspicuae veritatis,

non est improbandum studium, sed ad ordinem revocandum, ut a fide incipiat et bonis moribus nitatur pervenire quo tendit. Cf. *De Trinit., Study in St. Augustine* (St. Louis, Herder, 1954), p. 290.

21. Cf. Bourke, *Augustine's Quest of Wisdom* (Milwaukee, 1945).

22. XII, 7, 16: Haec sunt tria genera visionum . . .

23. This association of *beatitudo* with *sapientia* has cognitional as well as affective overtones. The theme is established in *De beata vita* and continued through the more mature works, such as *De civitate Dei*.

24. See V. Capánaga, "San Augustin en nuestro tiempo," Augustinus, II (1957), 155-175; A. C. Pegis, "The Mind of St. Augustine," *Mediaeval Studies*, VI (1944), 1-61. Both studies stress the *interiorism* of Augustine's psychology.

25. A much discussed recent work by B. Lonergan (*Insight*, New York: Philosophical Library, 1957) endeavors to relate the Thomistic theory of *intellectus* to the use of human understanding in contemporary science and metaphysics. Lonergan is influenced by the work of J. Maréchal.

26. This is made very clear in the essay by the eminent Thomist, Jacques Maritain "De la sagesse augustinienne," *Revue de philosophie*, 37 [1930], 715-741).

CHAPTER 5

Man's Approach to God

In his review of his own writings Augustine advises us to read his works in the order in which they were written, if we wish to follow the progress of his thought.[1] With that injunction in mind we propose to examine chronologically a remarkable series of texts illustrating Augustine's view on the spiritual growth of man in terms of the soul's movement toward union with God.[2] Two points in Augustine's thought will provide the context for our study of these passages: (1) his three-level ontology, and (2) his psychology of the tripartite soul.

As Augustine looked at the whole of reality he saw bodies existing on the lowest level of being, souls on the second level, and God dwelling at the top. There are only these three kinds of 'natures': the corporeal is subject to change in both space and time; the psychic changes temporally but not spatially; the divine nature is absolutely changeless. Furthermore, he insists that there is no intermediary nature between man's soul and God.[3] The spirit of man may choose to look upward to God and eternal verities (the *ratio superior*) or to look downward to bodies with their many changes (*ratio inferior*). This schematism is value oriented, for Augustine obviously thinks that the good life for man depends on his turning upwards to God (*conversio ad Deum*). As he says in *Letter* 18: "That highest [nature] is essential blessedness; the lowest, that which can be either blessed or wretched; and the intermediate nature lives in wretchedness when it stoops to that which is lowest, and in blessedness when it turns toward that which is highest."

Within the working of the human spirit, Augustine distinguishes three specific functions: mind (*mens*) is the soul as knowing; memory (*memoria*) is the soul retaining its contents; and will (*voluntas*) is the soul as acting in any way. These are not three distinct faculties, in the Scholastic sense of the term; they are simply three aspects of man's mental activity. Thus Augustine explains: "Since memory, understanding and will are not three lives but one life, nor three minds but one mind, it follows certainly that they are not three substances but one substance."[4] The human soul (in the broadest sense, *anima*) is called *animus* when Augustine wishes to stress its conscious features. It is called *ratio* (reason) when considered as looking toward any object: "*ratio sit quidam mentis aspectus*."[5] Finally, it is called *spiritus*, in Augustine's terminology, when one is thinking of its incorporeal nature and functions.

Having established these preliminaries, let us now examine a chronological series of passages dealing with the approach of man's spirit to God.

EARLY PERIOD: A.D. 388-400

In one of his youthful psychological treatises, *The Greatness of the Soul* (A.D. 388), Augustine described for the first time seven grades of soul energy.[6] The lowest level, animation (*animatio*) is that on which the soul gives life to its body, *praesentia sua vivificat*. A step higher is sensation (*sensus*), which is the soul perceiving through the sensory organs of the body. The third level is the use of artistic skills (*ars*), the force of the soul reasonably directing man's actions in all the arts of living, whether useful or fine. Fourth is the grade called evaluation or virtue (*virtus*) which involves the discernment of good things. This entails a purification of human effort and is the beginning of man's spiritual/moral growth. Next is the level of stabilization (*tranquillitas*) in which the soul rests quietly in itself, *in seipsa laetissime tenet*. Sixth is the grade of fixation (*ingressio*) in which the soul directs its attention toward the highest object of vision. Finally there is contemplation (*contemplatio*), the serene vision of truth.

By way of comment, we may note two things in this text. In the first place it is a cognitive analysis of man's ascent to Truth. And among these seven levels we have but four steps in man's spiritual progress, for that begins only at the fourth grade.

In another work of the same period, *On Genesis Against the Manichees* (A.D. 388-390), we find seven stages of spiritual development described allegorically.[7] Augustine suggests that the first day of creation signifies man's gaining the light of faith: *fidem Dominus visibiliter apparere dignatus est.* The second day means that man distinguishes things of the flesh from those of the spirit: *quo discernit inter carnalia et spiritalia.* The third day prefigures man freeing his soul from the stain of passions: *mentem suam . . . a labe et fluctibus tentationem carnalium . . . secernit.* He takes the fourth day to mean man's vision of spiritual truths in the light of the Immutable Truth: *videt quae sit incommutabilis veritas, quae tamquam sol fulget in anima.* The fifth day means man's acting to serve his brothers: *in actionibus . . . propter utilitatem fraternae societatis.* The sixth day suggests the submission of one's soul to the control of justice and reason: *anima . . . rationi et justitiae serviens.* Last, the seventh day stands for man's resting in the hope of lasting peace: *speret homo . . . quietem perpetuam.*

Noteworthy in these allegories are the facts that all seven steps are of spiritual significance, the introduction of divine illumination at stage four, and the stress on social activism in stage five. This is not so much a psychological analysis as it is a pious meditation on the flowering of faith within the soul. There is little doubt that the seventh step is some sort of union with God.

A year or so later, in the work *On True Religion* (A.D. 389-390), Augustine presented another cognitive series of steps.[8] (1) Immutable law is seen to be higher than reason itself: *At ratione praestantior lex immutabilis.* (2) God is this law: *Deus summa ista lex est, secundum quam ratio judicat.* (3) Unity in bodies is but a vestige of the unity seen by the mind: *Unitatis in corporibus est vestigium, sed ipsa unitas nonisi mente conspicitur.* (4) Eternal values, such as wisdom, beauty and goodness, are discovered above one's soul, in God: *noli foras ire, in teipsum redi, in interiore homine habitat veritas . . . transcende et teipsum . . . Illuc ergo tende, unde ipsum lumen rationis accenditur.* (5) As spiritual remedies, Augustine suggests that reflection will cure sensuality, and charity will take care of pride. (6) True religion (*religio*) is not a matter of fanciful imagery (*in phantasmatis nostris*); the worship of earthly or watery things (*terrarum cultus et aquarum*), or the perfected soul in itself (*vel ipsa perfecta et sapiens anima rationalis*). (7) Religion binds us to the one, omnipotent God; as Truth he abides above our minds with no intervening creature (*inter mentem nostram . . . et veritatem . . . nulla interposita creatura est*).

Here we may observe in the domain of reason another version of man's ascent to God. Even though he starts with immutable truth and recognizes quickly that this is divine, Augustine takes seven steps to make explicit the meaning of man's approach to God. This is a continuation of the theme of his earliest philosophical dialogues, in which thought moves from corporeal things to incorporeal.[9] Some interpreters regard this passage in the work *On True Religion* as a key analysis of man's spiritual progress.[10]

In *The Lord's Sermon on the Mount* (A.D. 393-394) we find a quite different seven step series toward blessedness.[11] (1) Fear is the beginning of blessedness: *initium autem sapientiae timor Domini.* (2) Meekness signifies a certain stability in one's eternal heritage. (3) The sorrow of those who mourn turns one from earthly joys to God. (4) Hunger makes us lovers of truth and immutable goodness. (5) Mercy brings the achievement of blessedness. (6) Clean-heartedness, purgation, prepares one for the vision of God. (7) Peacemaking brings us to perfection: *in pace perfectio est.*

What we have here is a combination of the Beatitudes with the gifts of the Holy Spirit. Much of the analysis of spiritual progress in this text involves affective dispositions,

such as fear and sorrow. No longer a set of stages in the life
of reason, it is an advance toward spiritual peace in the affective order. However, perfection in this final peace involves the subjection of man's emotional tendencies to the
direction of reason, of the mind, and of the spirit.[12]

A similar advance through the seven gifts of the Holy
Spirit is offered in *Christian Instruction* (A.D. 397)[13]: (1) Fear
turns one to the knowledge of God's will. (2) Piety leads to
respect for Holy Scripture. (3) Knowledge turns our love
toward God. (4) Fortitude brings one to take delight in eternal values. (5) Mercy cleanses sordid thoughts and turns one
to love of neighbor. (6) Cleanliness of heart leads us to the
vision of Truth, even though we see it obscurely. (7) Wisdom brings full enjoyment of final peace.[14]

It is noteworthy that the steps described in *The Lord's
Sermon on the Mount* and in *Christian Instruction* depart from the
psychological analyses of the earlier works. The first period
of his episcopacy finds Augustine devoting much time to the
study of Scripture. Although this turned his attention in part
from the Platonic psychology evident in the early dialogues,
Augustine did not abandon his efforts to discover a rational
explanation of the stages in man's spiritual journey to God.
The texts from his middle period, which we will now consider, exhibit the continuing influence of Plotinus and Porphyry as well as a growing competence in biblical exegesis.

MIDDLE PERIOD: A.D. 400-416

From the *Confessions* to *The Trinity* Augustine is of
course engrossed with the problem of man's spiritual growth
but no longer with seven stages of ascent. Rather, the pattern has been simplified to one that became commonplace in
medieval spiritual exercises. Ascent becomes a three-stage
schematism: withdrawal from the world of bodies, concentration on the soul in its most incorporeal features, and
elevation of attention to God above the soul.

A much-quoted sentence in the *Confessions* (A.D.
397-401) says precisely this: "thus admonished to turn back
to my very self, I entered into my innermost parts under
your guidance . . . and I saw . . . above my mind the immutable Light."[15] The pattern is clear: from outside the
mind, to inside the mind, to what is above my mind. It
would be possible to illustrate this triple-graded progress
from many other texts in the *Confessions* but there is another
passage in which seven steps may be seen.

> And so, step by step (*gradatim*) from (1) bodies, to (2)
> the soul which senses through the body, and thence to
> its (3) interior power to which the sense organs report
> about external things . . . further to (4) the reasoning
> power . . . which lifted itself to (5) its understanding
> . . . whence it discovered (6) the Immutable itself . . .
> and in the flash of a trembling glance (7) reached up to
> That Which Is.[16]

Later in the famous vision at Ostia, when Augustine
and his mother rose to some sort of spiritual contact with
God, the climax is reached "with a click of the heart" (*toto ictu
cordis*).[17] This suggests an affective, rather than a cognitive,
experience.

Whether there is also some indication of mystical experience in these and similar passages in the *Confessions* is
much debated. Dom Cuthbert Butler called these experiences "identical in kind with those described by the later mys-
tics."[18] Gerald Bonner agrees.[19] E. Hendrikx, on the other
hand, calls Augustine "a great enthusiast but no mystic."[20]
However this may be, it is quite clear that the theme of conversion to God, the volitional turning of one's will toward
the highest good, is the central theme of the *Confessions*.[21] We
are well beyond a purely rationalistic search for truth.

A dozen years later Augustine was asked by the Lady
Paulina to explain how one may 'see' God. His answer is a
lengthy letter important for our understanding of what may

happen in the final stage of man's approach to God.[22] He first distinguishes ocular vision — the soul seeing through the eyes of its body — from the mental vision of such facts as "that you are living, that you have a desire for God, that you wish to fulfill that desire, that you know that you are alive and willing and seeking, that you do not know that you are alive and willing and seeking, that you do not know how God may be seen," and so on.[23] Then, and not for the last time, Augustine faces two apparently conflicting texts from the New Testment: Mt 5:8 — "Blessed are the pure of heart: for they shall see God" — and, in contrast, Jn 1:18 — "No one has at any time seen God."[24] His solution to this puzzle suggests that while no one sees the nature of God, clearly and directly, in this life, some people may see God, in this life, through some sort of 'appearance' which conceals God's nature.[25] What Augustine now stresses is man's need *to will* that such a vision occur. He cites his older contemporary, St. Ambrose, in support of this claim that one must really wish to see God, before he can be seen, even obscurely.[26]

Etienne Gilson regarded this *Letter* 147, *to Lady Paulina*, as an important text for Augustine's differentiation of the natural intellectual seeing of truth from the supernatural vision of God. The whole second part of Gilson's classic *Introduction to the Study of St. Augustine* is an expansion of this theme of the approach to God, through willing.[27]

If the *Letter to Paulina* be dated A.D. 412/413, then within a year or so Augustine had returned to the problem of the vision of God in the last Book of his *Literal Commentary on Genesis* (A.D. 414). There, in an effort to explain St. Paul's rapture as a spiritual experience, Augustine takes the injunction, "You shall love your neighbor as yourself," as an example and then describes in relation to it three kinds of vision.[28] He says that we see the letters in which this precept is written by looking through the eyes of the body (*per oculos corporis*). On the second level of vision, we may see through the spirit (*per spiritum hominis*) the meaning of the word neighbor. This is an act of 'cogitating' a person (who is not present, as would be the case on the first level of vision) through images that are retained in interior sensation. It should be noted that this usage of 'spirit' is not identical with later Christian terminology but owes something to Pauline language and to Plotinian psychology. The third and highest level of human vision is accomplished through mental intuition (*per contuitum mentis*), whereby one sees immaterially the meaning of love, without having any image of it. This, according to Augustine, is imageless thought.

The implication of this discussion is that St. Paul saw God on the level of the third type of vision. There is a growing emphasis in this period of Augustine's thinking on the affective side of these higher experiences. Willing and loving add a new dimension to man's ascent to God.

In *The Trinity*, at about this same time (A.D. 412-416), Augustine examined analytically the union of the soul with God in the act of loving. At the start of the last Book (15) on *The Trinity*, he wrote:

> If we recall where it was in these Books that a trinity first began to show itself to our understanding, the eighth Book is what occurs to us; since it was there that, to the best of our power, we tried to raise the aim of the mind to understand that most excellent and immutable nature, which is not our own mind (*ad intellegendum illam praestantissimam naturam quod nostra mens non est*). But when we came to treat of love which in Sacred Scripture is called God (*ad caritatem quae in sancta scriptura Deus dicta est*) then a trinity began to dawn upon us a little, that is: the lover (*amans*), that which is loved (*quod amatur*), and love (*amor*).[29]

Going back to the eighth Book, written possibly some years earlier, we find this text:

> You certainly do not love anything except what is good, since good is the earth . . . an estate . . . a house . . .

a beautiful poem . . . This thing is good and so is that, but take away this and that and look at good itself (*et vide ipsum bonum*), if you can. So will you see God; not Good by a good that is other than Himself but the Good of all good . . . . So, God is to be loved, not as this and that good, but the good itself. For the good that must be sought for the soul is not one above which it is to fly by making a judgment but to which it is to cleave by loving (*bonum animae, non cui superuolitet iudicando sed cui haeret amando*) and what is this except God? Not a good mind, or a good angel, or a good heaven, but the good good (*sed bonum bonum*).[30]

These texts from *The Trinity* have been quoted at some length in order to show the context in which Augustine, in his middle period, puts spiritual progress in terms of the love of goodness itself. He still speaks of trying to understand God (*ad intellegendum illam praestantissimam immutabilemque naturam*) but this is now a movement within the ambit of divine charity.

LATE PERIOD: A.D. 418-429

We come finally to the time when Augustine began to stress the way in which divine grace affects man's spiritual life. In this period he became concerned with the teachings of Pelagius, whom he had hardly known before A.D. 415. Augustine felt that Pelagius was minimizing the role of God's grace in the growth of the human spirit. Since Pelagius claimed the support of Ambrose's writings, Augustine now turned to a more thorough study of the sermons and commentaries of the famous Bishop of Milan. The result of this anti-Pelagian activity is obvious in the treatise on *The Grace of Christ and Original Sin* (A.D. 418).[31] First Augustine states that men cannot avoid sin without the aid of grace (*agitur de auxilio gratiae, quo ad non peccandum adjuvamur*). Then he quotes and agrees with Ambrose's *Commentary on Luke* (2, 84) that "no man is able to undertake anything without the Lord" (*nemo custodire sine Domino*). He adds that Ambrose also taught that any growth in man's love of God results solely from the gift of grace (*etiam ipsam dilectionem, qua quisque amplius diligit, ad beneficium gratiae pertinere*). Augustine is now clearly teaching that only some people are called by God to spiritual beatitude. Quoting Ambrose again (*On Luke* 9:53) to the effect that God calls those whom he deems worthy (*quos dignatur vocat*) and makes any person religious whom he so wills (*et quem vult religiosum facit*), Augustine approves and adds: "For this reason, unless God enable one to do a deed, who can do it?" (*Quapropter, nisi a Deo fiat, ut hoc faciat, qui hoc facit?*)

Man's complete spiritual dependence on God is the theme of these mature years. Augustine placed less stress on the psychic *ascent* of the soul to God and more emphasis on God's *condescension* to man. These anti-Pelagian writings fascinated many theologians during the Reformation and induced some to dwell upon the weakness of the human will, left to itself, and to concentrate on the problem of predestination.

These emphases run throughout the *Enchiridion, on Faith, Hope and Charity* (A.D. 421). True liberty (*libertas*), he wrote, comes only from divine grace (*ista libertas unde erit . . . nisi redimat?*).[32] Quoting St. Paul (Ep 2:8), "By grace you have been saved through faith," Augustine adds that faith and liberty are both gifts from God, the whole thing is given by God (*totum Deo detur*). Eternal life, the reward of good works, is called the grace of God by the Apostle Paul.[33]

The City of God, in its last Book (A.D. 425-426), continues this teaching that spiritual progress depends entirely on divine condescension. Indeed we find here Augustine's own words for spiritual growth, *institutio spiritalis*:[34]

So then, in regard to spiritual growth (*institutio spiritalis*), whereby a man is formed in piety and righteousness, the Apostle says, 'Neither is he that planteth anything, nor he that watereth, but God that giveth increase' (I Co 3:7); so also must it be said that he who has intercourse and inseminates does nothing, but rather God gives the essential form (*nec qui concumbit, nec qui seminat, est aliquid; sed qui format Deus*). He alone, coupling and connecting in some wonderful fashion the spiritual and corporeal natures, the one to command, the other to obey, he makes a living being.

In such spiritual development seven steps may again be discerned: (1) animation (*anima*); (2) consciousness (*mens, ratio, intelligentia*); (3) intuition of truth (*perceptio veritatis*); (4) love of the good (*amor boni*); (5) wisdom (*sapientia*); (6) moral virtues (*prudentia, fortitudo, temperantia, justitia*); and (7) desire fixed on the highest good (*desiderium summi boni*).[35]

This remarkable text from *The City of God* draws together his sevenfold analysis of spiritual progress found in the early works and his mature emphasis on man's complete spiritual dependence on God.

Two writings from his last years maintain this view. In *Grace and Free Choice* (A.D. 426-427) we are told that, "God works in the hearts of men to incline their wills wherever he wills, whether to good deeds according to his mercy, or to evil after their own deserts."[36] And the theme of divine condescension is again stated: "God will give you understanding . . . Wisdom itself comes down from above, as the Apostle James tells us."[37] Then, in the *Predestination of the Saints* (A.D. 428-429), the elderly Augustine reminds us that all our accomplishments stem from God:[38]

Therefore in what pertains to religion and piety . . . if we are not capable of thinking anything is of ourselves, but our sufficiency is of God, we are certainly not capable of believing anything is of ourselves, since we cannot do this without thinking; but our sufficiency, by which we begin to believe, is of God (*sufficientia nostra qua credere incipiamus ex Deo est*).

He goes on to say that, like St. Cyprian before him, he had thought as a young man that faith is in us from ourselves (*a nobis esse in nobis*) but he now realizes that faith is preceded in us by God's grace.[39]

There is no doubt that Augustine was aware of a considerable shift in his views on moral and spiritual development. Yet we find six themes recurring throughout.

I. The threefold pattern: withdrawal from the world, concentration on the soul, rising above the soul to God.

II. Stress on religious conversion as man's will turning to God.

III. A suggestion of mystical experience, even if its character be somewhat ambiguous.

IV. The tendency to combine psychological ascent with divine descent.

V. Spiritual love (*caritas*) adds a new dimension to the highest understanding.

VI. The climax of spiritual growth comes in a final peace of the spirit, described in poetic rapture in the last Book of *The City of God*:

> What will the spirit of man be like, when it has no vice at all, and gives way to no one, nor yields to any, nor fights even a praiseworthy battle against anything—when it is perfected in the most peaceful virtue (*pacatissima virtute perfectus*)? How sure then will its knowledge be of the grandeur and beauty of all things—a knowledge without error or labor, in which the wisdom of God will be drunk from its very source (*ubi Dei sapientia de ipso suo fonte potabitur*), accompanied by the highest happiness and stripped of all trouble (*cum summa felicitate, sine ulla difficultate*)?[40]

Surely this is the elderly bishop trying to convey to his readers what he, and they, may look forward to in heaven.

NOTES

1. *Retractationes* 1, prologo: "Inveniet enim fortasse, quomodo scribendo profecerim, quisquis opuscula mea ordine quo scripta sunt legerit."

2. For the terminology of Augustine's spiritual teaching, see W.A. Schumacher, *Spiritus and Spiritual* (Chicago: Mundelein, 1957). Except for one article by Fulbert Cayré, the symposium edited by Agostino Trapé, *Sanctus Augustinus Vitae Spiritualis Magister* (Rome: Analecta Augustiniana, 1956) is of no great scholarly value.

3. *De musica* 6, 5, 13: "Oportet enim animam et regi a superiore, et regere inferiorem. Superior illa solus Deus est, inferius illa solum corpus, si ad omnem et totam animam intendas." Earlier in the same book (6, 1, 1) he had spoken of the one God, "qui humanis mentibus nulla natura interposita praesidet." For more texts on this three-level ontology, see my *Augustine's View of Reality* (Villanova, PA: University Press, 1964).

4. *De Trinitate* 10, 11, 18. This 'trinitarian' analysis of psychic activity runs throughout Books IX to XV.

5. *De quantitate animae* 27, 53. In this passage *ratio* is kept quite distinct from discursive reasoning, which Augustine calls *ratiocinatio*.

6. *De quantitate animae* 33, 70-76.

7. *De Genesi contra Manichaeos* 1, 25, 43.

8. *De vera religione* 30, 54; 31, 57; 32, 59; 39, 72; 42, 79; 55, 108; and 55, 113.

9. *Retractationes* 1, 6: "per corporalia cupiens ad incorporalia . . . ducere."

10. See M.F. Sciacca, *Sant' Agostino* (Brescia: Morcelliana, 1949) pp. 298-300.

11. *De sermone Domini in monte* 1, 1, 3; 2, 4; 2, 5; 2, 6; 2, 7; 2, 8; 2, 9.

12. Thus he speaks in the last text (*De sermone* 2, 9) of "omnes animi sui motus . . . componentes et subjicientes rationi, id est menti et spiritui."

13. *De doctrina Christiana* 2, 7, 9-11.

14. E. Gilson, *Introduction à l'étude de saint Augustin* (Paris: Vrin, 1949) p. 160, note 1, suggests that these seven grades in *De*

doct. Christ. parallel the last four steps in *De quantitate animae* 33, 70-76. i.e. *virtus, tranquillitas, ingressio* and *contemplatio*.

15. *Confessiones* 7, 10, 16: "Et inde admonitus redire ad memetipsum intravi in intima mea duce te . . . et vidi . . . supra mentem meam lucem incommutabilem."

16. *Conf.* 7, 17, 23: "Atque ita gradatim a corporibus ad sentientem per corpus animam atque inde ad eius interiorem vim, cui sensus corporis exteriora nuntiaret . . . atque inde rursus ad ratiocinantem potentiam . . . quae se quoque in me comperiens mutabilem erexit se ad intelligentiam suam . . . unde nosset ipsum incommutabile . . . et pervenit ad id quod est, in ictu trepidantis aspectus."

17. *Conf.* 9, 10, 24: "Nam fuisse et futurum esse non est aeternum. Et dum loquimur et inhiamus illi, attingimus eam modice, toto ictu cordis."

18. *Western Mysticism*, 2nd ed. (London: Constable, 1926) p. 46.

19. Gerald Bonner, *St. Augustine of Hippo* (Philadelphia: Westminster Press, 1963) p. 83, says that what is described in *Conf.* 7 might "be regarded as a mystical experience."

20. *Augustins Verhältnis zur Mystik* (Wurzberg 1936) p. 176.

21. See J. M. LeBlond, *Les conversions de saint Augustin* (Paris 1960) who stresses throughout the theme of *conversio ad Deum* in the *Confessions*.

22. *Ep.* 147, *De videndo Deo.*

23. *Ep.* 147, 1, 3.

24. *Ep.* 147, 6, 19: "Beati mundo corde: ipsi enim Deum videbunt," and "Deum nemo vidit umquam."

25. Ibid., the key sentence is: "Illi autem ideo viderunt, quicumque Deum viderunt, quia cui voluerit, sicut voluerit, apparet ea specie, quam voluntas elegerit, etiam latente natura."

26. Ambrose, *Super Lucam* 1, 1, 11; cited in *Ep.* 147, 6, 17-18.

27. See Gilson, *Introduction,* pp. 150-245. In English this book is entitled *The Christian Philosophy of St. Augustine*, translated by Larry Lynch (New York: Random House, 1960).

28. *De Genesi ad litteram* 12, 6, 15. My *Essential Augustine* (Indianapolis: Hackett, 1974) prints an English version by John H.

Taylor of this passage, pp. 93-95; the *Commentary* is now translated and will soon be published in the ACW series.

29. *De Trinitate* 15, 6; for the Latin see the critical edition by W. J. Mountain, in CC 50 and 50a (1968).

30. *De Trin.* 8, 3; CC, vol. I: 271-272.

31. *De gratia Christi et peccato originali* 1, 43, 46; 1, 43, 47; and 1, 46, 51.

32. *Enchiridion de fide, spe et caritate* 30.

33. Ibid. chapters 31-32 and 107.

34. *De civitate Dei* 22, 24.

35. Ibid. "Ipse itaque (1) animae humanae (2) mentem dedit, ubi ratio et intellegentia in infante sopita est quodam modo . . . excitanda scilicet atque exserenda aetatis accessu, qua fit scientiae capax atque doctrinae, et habilis (3) perceptioni veritatis et (4) amoris boni: qua capacitate haurit (5) sapientiam (6) virtutibusque praedita, quibus prudenter, fortiter, temperanter, et juste, adversus errores et cetera ingenerata vitia dimicet, eaque nullius rei (7) desiderio nisi boni illius summi atque immutabilis vincat." (Parenthetical numbers added.)

36. *De gratia et libero arbitrio* 43.

37. Ibid. 46; see Jm 1:17 and 3:17.

38. *De praedestinatione sanctorum* 2, 5.

39. Ibid. 3, 7.

40. *De civitate Dei* 22, 24, 5.

CHAPTER 6

The Problem of a World Soul

Attention has been directed to St. Augustine's interest in the possible existence of a cosmic soul (*anima mundi*) by two books dealing with a mediaeval controversy of the ninth century.[1] Actually, this dispute did not treat directly the question of a cosmic soul but rather the closely related theory of a universal soul for all men. What ties in the controversy with Augustine studies is the fact that both sides of the ninth-century dispute agree that the focal point of their discussion is a text from St. Augustine's *De quantitate animae*.[2]

It appears that Bishop Odo (consecrated in 861) became disturbed at the teaching of a theory of a universal soul by an anonymous monk of Beauvais who had written a treatise expounding the views of his teacher, Maccarius Scotus. According to Maccarius and his pupil, Augustine had intended to say in the treatise *De quantitae animae* that there is neither one soul only, nor simply many souls, but that soul is at once one and many.[3] At the insistence of Odo, Ratramnus of Corbie wrote a refutation of this interpretation of Augustine. Throughout Ratramnus' work (which is the *De Anima* edited by Lambot) the notion that Augustine held a universal soul for all men is strongly, and very properly, criticized. However, Ratramnus maintains also that, when Augustine speaks of soul as one, he is considering it as a *species*. Thus Augustine is made to talk of "soul" as if it were a universal concept. This makes good sense to Ratramnus, for he has a conceptualistic theory of universals[4] and he gives a clever explanation of Augustine's text in terms of this conceptualism. However sound Ratramnus' position may have been doctrinally, and pleasing to Bishop Odo, it does not appear that he was well informed historically on the position of St. Augustine.[5] That is why this controversy makes an excellent introduction to our present question: what precisely did Augustine write about the cosmic soul?

It is in a treatise written A.D. 387 that we find our first important text.[6] Augustine states that *species* are handed down to bodies *through soul*, and that body gets its subsistence and comes into being by receiving species through soul. Further, he says that body exists by the very fact that it is animated, either *universally* as in the case of the world, or *particularly* as in the case of individual animals in the world. Of course, this is a very important text. Reviewing his treatises, in 426-427, Augustine twice calls this passage a "rash" statement.[7] This later comment is the basis for the judgment of some Augustinian scholars, that Augustine eventually rejected the cosmic soul.

In the following year (A.D. 388) Augustine wrote the passage which became the bone of contention for our ninth-century controversialists.[8] With customary frankness, he admits that he does not know what to say on the number of souls. The claim that there is but one soul is disturbing because it is hard to explain how such a unique soul could be at once happy in one man and unhappy in another. On the other hand, to say that soul is at once one and many is to invite ridicule. Finally, Augustine concludes that to say that there are simply plural individual souls (apparently excluding completely any universal soul) is something which would make him laugh at himself.

Certainly there is much that is confusing in this text and it is no wonder that his readers in the ninth century were puzzled by it. He does not go on to explain why the third position is ridiculous (that there are many souls existing and no universal soul) nor does he return to the clarification or rejection of this passage at the time when he reviewed his works.[9] All that a careful reader may gather today is that, in the year 388, Augustine felt it was rather foolish to exclude the possibility that there exists a universal soul.

In 389, in the course of a lengthy discussion of the order, number, and consequent beauty of this world, Augustine remarks that the soul seeks constancy and eternity in this world but does not find it. For, he continues, the lower sort of beauty reaches perfection in the passing away of things. Whatever imitation of constancy is found in this lower beauty is conveyed *through soul* from the highest God. The reason for this is that the species (or form) which is mutable in time only [this type of species pertains to soul] is prior to the sort of species [that is, of bodies] which is mutable both in time and place.[10]

Now, there is no explicit reference to cosmic soul in this text, yet in his later comment on it Augustine shows that he had such a soul in mind when he wrote it. In a long review of the passage, he connects it with the previously noted text from *De immortalitate animae*.[11] He first points out that, if this text of *De musica* be understood as referring to the beauty of the bodies of men and animals, it is rationally evident that these animated bodies do receive their constancy, their order and beauty, through soul.[12] For the soul is that which holds the animated body together and keeps it, while alive, from the disintegration which appears at death. However, if this same lower beauty is meant to be that of *all bodies*, then this view *forces* one to believe that this world is an animal, in the sense that whatever imitation of constancy there be in this world is also conveyed to it *through soul* from the highest God.[13] Augustine adds that though Plato and many other philosophers have thought that this world is an animal (in other words, they did accept the existence of a cosmic soul) he has been unable to find rational proof of the theory, or any confirmation of it in Holy Scripture.[14] It is at this point in his comment that Augustine mentions again the passage in *De immortalitate animae* which we have examined. He repeats here that his statement was "*temere dictum.*" Then Augustine gives his exact position in the year 427: "I do not assert that this statement, that the world is an animal, is

false, nor do I understand that it is true."[15] Notice that this
is a formal explanation of the meaning of "temere dictum
est." He did not mean to reject the cosmic soul. What he intended to say was that he could find no firm ground for
either accepting or denying the world soul.

It is in 389 or 390 that Augustine turns to the religious
aspect of the cosmic soul theory. He now says that he can
see no religious error in accepting the world soul, provided
this cosmic soul is not taken to be God. Man's soul must
avoid giving divine worship to the cosmic soul, to bodies, or
to its own phantasms.[16] That he is definitely thinking of the
cosmic soul as the object which should not be worshiped
becomes clear from a reading of the comment on the passage
which Augustine gave in the *Retractationes*.[17] He plainly
states that he used "soul" (*animam*) in this text, *De vera
religione*, to name the whole incorporeal creation (*pro universa
creatura incorporali*) and he admits that this is not a biblical
usage. As Augustine understands it, whenever "soul" is used
in Scripture, not metaphorically, it means the vital principle
of mortal animals, in which genus men are included. In
other words, Augustine holds that in biblical usage "soul"
never means cosmic soul. He adds nothing more. He does
not say, as we might expect, that the cosmic soul is a foolish
myth of the pagans. He merely says what he knows: Holy
Scripture does not speak of a cosmic soul.

This is probably why little is said on the world soul
theory in the several famous commentaries on Genesis
which Augustine wrote. However we do find a passage in
the first of these treatises on Genesis suggesting that Genesis
I, 2 may be interpreted as favorable to the cosmic soul.[18]
Commenting on the phrase: *et spiritus Dei superferebatur super
aquam*, he says that this "spirit" of God may possibly mean
a vital creature which holds together and moves the visible
universe and all bodies in it. Augustine further submits that
this universal "spirit" may be the principle of all the opera-
tions in this bodily world. Thus it would be an invisible

creature, superior to all bodily things, and not absurdly called the "spirit" of God.

Lest we too hastily dismiss this *Incomplete Commentary on Genesis*, first written in 393-394, let us examine carefully Augustine's later comment on it.[19] He admits that it was the work of a novice in Scripture studies and is much less valuable than his *De Genesi ad litteram, Libri XII*. Then he states that he re-read the *Incomplete Commentary* when he was reviewing his treatises in the *Retractations* and revised the *Incomplete Commentary* for publication in 427.[20] It is noteworthy, then, that Augustine not only makes no criticism of this interpretation of the "spiritus" of God, in the *Retractations*, he allows the passage to stand for future readers.[21]

The year 400 is the approximate date of still another text in which Augustine refers to the cosmic soul.[22] He now mentions the view of certain pagan writers that Jove is the "soul" of the world, and that this cosmic soul, as well as the human soul, becomes wise by participation in the highest Wisdom. Augustine cannot approve this teaching about Jove, of course. Still he says that Catholic thinkers can agree and even insist on the point that all souls become wise through participation in the Wisdom of God. But whether there be a soul of the world as a whole is a great and profound question (*magna atque abdita quaestio*). Here again, the Bishop of Hippo speaks formally on the matter: "This opinion should not be affirmed unless it has been discovered with certainty that it is true; nor should it be denied unless it has been found with certainty to be false." Then he points out that it is far more important to understand that no soul is made happy by another soul, and that the only source of wisdom and happiness is God, than to know whether there is, or is not, a world soul. There is no comment on this text in Augustine's *Retractations*.[23]

At several points in the *City of God* we find allusions to this same pagan philosophic teaching, that the world soul is a god. Augustine invariably rejects this notion. In one place,

several lengthy chapters are devoted to an exposition and
criticism of Varro's natural theology.[24] Augustine firmly
condemns polytheism and with it the notion that the soul of
the universe is a deity. In place of all this nonsense about
souls being gods, he says, we Christians worship one God
who made heaven and earth.[25] It appears that this criticism
of Varro was written before the year 415.[26] In a later book,
dated about 416, he refers to Plato and Plotinus and their
belief in a soul of the whole of things (*universitatis anima*).[27]
Similar mentions of the views of Plato and the "philosophers"
on the cosmic soul as a deity occur in the portion of the
treatise done A.D. 418-420.[28] In all these texts Augustine
emphatically denies that the cosmic soul can be a god — but
he consistently refuses to commit himself on the question of
fact: is there, or is there not, a world soul?[29]

There are similar passages in the *Sermons*. On one occa-
sion Augustine was preaching on the resurrection of the
body and he went off on one of his famous *excursus*. Possibly
to the confusion of his not too learned audience, he began
to address the long-dead philosopher, Porphyry, with some
heat. I read your books, he said, you say that this world is
an animal and that the soul of this world is Jove. But you
[Porphyry] would kill the world. For, just as you say that my
soul should flee from my flesh, so do you say that Jove
should flee from heaven and earth.[30] Nowhere in the sermon
does he think of denying the possibility of a cosmic soul,
however.

Another *Sermon*[31] is considered spurious and relegated
to the *Appendix* in the Maurist and later editions of Augustine's works precisely because it teaches what we read in *De
Genesi ad litt. imperf.*[32] This sermon maintains that the "spirit"
of God which moved over the waters (*Gen.*, I, 2) may not
mean God (i.e. the Holy Spirit of the Trinity) but may sig-
nify the world soul.[33] Since the authenticity of this *Sermon* has
been questioned, it is not adduced here in order to prove
anything. However, since the only reason for doubting its

authenticity, given by the Maurist editors,[34] is this exegesis of *Genesis*, I, 2, it is worth mentioning in this study. Further study should be given the problem of sermons of this type which have been rejected on a supposedly doctrinal basis.[35]

The *Retractations* is the last work in which Augustine speaks of the cosmic soul. It is not necessary to repeat now the remarks which have been noted above in connection with each work which he reviewed.[36] Suffice it to say that, in 427, Augustine still felt that the existence of the cosmic soul was an open question. As Canon Bardy judiciously observes, the only way that Augustine could explain the ordering and beauty of the world of bodies was to posit a world soul. This is Augustine's position in the *Retractations* as it was in the Sixth Book on *Music*.[37] Augustine's hesitation on the point is due to his inability to find absolute proof of the existence of this universal soul.

He is always careful to say that the cosmic soul is not taught in Scripture but by many philosophers.[38] Historians of philosophy know that the cosmic soul appears in various forms in Plato, the Stoics, Plotinus, and many other classic philosophers.[39] Augustine's *City of God* references show that Varro and Porphyry were two of his immediate sources for the theory.

It is interesting to go for a moment to the thirteenth century and see what two of the great Schoolmen make of Augustine's hesitation on this question. Strangely enough, St. Thomas Aquinas does not rule out the cosmic soul completely. In fact, Aquinas knows St. Augustine's view quite accurately and reports it with precision. Because he knows more about the history of philosophy, Thomas is more sophisticated in handling the problem. We find him stating that the teaching of the *Philosophi* on the *anima orbis* is partly heretical and partly capable of Catholic support.[40] Heretical is the notion that the cosmic soul emanates from the First Intelligence. (It is clear that Thomas knows more about the *Psyche* and the *Nous* of Plotinus than Augustine, even though

Thomas may not have read as much of the *Enneads*). This emanation is not in accord with Catholic teaching because it contradicts the doctrine that God is the only Creator. Thomas has no objection to calling the angels *motores* of the heavenly bodies, but he will not agree that these angels are souls. Then Aquinas argues that *if* there be a cosmic soul it cannot be soul in anything but an analogous sense.[41] Like Augustine, he does not try to settle the question of the existence of a cosmic soul but limits the possible activities of such a soul to the vegetative level and does not speak with much approval of it.

On the other hand, St. Bonaventure, writing just a few years before St. Thomas, flatly states that it is the *communis sententia Sanctorum* that the heavens are not animated. Bonaventure claims that St. Augustine retracted his earlier view that the world is animated.[42] It is evident that Bonaventure has fallen victim to the same *a priori* approach to the history of thought which we find in some modern Catholic students of St. Augustine. These interpreters seem to reason: Augustine was a very good Catholic; no good Catholic could fail to reject the world soul; therefore Augustine did reject it.[43]

The only historically justifiable conclusion to make at the end of this reading of Augustine's texts on the cosmic soul is that he consistently refused either to affirm or deny its existence.[44] All that we can say is that St. Augustine was definitely opposed to any divinization of the world soul, if there is such a soul. It has not been the purpose of this study to attempt to revive the outmoded hypothesis of a cosmic soul. Both from the point of view of Catholic teaching and the findings of philosophy and science today, it is clear that there is no basis for acceptance of a cosmic soul. What we have seen is that St. Augustine could not bring himself to make such a categorical rejection of the hypothesis.

NOTES

1. Ratramne de Corbie, *Liber de Anima ad Odonem Bellova-censem*, texte inédit publié par D. C. Lambot, O. S. B. (*Analecta Mediaevalia Namurcensia*, 2), Namur-Lille, 1951, p. 159. Prior to this edition is the historical and analytical study of the same *De Anima*: Ph. Delhaye, *Une controverse sur l'âme universelle au IXe siècle* (*Anal. Med. Namur.* I), 1950, p. 72. This *De Anima* to Bishop Odon de Beauvais is not to be confused with another opusculum on the soul by Ratramnus, edited by Dom D. A. Wilmart in *Revue Bénédictine*, 43 (1931), pp. 207-223.

2. This text (32, 69) will be cited and discussed later: see *infra* notes 8 and 9.

3. See the fragment from Maccarius in Lambot, *op. cit.*, 17: "Haec autem ideo proposui, frater, ut sapias quod voluit Augustinus. Unam animam noluit, multas animas noluit; quod in medio posuit hoc voluit, hoc est, ut sit una anima et multa."

4. Delhaye, *op. cit.*, pp. 49-50, suggests that Ratramnus approaches an Aristotelian theory of universals. This judgment seems well founded and is important to future students of the problem of universals in mediaeval philosophy.

5. "Ratramne ne semble avoir aucune idée de l'arrière plan historique de l'opinion à laquelle il s'oppose. . .." Delhaye, *op. cit.*, p. 40.

6. "Hoc autem ordine intelligitur a summa essentia speciem corporis per animam tribui, qua est, in quantumcumque est. Per animam ergo corpus subsistit et eo ipso est, quo animatur, sive universaliter, ut mundus, sive particulariter, ut unumquodque animal intra mundum." *De immortalitate animae*, 15, 24. In the next section Augustine repeats this view: "Corpus enim nullum fit, nisi accipiendo per animam speciem." *Ibid.*, n. 25.

7. *Retractationes* I, 5, 3: "temere dictum est."

8. "De numero vero animarum, nescio quid tibi respondeam, cum hoc ad istam quaestionem pertinere putaveris: citius enim dixerim non esse omnino quaerendum, aut certe tibi nunc differendum, quam vel tam involutam quaestionem modo a me tibi posse expedire. Si enim dixero unam esse animam, conturbaberis, quod in altero beata est, in altero misera; nec una res simul et beata et misera potest esse. Si unam simul et multas

dicam esse, ridebis; nec mihi facile, unde tuum risum comprimam, suppetit. Si multas tantum modo esse dixero, ipse me ridebo, minusque me mihi displicentem, quam tibi perferam." *De quantitate animae*, 32, 69.

9. *Retract.*, I, 8, review *De quant. animae* but without any attention to this text.

10. "Quod enim in illo anima quaerit, constantiam scilicet aeternitatemque, non invenit; quoniam rerum transitu completur infima pulchritudo, et quod in illa imitatur constantiam, a summo Deo per animam trajicitur; quoniam prior est species tantummodo tempore commutabilis, quam est ea quae et tempore et locis." *De musica*, 6, 14, 44.

11. *Supra* footnote 6.

12. *Retract.*, I, XI, 4.

13. "Si autem ipsa pulchritudo in omnibus corporibus intelligatur, cogit ista sententia etiam ipsum mundum animal credere, ut etiam in ipsum, quod in illo imitatur constantiam, a summo Deo per animam trajiciatur." *Ibid.*

14. "Sed animal esse istum mundum, sicut Plato sensit aliique philosophi quamplurimi, nec ratione certa indagare potui, nec divinarum Scripturarum auctoritate persuaderi posse cognovi." *Ibid.*

15. "Non quia hoc falsum esse confirmo, sed quia nec verum esse comprehendo, quod sit animal mundus." *Ibid.*

16. "Quamobrem sit tibi manifestum atque perceptum, nullum errorem in religione esse potuisse, si anima pro Deo suo non coleret *animam*, aut corpus, aut phantasmata sua, aut horum aliqua duo conjuncta, aut certe simul omnia." *De vera religione*, 10, 18. (The underlining of *"animam"* is supplied by the present writer to indicate the term which refers to cosmic soul, as is explained *infra*, note 17).

17. "Hic animam pro universa creatura incorporali posui, non loquens more Scripturarum, quae animam, quando non translato verbo utuntur, nescio utrum velint intelligi nisi eam qua vivunt animalia mortalia, in quibus et homines sunt, quamdiu mortales sunt." *Retract.*, I, 13.

18. "Potest autem et aliter intelligi, ut Spiritum Dei, vitalem creaturam, qua universus iste visibilis atque omnia corpora contineur et moventur, intelligamus; cui Deus omnipotens tribuit vim

quamdam sibi serviendi ad operandum in iis, quae gignuntur. Qui spiritus cum sit omni corpore aethereo melior, quia omnem visibilem creaturam omnis invisibilis creatura antecedit, non absurde spiritus Dei dicitur." *De Genesi ad litteram, liber imperfectus*, 4, 17.

19. *Retract.*, I, 18.

20. "Sed in hoc opere, cum mea opuscula retractarem, iste ipse, ut erat imperfectus, venit in manus . . . Verum et hunc posteaquam retractavi, manere volui ut esset index, quantum existimo non inutilis, rudimentorum meorum in enucleandis atque scrutandis divinis eloquiis, eiusque titulum esse volui, De Genesi ad litteram imperfectus." *Retract.*, I, 18; cf. G. Bardy (ed.) Saint Augustin, *Les Révisions* (Paris, 1950), p. 571, where this revision in 427 is also noted.

21. Observe that Augustine does not say that the Holy Spirit, the third Person of the Trinity, is the world soul (a view condemned by the Council of Soissons, A.D. 1121, and of Sens, A.D. 1140, *vide* Denziger-Bannwart-Umberg, *Enchiridion symbolorum, definitionum et declarationum,* Freiburg i. Br. 1937, no. 370.) In this interpretation, which Augustine suggests only as an alterative to several others, the *spiritus Dei* could be regarded as merely a creature. It goes without saying that Augustine did not know the later theological objections to such an interpretation.

22. "Neque enim ullam animam rationalem sapientem fieri disputant, nisi participatione summae illius incommutabilisque sapientiae; non solum cujusquam hominis animam, sed ipsius etiam mundi, quam dicunt Jovem. Nos vero, esse quamdam summam Dei sapientiam, cujus participatione fit sapiens quaecumque anima fit vere sapiens, non tantum concedimus, verum etiam maxime praedicamus. Utrum autem universa ista corporalis moles, quae mundus appellatur, habeat quamdam animam, vel quasi animam suam, id est rationalem vitam, qua ita regatur sicut unumquodque animal, magna atque abdita quaestio est: nec affirmari debet ista opinio, nisi comperta quod vera sit; nec refelli, nisi comperta quod falsa sit. Quid autem hoc ad hominem, etiam si semper eum lateat? Quandoquidem nulla anima fit sapiens vel beata ex alia quacumque anima, se ex illa sola summa atque incommutabili Dei sapientia." *De consensu evangelistarum*, I, 23, 35. On the date of this work, see Bardy, *Révisions*, p. 580.

23. See *Retract.*, 2, 16, where *De consensu evangelistarum* is reviewed.

24. *De civitate Dei*, 7, cap. 6-29.

25. "Nos Deum colimus, non caelum et terram, quibus duabus partbus mundus hic constat: nec animam vel animas per viventia quaecumque diffusa; sed Deum qui fecit caelum et terram et omnia quae in eis sunt." *Ibid.*, cap. 29.

26. Cf. Bardy, *Révisions*, pp. 56-57, for the chronology of the various books of the *City of God*.

27. *De civ. Dei*, 10, 2.

28. *De civ. Dei*, 13-16-17.

29. "Plato . . . etiam de ipso universo mundo, tamquam uno animali maximo, quo cuncta cetera continerentur animalia, instanter affirmat. Sed haec, ut dixi, alia quaestio est, quam nunc discutiendam non suscepimus." *De civ. Dei*, 13, 16, 2.

30. *Sermo* CCXLI (De resurrectione corporum, contra Gentiles), cap. 7, 7.

31. *Appendicis Sermo* CLVII (in Vigilia Pascha, I, de verbis Genes. I: "In principio fecit Deus," etc.) *Opera Omnia* ed. Bened. S. Mauri (Venetiis 1731) t. V (2), pp. 279-280.

32. See *supra*, note 18.

33. "Hic ergo spiritus qui superferebatur aquas, seminarius est animandae conditionis . . . alterum esse spiritum Dei, qui Deus est: alterum spiritum hujus mundi, quo animantur universa." *Sermo cit.*, I, 3, col. 280.

34. See their prenote to the *Sermo cit.* t. V (2), col. 279.

35. Actually, the Maurists asserted that this *Sermon* is in conflict with the teaching of *De diversis quaestionibus ad Simplicianum*, 2, 5. This assertion is repeated by G. Verbeke, *L'evolution de la doctrine du Pneuma* (Paris-Louvain, 1945), p. 496. What Augustine says (*De divers. quaest.* 2, 5) is that he finds nothing intrinsically evil in understanding the *spiritus Dei* to be some invisible creature. It appears to be the same teaching as in *Sermo CLVII in Append.*

36. See *supra*, notes 7, 12-15, 17.

37. "La seule réponse satisfaisante que trouve Augustin à ce difficile problème reste, lorsqu'il écrit les *Révisions*, celle qu'il avait déjà donnée dans le *De musica*: il faut, pour cela, que le monde soit animé." G. Bardy, *Les Révisions*, Introduction, p. 157.

38. The philosophic background of the world soul theory is

adequately sketched by P. Delhaye, *op. cit.*, pp. 7-14. Other general studies of the history of the theory, by P. Thevenaz, J. Moreau, and the study of Verbeke cited above, are noted by Delhaye.

39. *Timaeus* 34B, 38C, 40A, 41A; *Phaedo* 103B-107B; *Laws* 967A-B. Numerous references to the Stoic fragments and the Roman Stoics are given by Verbeke, *op. cit.*, pp. II-174. One of the classic passages in the *Enneads* is IV, 8, 6; ed. Bréhier (Paris, 1927), t. IV, pp. 216-235.

40. S. Thomae Aq., *In II Sententiarum*, 14, I, 3, resp.: "dicunt [philosophi] esse animam orbis . . . Haec autem positio partim est haeretica, et partim catholice sustineri potest."

41. *Ibid.* ad 3ᵐ: "secundum philosophos non dicitur univoce anima coeli et hominis." Cf. S.T., I, 3, 8 c., where Thomas speaks directly of the *anima mundi* and cites favorably Augustine's *De civ. Dei*, 7, 6. See also C.G., I, 27; II, 42; and III, 120, where Thomas insists with Augustine that if there be a world soul it cannot be divine.

42. S. Bonaventurae, *In II Sententiarum*, d. 14, Pars I, art. 3, q. 2, resp.: "Augustinus retractat illud verbum . . . quod mundus animatur."

43. Thus R. Allers, *Microcosmus from Anaximander to Paracelsus, Traditio* II (N.Y., 1944), p. 360. "Augustine was not in favor of the *anima mundi* theory." Cf. G. Verbeke, *op. cit.*, pp. 496-497, is none too clear on the point but he speaks of the interpretation of the *spiritus Dei* as, "le principe vital qui anime l'univers." Then he adds, "cette doctrine est rejétée explicitement dans les autres ouvrages de saint Augustin . . . ."

44. "Incertus Augustinus fuit de anima mundi, sed certissimus mundum aliud esse a Deo." J. Cappello, *Introd.* p. XL, to *Confessionum Lib. III* (Torino-Roma, 1948). For similar accurate reports of Augustine's position, see E. Portalie, "Augustin," *Dictionnaire de Théologie Catholique* (ed. Vacant et al.) I, col. 2331; E. Gilson, *Introduction à l'étude de Saint Augustin* (Paris, 1943), p. 274.

III
Morality and Values

CHAPTER 7

The Roots of Moral Values*

Some years ago a keen critic of the human condition wrote the following gloomy lines:

The world itself now bears witness to its approaching end, by the evidence of its failing powers. There is not enough rain in winter to germinate the seeds; nor is there enough heat in summer to mature them. Spring is no longer mild and autumn is not rich in fruit. Less marble is quarried from the depleted mountains and the dwindling supplies of gold and silver show that the mines are worked out, for their meagre veins of metal grow narrower and smaller from day to day. The farmer is failing and leaving his fields; the sailor from the sea, the soldier from his camp, uprightness from the forum, justice from the court, mutual trust from friendships, skill from the arts and discipline from morals. Can anything that is old keep the same powers that it had in the prime and vigor of its youth? Inevitably whatever is on the road to decay and nearing its finish must decrease in strength, as do the setting sun, the waning moon, the dying tree and the failing stream. This is the judgment passed on this world: it is God's law, that all that has gone up must come down, all that has grown to maturity must decline into senility, the strong must grow weak, the great become small — and when they have been weakened and diminished, they must reach their termination.[1]

*This chapter was originally the J. H. Taylor, S.J., Annual Lecture at Gonzaga University, Spokane, Washington on November 13, 1974.

The claim that our natural resources are depleted and
that the moral standards of mankind are degenerating is
heard on every side today. Actually, the foregoing long
quotation was written more than seventeen hundred years
ago, by an African, St. Cyprian the Bishop of Carthage.
Both before and after his time in the third century many
famous writers spoke of us moderns as pygmies standing on
the shoulders of the ancients who were giants. The optimists
claimed that we dwarfs can see farther than our predeces-
sors, even though they were of greater stature than we.[2] But
the pessimists who used this conceit bemoaned, as does
Cyprian, the shrinking up of the cosmos and of man's power
to distinguish good from evil. Certainly there are many in
our own era who think that the world is going to the dogs —
and that the good people are outnumbered by the bad.

Fortunately, as far as the present status of our moral
ideals is concerned, we are not wholly dependent on the examples set by some of the leading men in the world today.
Nor need we rely on the teaching of academic ethicists, for
they have little to tell us about how we should live our actual
lives. The sources of our moral convictions are found in
many different places: in the great world religions, in much
serious literature, in the classic tradition of art, even in the
folk-sayings of popular life and the myths of national greatness. But the roots of our moral values may be traced back
to a few great men in the past who have thought with seminal minds and left a heritage that is morally enriching.[3]

It can hardly be doubted that Augustine of Hippo,
another African Bishop, was one of these paradigmatic individuals. Little in his family antecedents would suggest that
he could become the Adam of Christendom, as he has been
called. Yet in his voluminous works are to be found the seeds
of most of the moral ideals that have sustained more than fifteen centuries of western culture.[4]

A few years ago, a very famous Augustine scholar,
Henri Marrou, undertook to explain Augustine's impact on
human values in later tradition.[5] His emphasis fell chiefly on

the fact that the Christian teaching concerning the resurrection of the human body enabled Augustine to react against
the Neoplatonic contempt for the body. Hence, Marrou
claimed, it is high time that Christian scholarship recognize
the worth of the human body in the economy of life and
salvation. All of this is true — and Marrou has demonstrated
his conclusion very completely. No one who has looked at
Augustine's treatise *On the Nature of the Good* could doubt that
he cherished all of God's creatures, including the human
body.

However, as Marrou realized, the primary impact of
Augustine's moral outlook falls elsewhere. In point of fact,
Augustine opened up to western man the importance of the
spiritual. At the end of his study, Marrou quite fittingly concludes: "The true human values are those spiritual values at
which we have finally arrived: contemplation, praise, love."[6]
It is this emphasis on the values of the spirit that I propose
to stress here.

Just what spirit means was not entirely clear in ancient
philosophy, in the Old and New Testaments, or among the
first Fathers of the Church. The Greeks called it *pneuma*, and
the Latins *spiritus*, but the primary meaning fluctuated. At
first spirit meant the warm breath which nearly all primitive
peoples regard as the vital principle in men and beasts. Then
there developed an intermediary meaning in which spirit
was understood to be a sort of half-way house between mind
and matter. From the time of the earliest Greek physicians
down to Descartes, Sir Kenelm Digby, Doctor F. A. Mes-
mer and Sir Arthur Conan Doyle, there has been a prevalent notion that a "spirit" is some sort of thin gas.[7] Some people even try to take the pictures of such spirits; others see
and feel them in haunted houses. Even St. Augustine uses
the term *spiritus* to name "a power of the soul, inferior to the
mind, in which the likenesses of bodily things find expression" (*vis animae quaedam, mente inferior, ubi corporalium rerum
similitudines exprimuntur*[8]).

As Gérard Verbeke of Louvain has show in an impressive work of historical research,[9] the significance of spirit evolved from the primitive notion of living breath, through the vague second meaning of a ghostlike gas, eventually to a purified third sense where spirit signifies a dynamic reality that is entirely immaterial. Augustine marks the climax of this evolution in usage: even in the two centuries immediately preceding him there were prominent Christian thinkers, like Tertullian and Origen, who were not clear as to the incorporeal character of the human spirit. In the mature works of Augustine, the primary meaning of spirit is identified with the unchanging God. As he says: "For spirit is even God Who cannot be renewed, for He cannot grow old."[10] Or, as we read in the last book of his *Literal Commentary on Genesis*, "*dicitur spiritus etiam Deus.*"[11] In the *City of God* Augustine adds: "The spirit of life, which quickens all things and is the Creator of everyone, and of every created spirit, is God Himself, the uncreated Spirit."[12]

Of course the Bible is the important source for this conception of spirit as divine. The Book of Genesis speaks of the Spirit of God hovering over the waters.[13] And the third Person of the Trinity is called *pneuma* in Greek and *Spiritus* in Latin.[14] The psychology of Plotinus and Porphyry popularized and reinforced the dynamic and immaterial character of this highest meaning of spirit.

However, it is Augustine with his introspective analyses of the contents of personal consciousness who gives a positive significance to this immaterial meaning of spirit. One place in which he does this is in the twelfth Book of his *Literal Commentary on Genesis*.[15] There Augustine starts with St. Paul's enrapture to the third heaven and his talk about seeing and praying in the spirit. There are three levels of human vision, Augustine argues: the lowest is seeing through the eyes of the body, the middle vision is accomplished in that kind of thinking that employs images, but the highest kind of vision sees the objects of understanding without any images. Psychologists still dispute today whether imageless thought is even possible. Augustine felt that it is. By this claim he opened the way for a whole new dimension of human experience.

To appreciate this point, let us look at a famous passage in the tenth Book *On the Trinity*,[16] where Augustine begins by criticizing those philosophers (Stoic and Epicurean) who thought that man's soul is corporeal. Rather, he argues, the mind of man (and he uses the word *mens*, from the Latin Bible) discovers itself through an experience that is quite different from bodily perception. The human intelligence (*intellegentia*) obeys the classic injunction, "know thyself," by attending to its own act of understanding. My mind is able to discover itself (the Latin *invenire* suggests coming into itself) by seeing that it exists, that it lives, and that it understands. This psychic progression from *esse*, through *vivere*, to *intellegere*, does not begin from the consciousness of extra-mental things but from within the mind. This is the famous "interiorism" of St. Augustine, of which so much has been written.[17]

Thus far, our passage is a purely cognitive analysis of what one finds in internal consciousness. Next Augustine explains that the mind also becomes aware of itself as remembering and willing. This is the entrance into the warm domain of affective experience. Here we find a sentence that shows how ridiculous it is to regard Augustine as an enemy of love, as some recent writers claim.[18] What Augustine says is: "For the mind that loves eagerly (*animus vehementer amans*) is then to be praised, when it loves that which ought to be loved eagerly."[19] Obviously not all objects are equally worthy of being loved. The goods of the mind, of spiritual experience, are most valuable for men and most to be cherished.

If we return to his *Commentary on Genesis*, we find him saying:

> So also, among the objects of the understanding there are some that are seen in the soul itself: for example, the virtues (to which the vices are opposed), either vir-

tues that will endure, such as piety, or virtues that are
useful for this life and not destined to remain in the
next, as faith . . . hope . . . patience . . . they are seen
with the understanding.[20]

These virtues that are indicative of the highest goods for
human love are not exhaustively discussed in this *Commentary*. Further details are given in a letter that Augustine
wrote to a man named Macedonius, in the year 414.[21]

In this life [Augustine writes], although there is no virtue save that of loving what ought to be loved (*diligere
quod diligendum est*), prudence lies in choosing it, fortitude in not being turned away from it by any troubles,
temperance in being allured by no seductions, justice
in the absence of pride. But what ought we to choose
as the object of our principal love but that which we
find to be better than anything else (*quo nihil melius
invenimus*)? This object is God: and to set anything
above, or even equal to, Him is to show that we do not
know how to love ourselves. For our good becomes
greater the closer we approach Him, than whom there
is nothing better.[22]

Our moral behavior (*mores*), Augustine adds, is not to
be judged on the basis of some bit of knowledge that a person may have, but from the object that one loves. Nothing
makes conduct good or bad, except good or bad loves.[23]

Clearly Augustine is telling us that we may discover the
standards of good conduct by consulting those evident truths
that are above our minds but which can be seen by all men
who will make the effort. Early in his life, in his dialogue on
Free Choice, Augustine spoke of an unchanging truth "more
excellent than our minds." It enables us to judge that some
minds are as they ought to be, and others are not, just as our
intelligence appraises our own conduct (*sicut nostrorum morum
se ratio tulerit*). We make such judgments on the basis of those
interior rules of truth that we discern in common with

others; for example, that eternal things are more important than temporal ones, or that seven plus three are ten. One does not question the truth of such standard rules but simply rejoices to have discovered them.[24] For Augustine, the source of moral values lies in our mind's native ability to recognize what is right and good in our higher mental experience. We are all familiar with the famous description of the contents of memory in the tenth Book of the *Confessions*.

In several of his sermons Augustine contrasts the outlook of the pagan philosophers with that of Christianity. The Epicureans cherish bodily perfection and enjoyment and the Stoics exalt that steadfastness of character which stems from a disciplined mind (*virtus animi*). But Christians look to eternal life as their greatest chance for satisfaction. It is not that bodily and mental values are bad: they are simply incomplete, as Augustine sees it.[25] At another point in his preaching, Augustine explains that the philosophers get their knowledge of God in two ways: first, by starting with the beauties of all things in nature and rising to a vision of changeless Beauty; second, by studying man himself, in all his imperfections, and then concluding to the necessary existence of a perfectly unchanging reality, God.[26] Then he sets up a scale of human values: important, but the lowest kind of goods for man are health, strength and bodily satisfactions; on the second level are perfections of conscious personality, things like knowledge and strength of character; at the top lies happiness with God.

Still another sermon is concluded with a little meditation on the Psalmist's query: "Who will give me wings like a dove?"[27]

> One of these wings [Augustine explains] is to be found in the words: 'Thou shalt love the Lord thy God with thy whole heart, with thy whole soul, and with thy whole mind' (Mt 22:37). But do not limit yourself to one wing. For if you think that you have one wing, you do not even have that. 'Thou shalt love thy neighbor as

thyself' (Mt 22:39). If you fail to love your brother,
whom you see, how can you love God, whom you cannot see?[28]

The injunction to love is not enough: people must learn *what*
to love, what are the most valuable objects for our concern.
The supreme Value is, of course, God. And the next highest
values lie in the perfection of the human spirit, individually
and collectively.

This truth about the importance of the spirit was
brought home to me a few years ago, at an international
Congress of philosophers in Venice. The Soviet Union had
sent a large delegation, including smart girl translators and
several hard-faced commissars. The head of the group of
about fifty was a man named Mitin whom I had met at other
meetings. He has since fallen into disgrace in Russia but at
that time he did most of the talking for the Soviet philosophers. One of the things that he kept insisting on was that
Russian Marxism is not crudely materialistic. True, they
still call their practical philosophy dialectical materialism but
the term "materialism" is used to distinguish their world-
view from the dialectical idealism of Hegel. Emphatically
Professor Mitin stressed the claim that Communist philosophy embraces the life of the "spirit". It is well to remember
how much Marx was influenced by earlier German idealism, in which the Spirit (*Geist*) is reality itself. Communist
theoreticians value the workings of the human mind in the
arts of music, poetry, the dance and other esthetic fields.
They foster the competitive spirit that comes to the fore in
active games and sports. They encourage that intercom-
munication of minds which is achieved in knowledge and
science.[29]

Soviet thinkers particularly value the satisfactions of
shared community life. It became clear to me in Venice that
these twentieth-century Russians were far removed in their
sense of human values from the rigid corporealism of the
mid-nineteenth century. Adam Schaff, from Poland and a

highly intelligent Marxist, gave the most effective expression
to this openness of recent Marxism to the ideals of the
human spirit.

Then our Congress moved for one day from the sensual splendors of Venice to the Franciscan austerity of
Padua. It was immediately evident that Paduan spirituality
was baffling to the Russians. Somehow or other, the soul of
Mother Russia was not comfortable with the religiosity of
St. Anthony. This piety was a dimension of the human spirit
with which they could not cope. The paper delivered by the
Russian speaker in the great Municipal Hall of Padua struck
a discordant note. It dealt with an obscure medical doctor in
the Paduan Renaissance Lucilio Vanini, who turned out to
be a bit of an atheist. The notion that man's spirit may extend to higher than natural values had no meaning for them.
Indeed, vast numbers of otherwise intelligent people on
earth today lack all appreciation of spiritual values. This is
so in our own country and throughout the world.

It was only yesterday that avant-garde Christian theologians were echoing Nietzsche's cry that God is dead. In a
sense, God is still not a living reality for many of us. We
should face up to this fact: if St. Francis, or St. Anthony,
or St. Clare, come back to visit us at the average Catholic
university today they might feel no more at home than the
Marxists at Padua. The same thing could be said of St.
Augustine. His world was a pluralistic culture like ours — but
his sense of values, his love of the highest good, was different
from our kind of love.

Think of the broad themes of Augustine's great works.
The early dialogue *On Free Choice* tells us that man's freedom
is the greatest personal good that God has given us. Then
the *Confessions* stress the lack of meaning in a human life that
is not committed to the love of God. Augustine's long *Commentary on Genesis* keeps reminding us that this reasonably
made world finds its ultimate ground in the divine Ideas, the
rationes aeternae which constitute God's plan for creation. The

longest work, both in volume and the time that it took to produce, is the *Enarrationes in Psalmos*, a vast hymn to divine beauty and a poetic expression of the dignity of the human person under God. His treatise on *The Trinity* tells us how psychological introspection finds a dozen created "trinities" within man's soul — all imperfectly imaging the perfection of God. And Augustine's most influential work in the social order, the *City of God*, describes the progress of spiritual creatures (men and angels) through history, divided into two great societies, the one animated by the love of temporal goods, the other, the heavenly City, inspired by the love of God and eternal values. This is what the good life means to St. Augustine: to live with one's mental gaze ever directed toward eternity.

In a recent study of the Catholic novel, Gene Kellogg comments on the growing tendency of Christians, and of Catholics in particular to merge their values with those of the surrounding secular culture. First there was convergence and now we are reaching confluence. Kellogg writes:

> For many Catholics, confluence by the mid-1960s became so complete that they were no longer sure what the true Catholic essence was. The primary and defiant Catholic emphasis upon the spirit, which for so many generations had caused the creative spark between Catholic communities and the secular environment, virtually ceased.[30]

We must admit that for many members of the Church it is no longer very distinctive to be a Catholic. Nor is it something very special to be a Christian. We are uncertain about the values of our moral and religious heritage. Nowadays we are not sure whether there are any intrinsically evil human actions. We criticize our public officials for cheating and lying and deceiving us — but what are the moral standards that we use to judge them? Do we use the same strict standards to judge our own acts?

Perhaps we can regain some moral direction, recover the roots of our ethical heritage, by a return to the spirit of St. Augustine. He well knew the difference between a pagan and a Christian. As Yves Congar has so well said, he nourished most of the spiritualist currents in Western culture.[31] And since I began with a complaint about Henri Marrou's emphasis on the value of the body, may I close with his final judgment on the status of Augustine's views on human values.

> On this level [Marrou writes] all schools of spirituality meet. Recourse to St. Augustine does not enclose us in a dark and exclusive 'Latinism' . . . The wisdom which St. Augustine teaches us does not differ greatly from that of the great spiritual writers of the Eastern Church.[32]

I would simply add that the moral wisdom of St. Augustine is not outmoded in twentieth-century America. It remains a fertile source for the revitalization and growth of our confidence in the ideals that have always distinguished what is finest in human culture.

NOTES

1. St. Cyprian, *Ad Demetrianum*, cap. 3 (CSEL III, 355; PL IV, 546; written *circa* A.D. 250). Translation revised by V.J.B.

2. Cf. Bourke, "The Quarrels of the Ancients and the Moderns," *The Classical Bulletin* (St. Louis) X, 5 (1934) 33-34.

3. Thus Max Scheler speaks of "moral Prometheuses in whose vision a moral value suddenly appears which has never been known before." See his essay, "Zum Phänomen des Tragischen," in *Vom Umsturz der Werte*, 4 Aufl. (Bern: Francke, 1955) p. 166. Karl Jaspers has a similar view. Cf. A. Cua, "Morality and Paradigmatic Individuals," *American Philosophical Quarterly* VI, 4 (1969) 324-329.

4. Cf. Christopher Dawson, "St. Augustine and His Age," in *Saint Augustine*, by M. C. D'Arcy et al. (New York: Meridian

Books, 1957) pp. 15-77; and John O'Meara, *The Charter of Christendom: the Significance of the* City of God (New York: Macmillan, 1961).

5. H.I. Marrou, *The Resurrection and Saint Augustine's Theology of Human Values* (Villanova: Villanova University Press, 1966).

6. *Ibid.* p. 35.

7. In his *Discours de la méthode* (ed. E. Gilson, Paris: Vrin, 1930) p. 54, Descartes speaks of "esprits animaux, qui sont comme un vent très subtil."

8. *De Genesi ad litteram* XII, 9, 20, where he is discussing St. Paul's statement (I Cor, 14:14) "For if I pray in a tongue, my spirit prays, but my understanding is unfruitful."

9. *L'Évolution de la doctrine du pneuma, du Stoicisme à saint Augustin* (Louvain-Paris: Desclée, 1945).

10. "Est enim spiritus et Deus qui renouari non potest quia nec ueterescere potest." *De Trinitate*, XIV, 16, 22 (ed. C. J. Mountain, Turnholti: Brepols, 1968, p. 452).

11. *De Gen. ad lit.* XII, 7: for a portion of Father John Taylor's translation of this important book, see my anthology, *The Essential Augustine* (Indianapolis: Hackett, 1974) pp. 93-97.

12. *De civitate Dei* V, 9.

13. See *De Gen. ad lit.* I, 18, 36; for my discussion of some difficulties in Augustine's interpretation, consult "St. Augustine and the Cosmic Soul," *Giornale di Metafisica* IX (1954) 431-440.

14. For these terms in Graeco-Latin versions of the early *Creeds*, see Appendix C, pp. 558-567, in Mountain's edition of Augustine, *De Trinitate,* cited above in note 10.

15. Cf. J. H. Taylor, S.J., *St. Augustine; De Genesi ad litteram, Book* XII, St. Louis University Dissertation, 1948.

16. *De Trinitate*, X, 7-12 (ed. Mountain, pp. 322-332.).

17. A.C. Pegis, "The Mind of St. Augustine," *Mediaeval Studies* VI (1944) 1-61, is a good example.

18. Daniel C. Maguire, "Moral Absolutes and the Magisterium," in *Absolutes in Moral Theology*, ed. Charles Curran (Washington: Corpus Books, 1968) pp. 64-66, makes the odd charge that Augustine opposed love because he was influenced by the Stoics.

19. *De Trin.* X, 11, 17 (ed. Mountain, p. 330).

20. *De Gen. ad. lit.* XII, 31, 59; Taylor translation in *The Essential Augustine*, pp. 97 f.

21. *Epistula* CLV, 4, 13; see Bourke, *History of Ethics* (New York: Doubleday, 1968) pp. 57-58.

22. Anselm of Canterbury echoed these lines in his famous definition of God as, "quo maius cogitari non possit." *Proslogion*, cap. 2.

23. "Mores autem nostri, non ex eo quod quisque novit, sed ex eo quod diligit, dijudicari solent. Nec faciunt bonos vel malos mores, nisi boni vel mali amores." *Epist.* CLV, loc. cit.

24. *De libero arbitrio* II, 12, 34.

25. *Sermo* 150; see an excellent translation in *Selected Sermons of St. Augustine*, ed. Quincy Howe, Jr., (New York: Holt, Rinehart and Winston, 1966) pp. 93-94.

26. *Sermo* 241; in the Howe translation, pp. 102-104.

27. *Psalm* 54:7.

28. *Sermo* 30 (Mai 126); in the Howe translation p. 234.

29. When we reprinted the complete works of Thomas Aquinas in Latin twenty-five years ago, the Moscow Academy of Science bought one of the first sets, at four hundred dollars.

30. From *The Vital Tradition: The Catholic Novel in a Period of Convergence* (Chicago: Loyola University Press, 1970), quoted in R. E. Lauder, "The Catholic Novel and the 'Insider God' ," *Commonweal* CI, 4 (Oct. 25, 1974) p. 78.

31. "Saint Augustin a également alimenté la plupart des courants spiritualistes de l'Occident . . ." *L'Église. De saint Augustin à l'époque moderne* (Paris: Cerf, 1970) p. 23.

32. Marrou, *op. cit.* pp. 37-38.

CHAPTER 8

Moral Illumination

St. Augustine's teaching on divine illumination is widely recognized as an important attempt to explain how men come to know some truths (such as the axioms in Euclidean geometry) with absolute certitude. But in addition to the epistemological role of God's light there are two other areas in which it functions for Augustine. Stemming from the *fiat lux* of Genesis, Augustine's meditations on the light theme led to an ontological theory of reality. Physically and metaphysically light was envisioned as a dynamic principle working throughout the created world.[1] Eventually this light-metaphysics originating in Augustine was developed and refined in the thirteenth century by thinkers such as Witelo and Robert Grosseteste. But the third field in which Augustine used light as an explanatory device was ethics. He had a theory of moral illumination which has not yet been studied adequately.[2] The present article will attempt to open up some of the possibilities inherent in this part of Augustine's ethical thinking.

I. COGNITIVE ILLUMINATION IN GENERAL

It is in the theory of knowledge that most studies of Augustine's illumination doctrine are concentrated. There are many different interpretations of this teaching.[3] The broad outline of his explanation of human knowing is not, however, subject to much dispute. Augustine saw man as an

immaterial soul, giving life and regulation to an organic
body. This soul is capable of three kinds of vision: corporeal,
imaginative and intellectual.[4] The first way of seeing works
through the eyes of the body: its objects are the sensible ap-
pearances (*species*) of material objects in man's environment.
Such perception is an activity of man's soul, forming images
of things that impress the various sense organs. The imaginative level of vision is cogitation, an act of thinking in
terms of the images formed by the soul in the lowest kind of
perception. Thus, when Augustine saw his mother in person
he was using bodily vision, but when he thought of her in
Monica's absence, or when he combined other images with
his basic view of her, he was cogitating. The third kind of
seeing is purely mental and imageless: by it the human soul
sees non-material objects (*rationes*) that have changeless
meanings. These are items such as unity, equality, mother-
hood, love and (as we shall note later) many standards of
esthetic and moral judgment. There is a light that is appropriate to each level of vision but the one that is most distinctive of Augustine's thought is the third, the immaterial light
of the mind (*lumen mentis*) which enables man to see eternal
truths.

Cognitive illumination appears in Augustine's earliest
works and continues into those that are most mature. By
A.D. 389 it is well developed in the dialogue *On the Teacher*,
where we read:

> But when there is a question of those things which we
> perceive in the mind, that is, by means of understand-
> ing and reason, we speak truly of the things that we
> behold as present in the interior light of truth (*in illa in-
> teriore luce veritatis*), by which he who is called the inner
> man is enlightened (*illustratur*) and whence also comes
> his joy: but then our hearer, if he also himself sees
> those things with the simple and unseen eye, knows
> what I say, not by means of my words but by his own
> intuition (*sua contemplatione*).[5]

At about the same time, in the dialogue *On Free Choice*,[6] Augustine calls this inner light of the mind "mysterious and universal" (*secretum et publicum lumen*), implying that it is available in common to all men.

Much interpretive dispute has centered on the nature and precise function of this inner light of man's soul. *The Trinity* has a notorious text in which we read that the soul sees intelligible truths "in an incorporeal light of a unique kind" (*in quadam luce sui generis incorporea*).[7] Through the centuries, this has been interpreted in at least three distinct ways. Some readers have thought that this "light" is God Himself, as present and working within man's mind. Sometimes Augustine seems to say just that. Thus a letter dated A.D. 408/9 quotes John 1:5, "God is light, and in Him is no darkness," and Augustine adds, "this light is God Himself" (*lux illa Deus ipse est*).[8] However, it appears that he is here contrasting the vision of God in heaven with the sort of vision that is appropriate to earth dwellers. In general the weight of Augustine's texts is against the claim that man sees God directly in this life and knows general truths through this divine vision.[9] In other words, the ontologistic interpretation associated with the name of the Abbé Malebranche is not accepted by many present-day scholars.

A second interpretation makes Augustine's inner light simply a special power that is innate in man's soul. Perhaps the most famous example of this view is Thomas Aquinas' identification of the light of the soul with the agent intellect, one of the natural potencies of understanding.[10] Very few modern students of Augustinian thought embrace this so-called Thomistic explanation.

A third way of explaining what Augustine meant by the light of the mind focuses on judgment as the central activity of human understanding. In this explanation (which Ronald Nash in a very thorough survey of the possibilities has called the "formal" approach[11]), the intellectual light provides a ground for the certitude of some of man's judgments.

We are said to "consult" the Truth that dwells within our minds (*intus ipsi menti praesidentem consulimus veritatem*).[12] Thus, if I judge that "seven plus three equals ten," I am sure that this is correct but I may not be able to define the principle of equality, or the nature of the number system, in which this proposition is grounded. Similarly, if I think that "p" is "q" and that "p" cannot be "not-q," I am guided by the eternal truth of non-contradiction, even though I am not fully aware of its logical character. That is to say, Augustine felt that "God illumines the mind, not by impressing the divine Ideas upon it, but rather by making evident the truth of necessary judgments, in a formal and regulative manner."[13] This formal explanation seems to me to come closest to the core meaning of Augustine's texts on the role of the inner light in the area of cognition.[14]

Precisely *what* is seen by the aid of this inner light is stated in a number of ways. Augustine agreed with Plato that there are certain ideal forms, in accord with which all things are made and all true judgments accomplished. Unlike Plato, however, Augustine placed these exemplars in the mind of God.[15] For the Bishop of Hippo they are the *rationes aeternae*, the everlasting principles of reality, of knowledge, and of the good life.[16] It is not that man on earth sees God and knows these forms through that immediate vision. Augustine says quite plainly that the direct seeing of God in Himself (*in illa specie qua Deus est*) is possible to no man in this life (*nemo videns vivet vita ista*).[17] Rather, every man is helped by God to understand within his own mind certain meanings that are not derived from sense experience. Frequently Augustine uses mathematical definitions and axioms as examples of the kind of non-physical truths that are the objects of intellectual vision. A letter of the period 413/414 states that you see with the gaze of your mind, "your life, will, thought, memory, understanding, knowledge, faith."[18] These are what other thinkers might call abstractions or universals — but there is no place for intellectual abstraction in Augustine's epistemology. He regarded these *rationes* as immaterial realities.

II. MORAL ILLUMINATION AND VIRTUE

At times, however, Augustine speaks of another type of divine illumination which regulates the ethical judgments and activities of men. The objects of its enlightening are norms of moral judgment. The *Literal Commentary on Genesis* has a lengthy text which brings this out. In part it states that, "just as man works the soil, so that it becomes cultivated and fruitful . . . so does God work the just man, in order to justify him . . . and thus man is enlightened by God's very presence to him."[19] Commenting on this, Etienne Gilson calls it an "illumination of the will by grace." Indeed, Augustine does say (later in the same long sentence) that without this moral illumination the soul departs from rectitude by a turning away of the will (*voluntatis aversione disceditur*).[20]

This ethical dimension of mental illumination is present in even the first works that Augustine wrote. The dialogue *On Order* discusses the soul's knowledge of the foundations of mathematics and notes a similar fundamental awareness of the principles of right living: "By degrees the soul leads itself toward good habits and the best life (*ad mores vitamque optimam . . . perducit*), not only through faith but by sure reasoning" (*certa ratione*).[21] And in the treatise *Against Faustus the Manichee* (A.D. 400) we find this explanatory text:

> Far different from the cogitation whereby I think about limited and familiar bodies is that incomparably distinct cogitation in which I understand justice, chastity, faith, truth, charity, goodness, and whatever else is like these. Now tell me, if you can, in regard to this cogitation known by trustworthy evidence, what kind of illumination is identified with this cogitation, whereby all those things that are not this light are both distin-

guished among themselves and shown to be different
from the light. Yet even this light is not the Light that
is God: the former is created, the latter is the Creator.
. . . From it come the beginning of our act of being
(*initium existendi*), the principle of our act of knowing
(*ratio cognoscendi*), and the law of our act of loving (*lex
amandi*).[22]

Note how this passage distinguishes the three functions of
divine illumination: the metaphysical, the epistemological,
and the moral. It also relates the light of the mind to law (*lex*)
and to loving (*amandi*). This connection we shall examine
later.

Fifteen years later, in *The Trinity*, Augustine asks
where the rules (*regulae*) of moral righteousness are to be
found. He suggests that they are available to all men, even
the unjust. They do not originate from men's minds (*nec in
habitu suae mentis*)[23] but stem from the immutable Truth
above.

Where indeed are these rules written, wherein even the
unrighteous man recognizes what is right, wherein he
discerns that he ought to have what he himself lacks?
Where, then, are they written, if not in the book of that
Light that is called Truth? Whence every righteous law
is copied and transferred . . . to the heart of the man
that worketh righteousness, as the impression from a
ring passes into the wax, yet does not leave the ring.[24]

Much the same explanation is offered in the *Treatise on St.
John's Gospel*, where we read that unless the "eye of the mind"
be irradiated with the light of Truth, it will be unable to
achieve either wisdom or justice (*nec ad sapientiam nec ad
justitiam poterit pervenire*).[25]

Toward the end of his life, Augustine was still speaking
of moral illumination, but now he stresses the affective and
loving aspects of this experience. "When the mind has been
imbued with the beginning of the faith 'that works through

love' " (*per dilectionem*, Gal. 5:6), he explains, "then it tends by right living (*bene vivendo*) . . . toward the beatific vision which constitutes supreme happiness."[26] Progress in right living is accomplished through the development of the moral and theological virtues. Of course the four cardinal virtues were well known to the ancient Greeks and Romans, and Augustine frequently borrows their definitions of these virtues. He thus shows that he was convinced that the ancients shared in the benefits of moral illumination. A famous passage in the *City of God* discusses and approves these philosophical meanings.[27] Temperance (the Greek *sophrosyne*, as he notes) "bridles carnal lusts and prevents them from winning the consent of the spirit to wicked deeds." Prudence distinguishes "good from evil things." Justice "renders to every man his due." And Fortitude enables man "to bear patiently" the ills of life.[28] The rightness of these definitions of natural virtue, which Augustine regards as universally known and accepted by mankind, is guaranteed by the light of reason working in all men.

That these natural virtues, together with such supernatural ones as faith, hope and charity, are known to men through the divine light is beautifully explained in the following little-known text from the *Literal Commentary on Genesis*:

> So also among the objects of the intellect there are some that are seen in the soul itself: for example the virtues (to which the vices are opposed), either the virtues which will endure, such as piety, or virtues that are useful for this life and not destined to remain in the next, as faith, by which we believe what we do not see, and hope, by which we await with patience the life that shall be, and patience itself, by which we bear every adversity until we arrive at the goal of our desires. These virtues, of course, and other similar ones, which are quite necessary for us now in living out our exile, will have no place in the blessed life, for the attainment

of which they are necessary. And yet even they are seen with the intellect; for they are not bodies, nor have they forms similar to bodies. But distinct from these objects is the light by which the soul is illumined, in order that it may see and truly understand everything, either in itself or in the light. For the light is God himself, whereas the soul is a creature; yet, since it is rational and intellectual, it is made in His image. And when it tries to behold the Light, it trembles in its weakness and finds itself unable to do so. Yet from this source comes all the understanding it is able to attain. When, therefore, it is thus carried off and, after being withdrawn from the senses of the body, is made present to this vision in a more perfect manner (not by a spatial relation but in a way proper to its being), it also sees above itself that Light in whose illumination it is enabled to see all the objects that it sees and understands within itself.[29]

We may observe in this key text Augustine's forthright claim that all our higher knowledge depends on divine illumination and that the source of the intellectual light is God. However, he is careful to say that we wayfarers on earth do not see God: when the soul "tries to behold the Light, it trembles in its weakness and finds itself unable to do so."

III. JUDGMENT AND MORAL EVALUATION

We have already noted how central the act of judgment is in Augustine's theory of knowledge. He knew the literal signification of the Latin word *judicare*: to declare what is right. And it is not so much the logical meaning of judgment (although that is involved) as the legal usage which is primary to Augustine. When a judge pronounces sentence on a convicted criminal, this is a *judicium* in the strong Augustinian sense. This is why he says so frequently that the judge is always superior to the object of his judgment.[30]

Of course it is possible for a person to know (*cognoscere*) in a preliminary way without making a judgment (*judicare*). To know is simply to see that something is so, or is not (*videamus ita aliquid esse vel non ita*): this is the awareness of facts. To judge is to add the dimension of "oughtness"; in judging we say, "this is how it ought to be" (*ita esse debet*).[31] Such normative judgments are made by craftsmen (*artifices*) who appraise their products and decide that they are well or ill made. Similar practical judgments enable men to regulate their moral lives. One *knows* but does not judge the eternal law of God; one judges human actions in the light of one's knowledge of God's law:

> So, in regard to our minds, we not only know that they exist in a certain manner but oftentimes that they also should be such and such (*ita esse debere*). . . . And we judge these according to the inner rules of truth (*interiores regulas veritatis*) which we discern in common.[32]

Augustine frequently expounds his theory of moral illumination in conjunction with his views on artistic judgment. At one point in *The Trinity*[33] he asks how the ardor of brotherly love for a good man is kindled in a person. He suggests that this specially approbative love stems from taking counsel with the eternal exemplar (*ratio*) of human goodness, by means of the intellectual light (*eadem luce*). Then, by way of explanation, he adds this esthetic parallel:

> When I recall to mind some arch that is beautifully and symmetrically rounded, let us say one that I saw in Carthage, a certain reality made known to the mind through my eyes and transferred to memory causes this imaginative vision. But I behold in my mind yet another thing, in accord with which that work of art pleases me; whence also, if it displeased me, I should correct it. We judge therefore of these particular things in accord with that [form] (*de istis secundum illam judi-*

camus), and we discern it by the insight of a rational mind (*et illam cernimus rationalis mentis intuitu*).

What we have, in this passage from *The Trinity*, is a normative intuitionism, depending on a theory of divine exemplarism. In the moral order it terminates in an ethical judgment which takes the pattern: "This act is good and approvable in terms of these eternal norms of judgment."

As Benoit Garceau has observed, there are two special characteristics of Augustinian judgment: 1) it is the distinctive function of the human mind, as contrasted with the sense awareness of non-rational animals; and 2) judgment is the termination of a moral progression toward an ideal, in which advance one comes closer and closer to the light of unchanging truth.[34]

In the language of the twentieth-century ethics, Augustine has a theory of moral evaluation, an axiology. One of his terms for a value judgment is *aestimatio*. To estimate, he says, is to set a price on anything.[35] God is, of course, the supreme Evaluator, but man is able to share to some extent in making judgments on the worth of both things and human activities. The treatise on *Christian Instruction* says that the person who lives in accord with the ideals of justice and holiness is the evaluator (*aestimator*) who views the whole of things (*rerum integer*). This is not merely a cognitive appraisal: it involves affective consciousness. Thus Augustine adds that the person who makes a sound value judgment is:

> he who has a love that is ordered (*ordinatam dilectionem*), lest he love what should not be loved, or not love what should be loved, or love too much what should be little loved, or give more or less love to that which should be loved equally.[36]

There might appear to be something of a circle in this teaching, for Augustine says that one must live a good moral life in order to be able to intuit the highest standards of ethical judgment. Yet he also says that one cannot live well

without the guidance of the eternal truths of morality that
are seen in the divine light. What he seems to mean is that
all men initially have the opportunity to grasp something of
the elementary values of justice, courage and right thinking; or, if they are deprived of such beginnings of moral
judgment, because of immaturity, insanity, or other impedi-
ment, then they are not responsible agents. Moreover, Augustine envisions a sort of progress in the capacity to make
sound moral judgments; this progress depends on one's continued efforts to live well and to treat others decently.
Augustine's *Sermons* often bring out this point in simple language. In one that dates from the decade 410-420, we find
this typical explanation:

> Let us try, Brethren, to think about the light of truth,
> the light of wisdom, how it is present everywhere to all;
> let us try to think of the light of justice, present to every
> thinker. What indeed is the object of this cogitation?
> . . . . Justice is right there: it is ready at hand for the
> one who lives justly. Such people see how they live
> justly in accord with its rule; as the just see it by living
> properly, so the unjust do not see it, because they live
> badly . . . it is not in any place, yet it is everywhere:
> thus is justice, wisdom, truth, purity. Let us strive,
> then, to see this sort of light; but you are not able, the
> gaze of the mind falters; let it be cleansed so that we
> may see.[37]

Such striving to do one's best requires great effort of
will. One does not try very hard to attain some objective
unless one loves it. This brings us to Augustine's analysis of
various kinds of love; for, after all, he is the man who wrote:
"Love, and do what you will."[38]

IV. LOVE AND LAW

Augustine did not mean that it is morally approvable
to do whatever you wish, provided you act with a feeling of

benevolence.[39] A sentence after the much-quoted injunction, "Love, and do what you will," he explained that love does not take the place of law but goes along with it. "You say that you love Christ," Augustine writes, "then keep his commandment (*serva mandatum ejus*) and love your neighbor."[40] At the same place he rebukes the person who says, "I love the Emperor but I hate his laws" (*Diligo imperatorem, sed odi leges ejus*). To Augustine's mind this is a practical self-contradiction: love and law are mutually supportive.

The love language in Augustine's writings is complicated.[41] For love in the broadest sense of any sort of attraction, psychic or physical, he uses *amor*. A high-minded spiritual love is usually called *dilectio* (as in the preceding paragraph). The highest kind of love is *caritas*: one's love for God, or for other beings as creatures of God. Love culminating in the joyful attainment of union with God is *fruitio*.[42] For any kind of love that gives pleasure (but usually for sensual satisfaction) Augustine uses *voluptas*. Always designating fleshly lust are the terms *libido* and *cupiditas*. Since he had no verb cognate for the noun *caritas*, he used the verb *diligere* for the act of charitable loving.[43] So the command, "love (*dilige*) God and neighbor," is expressed in the language of the purest and highest sort of love. It is not a precursor of situationist ethics.[44]

Virtue is, indeed, nothing but the supreme love of God (*summum amorem Dei*) but such love is specified in four ways in the good human character. Temperance is "a love that maintains its integrity before the object of its love"; fortitude is "a love that endures all things for the sake of its object"; justice is "a love that serves its beloved alone and thus rules all else rightly"; and practical wisdom (*prudentia*) is "a love which distinguishes wisely between those things that help and those that hinder" man's quest for God.[45] Thus, morally good love must be "ordered" to man's Creator. The simplest definition of virtue, for Augustine, is that it is the "*ordo amoris*."[46]

That which "ought to be loved" is determined by the

rules of virtue. These principles (which are also moral laws) are made available to man through moral illumination.[47] Basic to Augustine's understanding of such "oughtness" are the two precepts of charity from the New Testament. Early in his writing career Augustine connected the precept, love God and neighbor (Matt. 22:37-40), with the natural inclination to love self. Thus the divine precepts are taken as an extension of, or addition to, the law of nature (*inconcussa naturae lege*).[48] But in the later, anti-Pelagian treatises this emphasis on natural law decreases and is partly replaced by an agapistic teaching that God offers immediate moral guidance to man's soul, without much need of legalistic rules.[49] It was not that the elderly Augustine rejected the notion of moral law but rather that he came to stress the role of faith and charity in man's ready acceptance of moral ideals. In other words, moral illumination became more closely associated with the presence of grace in men's souls.

In the *Spirit and the Letter*[50] he relates this role of sanctifying grace to moral illumination. Speaking of pre-Christian thinkers, he writes:

> For they too were men, and there was inherent in them that power of nature, which enables the rational soul both to perceive and to do what is lawful (*qua legitimum aliquid anima rationalis et sentit et facit*); but the godliness (*pietas*) which transfers to another life happy and immortal has "a spotless law, converting souls" (Ps. 19:7), so that by the light thereof they may be renewed (*ex illo lumine renoventur*), and that be accomplished in them which is written, "There has been manifested over us, O Lord, the light of Thy countenance" (Ps. 4:6). Turned away from which, they have deserved to grow old, while they are incapable of renovation except by the grace of Christ (*gratia Christiana*).

Here we see developing, by the year 412, a use of divine light in the explanation of the moral impact of God's grace.

However, Augustine often cites the golden rule (usually in the negative formula: *"quod tibi non vis fieri, noli alteri facere"*[51]) as evidence for the fact that even those who are not of the Christian faith share in moral illumination. In one of his meditations on the Psalms (A.D. 418), he makes this point:

> Now there is no one who injures another who does not resent having injury done to himself. And in so doing he trangresses the law of nature, which one is not permitted to ignore, in view of his unwillingness to suffer what he is doing. . . . Now was this natural law present in the people of Israel? Certainly it was, since they were human too; they would have been without natural law, only if they could have existed outside the nature of mankind.[52]

Augustine was a classical eudaimonist, in the sense that he was firmly convinced that all men desire to be happy. Ultimate well-being (*eudaimonia*) is also, for Augustine, the basic reason for philosophizing. This is evident in his early *De Beata Vita*; the theme runs through the works of the middle period; and toward the end of his life he concluded: "Man has no reason for devoting himself to philosophy, other than to become happy."[53]

Now the way in which man achieves a dynamic level of ultimate satisfaction is described in Augustine's theory of fruition.[54] Briefly, man's will is attracted to some objects for their own sakes: his love for these intrinsic goods (all of which center in God) is designed to take joy (*frui*) in them. On the other hand, the will is attracted to other secondary goods that are useful means to the attainment of ultimate joy: man's love for these lower goods unfolds in the act of using (*uti*) them as proper means.[55] Obviously Augustine thinks that moral illumination helps men to differentiate intrinsic goods from utility goods.

Love reaches its well-ordered climax in the continued

act of enjoying the greatest good. That this object is God was something that Augustine firmly believed and strove to understand with full certainty. In fact the famous argument for the existence of God, in the second book of *De Libero Arbitrio*, is but an expansion of the view that the certitude of some of our intellectual judgments (including those in the area of morals) necessarily requires an existing supreme Truth (God) to guarantee these judgments. Such grounding of absolutely certain judgments in a supreme being is but another aspect of the theory of moral illumination.

V. THE PRESENT RELEVANCE OF THIS TEACHING

Clearly this Augustinian theory of moral illumination is completely theocentric. Without God and divine providence Augustine's ethics would amount to nothing. But he does not intend it as an exclusively Christian ethics. Just as the sun's light gives life to all, so does the Augustinian God of Lights shine forth and spiritually enliven all human souls. In our present age, not notable for its belief in a supreme being and in unchanging moral values, divine illumination may not find ready acceptance. Yet there is today an undercurrent of general concern for the re-establishment of stable values in human living. Perhaps Augustine's confident espousal of absolute ideals, without the expectation of perfect goodness in the actual lives of men, may point the way to a high-minded ethics of the future.

We have already noted that this ethics resembles a moral intuitionism. But there is at least one great difference between Augustinian illuminationism and the insight theories of modern ethics. Generally speaking, the present-day intuitionist offers an ethics claiming the ability to discern by immediate inspection the difference between a good and a bad *deed*. This is the sort of approach espoused by G. E. Moore in the first chapter of his *Principia Ethica*. The focal point of ethical attention is for the modern intuitionist the individual human action. But Augustine stressed the ideal standard, the *ratio aeterna*, of moral goodness. His ethical insight was directed toward general norms, rules, patterns of approvable behavior. His divine light was primarily for the vision of higher truths, rather than for the appraisal of concrete activities. Of course he felt that particular judgments of conscience are enlightened by previous or concomitant moral illumination of the standards of judgment. But the primary role of Augustine's moral illumination was not in the area of a deed-ethics.

Another emphasis in Augustine's ethics tends to counteract what might appear as an abstract universalism in the preceding paragraph. He actually shared many of the concrete concerns of the more serious existentialists of the twentieth century. This is a feature much stressed by modern German interpreters. People like Franz Koerner and Caroline Schuetzinger, among others, have drawn attention to many resemblances between phenomenology and the moral viewpoint of Augustine.[56] Here the similarities lie in the stress on the affective and loving side of good actions and in the Augustinian tendency to teach by means of examples and biographical studies of good men. Certainly the notion that Augustine's ethics is simply a legalistic code of conduct is in contrast to this quite valid existential interpretation.

NOTES

1. A large part of *De Genesi ad Litteram* is concerned with this ontological role of light; see my *Augustine's View of Reality* (Villanova, 1964) for details.

2. *De Civitate Dei* VIII, 4, speaking of Plato and other philosophers, says: "aliquid tale de Deo sentiunt, ut in illo inveniatur et causa subsistendi, et ratio intelligendi, et ordo vivendi. Quorum trium, unum ad naturalem, alterum ad rationalem, tertium ad moralem partem intelligitur pertinere." Etienne Gilson, *Introduc-*

tion à l'étude de saint Augustin, 3rd ed. (Paris, 1949), pp. 167-168, points to this triple role of divine illumination: "Il y a donc dans l'augustinisme une illumination physique et une illumination morale comparables en tous points à l'illumination intellectuelle, et qui reposent sur les mêmes bases métaphysiques."

3. Ronald H. Nash, *The Light of the Mind: St. Augustine's Theory of Knowledge* (Lexington, Ky., 1969), Chap. vii, discusses three main interpretations. For a good collection of the key epistemological texts in Latin, see L. W. Keeler, ed., *Sancti Augustini Doctrina de Cognitione* (Rome, 1934).

4. These three levels of vision are discussed in *De Genesi ad Litteram* XII, 6-11; the passage is in English in my *Essential Augustine* (Indianapolis, 1974), pp. 93-96.

5. *De Magistro* 12, 40, in *Oeuvres de s. Augustin*, Bibliothèque Augustinienne (Paris, 1947-   ) (hereafter cited as BA), Vol. 6, p. 106. The English is a revision of J. Mourant, *Introduction to the Philosophy of Saint Augustine* (University Park, Pa., 1964), p. 198. Unless otherwise indicated, later English translations are my own.

6. *De Libero Arbitrio* II, 12, 33 (BA, Vol. 6, p. 278).

7. *De Trinitate* XII, 15, 24, in *Corpus Christianorum*, Vol. L (Tournhout, 1968) (hereafter cited as *CC*, Vol. L), pp. 377-78.

8. *Epistola 92, ad Italicam*, Sect. 2, in *Corpus Scriptorum Ecclesiasticorum Latinorum* (Vienna, 1866-   ) (hereafter cited as *CSEL*), Vol. XXXIV (II), p. 437.

9. For the texts of Augustine that run counter to the Ontologistic interpretation, see L. W. Keeler, *S. Augustini de Cognitione*, pp. 61-64.

10. S. Thomas Aquinas *Summa contra Gentiles* II, cap. 79, where he speaks of "anima humana, cujus lumen est intellectus agens." Note, however, that Aquinas also admits the possibility of human participation in the light of the highest Truth, either on the level of nature or of grace. Cf. *Summa Theologiae* I, q. 88, 3, ad primum.

11. Nash, *The Light of the Mind*, p. 98.

12. *De Magistro* 11, 38 (BA, Vol. 6, p. 102).

13. Keeler, *S. Augustini de Cognitione*, p. 64, comments: "Deus mentem illuminat, non ipsas ideas ei imprimendo, sed modo dumtaxat formali et regulativo, manifestando veritatem judiciorum necessariorum." This is the explanation also offered by Gilson, *Introd. à l'étude de s. Augustin*, pp. 110-41. For the frequently

used example, seven plus three equals ten, see *Confessiones* VI, 4, 6; and *De Libero Arbitrio* II, 8, 21.

14. Cf. Bourke, "Wisdom in the Gnoseology of St. Augustine," *Augustinus* (Madrid), 3, 10-11, (1958), pp. 331-36.

15. *De Diversis Quaestionibus 83*, q. 46 (BA, Vol. 10, pp. 122-28): "Has autem rationes ubi arbitrandum est esse, nisi in ipsa mente Creatoris?"

16. For a discussion of the *rationes aeternae* as principles of existing things, see my *Augustine's View of Reality*, pp. 4-23.

17. *De Gen. ad Lit.* XII, 27, 55, in *Patrologia Latina* ed. J. P. Migne (Paris, 1844-80), 34: 478.

18. *Epistola 147, ad Paulinam* cap. 4: "ita videas mentis intuitu, ut vides vitam, voluntatem, cogitationem, memoriam, intelligentiam, scientiam, fidem tuam."

19. *De Gen. ad Lit.* VIII, 12, 26 (*Patrologia Latina* 34:383): "sicut operatur homo terram ut culta atque fecunda sit . . . ita Deus operatur hominem justum, id est justificando eum . . . sic homo Deo sibi praesente illuminatur."

20. Gilson, *Introd. à l'étude de s. Augustin*, p. 111, note 3.

21. *De Ordine* II, 19, 50 (BA, Vol. 4, p. 450).

22. *Contra Faustum Manichaeum* XX, 7 (*Patrologia Latina* 42:372).

23. The fact that moral values are not innate in the human mind, for Augustine, demarcates his ethics from Kant's apriorism. Many German interpreters miss this difference.

24. *De Trinitate* XIV, 15, 21 (*CC*, Vol. L, pp. 450-51). The translation is by Marcus Dods (Edinburgh, 1887).

25. *In Joannis Evangelium* Tract. XXXV, 8, 3 (*Patrologia Latina* 35:1658).

26. *Enchiridion* 1, 5 (BA, Vol. 9, pp. 106-08).

27. *De Civitate Dei* XIX, 4 (BA, Vol, 37, pp. 66-70).

28. The English definitional phrases are from the Dods translation.

29. *De Gen. ad Lit.* XII, 31, 59 (*Patrologia Latina* 34:479-80); the English version by J. H. Taylor, S.J., is from *The Essential Augustine*, p. 97.

30. *De Vera Religione* 29, 53 (BA, Vol. 8, p. 98): "Jam vero illud videre facillimum est praestantiorem esse judicantem, quam illa res de qua judicatur." Cf. *De Lib. Arb.* II, 12, 33-34 (BA, Vol. 6, pp. 278-80).

124 Morality and Values

31. *De Vera Relig.* 31, 58 (BA. Vol. 8, p. 108).

32. *De Lib. Arb.* II, 12, 34 (BA, Vol. 6, p. 280).

33. *De Trinitate* IX, 6, 11 (*CC*, Vol. L, p. 303).

34. Benoit Garceau, *Judicium: Vocabulaire, sources, doctrine, de saint Thomas d'Aquin* (Montréal-Paris, 1968), p. 58: "pour le Maître d'Hippone, le jugement comporte deux caractéristiques: il est l'acte propre de l'esprit, la fonction qui distingue l'homme de la brute, la connaissance intellectuelle de la représentation sensible; et il constitue le but d'une démarche morale, un idéal dont on s'approche en se conformant toujours mieux à la lumiére immuable, qui est au-dessus de l'œil de l'âme, la vérité." Much the same interpretation of judgment in Augustine is found in Knut Ragnar Holte, *Béatitude et sagesse* (Paris, 1962), pp. 63-70.

35. *Enarrationes in Psalmos* 143, 10 (*Patrologia Latina* 37:1863): "Aestimatio enim est, quanti pretii sit quidque." For *aestimatio* as an act of reason, see *De Musica* VI, 9, 23 (BA, Vol. 7, pp. 110-112).

36. *De Doctrina Christiana* I, 27, 28 (BA, Vol. 11, p. 214).

37. *Sermo IV, De Jacob et Esau*, 6, 7 (*Patrologia Latina* 38:36).

38. *In Epistolam Joannis ad Parthos* Tract. 7, 4, 8 (*Patrologia Latina* 35:2033): "Dilige, et fac quod vis."

39. See my criticism of such an interpretation by recent situationists, in "Saint Augustine and Situationism," *Augustinus* (Madrid), 12 (1967), 117-23.

40. *In Epist. Joan.* Tract. 9, 4, 11 (*Patrologia Latina* 35:2053).

41. Of the many secondary studies the most helpful are: Hélène Pétré, *Caritas: Etude sur le vocabulaire Latin de la charité chrétienne* (Louvain, 1948), pp. 95 ff.; Hannah Arendt, *Die Liebesbegriff bei Augustinus* (Berlin, 1929); Josef Brechtken, *Augustinus Doctor Caritatis: Sein Liebesbegriff* (Meisenheim am Glan, 1975); and John Burnaby, *Amor Dei: Augustine on the Love of God* (London, 1947). See my *Joy in Augustine's Ethics* (Villanova, 1979).

43. *De Div. Quaest. 83*, q. 36, 1 (BA, Vol. 10, p. 104).

44. Cf. my "Augustine and Situationism," pp. 117-23.

45. *De Moribus Ecclesiae Catholicae* I, 15, 25 (BA, Vol. 1, pp. 174-76).

46. *De Civ. Dei* XV, 22 (BA, Vol. 36, p. 140). See Norbert Hartmann, "Ordo amoris. Zur augustinischen Wesensbestimmung des Sittlichen," *Wessenschaft und Weisheit*, 18 (1955), 1-23, 108-21.

47. *De Div. Quaest. 83*, q. 35 (BA, Vol. 10, pp. 100-04), which asks, "Quid amandum sit?" And *Epistola 167*, 3, 11 to 4, 15, where he concludes that "virtue is the love with which that which ought to be loved is loved." See the English in Mourant, *Introduction*, pp. 290-93.

48. *De Doct. Christ.* I, 26, 27 (BA, Vol. 11, p. 212); compare *De Sermone Domini in Monte* II, 9.

49. See my article, "Voluntarism in Augustine's Ethico-Legal Thought," *Augustinian Studies*, 1 (1970), 3-17. The shift from a natural-law ethics was noted earlier in Guido Fasso, *Le legge della ragione* (Bologna, 1964), pp. 29-46.

50. *De Spiritu et Littera* 27, 48 (*Patrologia Latina* 44:229-30); the English is P. Holmes' from the *Nicene and Post-Nicene Fathers*, reprinted in Whitney Oates, *Basic Writings of St. Augustine* (New York, 1948), I, 499.

51. *En. in Ps.* 57, 1 (*Patrologia Latina* 36:673-74).

52. *En. in Ps.* 118, *Sermo* 25, 4 (*Patrologia Latina* 37:1574). Cf. *Epist. 157*, 15 (*Patrologia Latina* 33: 681).

53. *De Civ. Dei* XIX, 1, 3 (BA, Vol. 37, p. 58): "Nulla esset homini causa philosophandi, nisi ut beatus sit."

54. My book *Joy in Augustine's Ethics* explores this *frui-uti* theme.

55. The most important explanation of fruition and use as aspects of love is in *De Doct. Christ.* I, 3,3 to 5,5 (BA, Vol. 11, pp. 182-86).

56. Cf. Franz Koerner, *Vom Sein und Sollen des Menschen: Die existential-ontolologischen Grundlagen der Ethik in augustinischer Sicht* (Paris, 1963); and C. E. Schuetzinger, *The German Controversy of St. Augustine's Illumination Theory* (New York, 1960).

CHAPTER 9

Situationism and Augustine's Ethics

In some recent treatments of situation ethics (or the so-called *New Morality*) St. Augustine is cited as a patristic supporter of this kind of moral teaching. The present brief study is devoted to the examination of this odd claim. We will look at the ethical position of the situationists and compare it with the key text in Augustine's *Tractates on St. John's First Epistle*. We will recall certain points in the general ethical position of the Bishop of Hippo to see whether he is actually a patron of Christian *Situationsethik*.

A recent book by Joseph Fletcher quotes the famous Augustinian phrase, *Dilige et quod vis fac*, and then suggests that this is an expression of situationism.[1] The author is careful to note that Augustine's view is not antinomianism but is a Christian morality stressing charity and opposing the legalism of later Catholic moral doctrine. Fletcher's version of the new morality has attracted much attention in American Catholic circles, partly because of the publication of his article, *"Love is the only measure,"* in a Catholic weekly magazine.[2] No one, as yet, has challenged Fletcher's allegation that St. Augustine was a situationist.

It was in 1952 that Pope Pius XII drew the attention of the Catholic world to what he called the "morality of the situation."[3] His Holiness bluntly condemned this new moral theory. Various Catholic journals soon produced articles explaining the history and basic teaching of "situation ethics."[4]

In 1928 a little known German ethician published a book which has been regarded as the first in the European school of situation ethics.[5] Basically, the view of the situationists is comparatively simple. Every individual moral problem must be decided by the decision of the person involved. There are no absolutely true moral laws or rules. All that is needed for a good moral decision is the motivation of love. As Fletcher states it:

> Only one 'general' proposition is prescribed, namely, the commandment to love God through the neighbor . . . All else, all other generalities (e.g. 'One should tell the truth' and 'One should respect life') are at most only *maxims*, never rules. For the situationist there are no rules — none at all.[6]

In point of fact, ethical relativism is by no means a new theory. To indicate many advocates of this position in the history of ethics would be an easy task. Let us consider but one instance, John Dewey. In his middle period as a writer on ethics, Dewey frequently argued that universal laws of morality have no value. What is important is an honest and reflective appraisal of each moral situation as it arises in its concrete circumstances and with its apparent consequences. As he put it in a book written before 1920:

> The blunt assertion that every moral situation is a unique situation having its own irreplaceable good may seem not merely blunt but preposterous. For the established tradition teaches that it is precisely the irregularity of special cases which makes necessary the guidance of conduct by universals . . . Let us, however, follow the pragmatic rule, and in order to discover the meaning of the idea ask for its consequences. Then it surprisingly turns out that the primary significance of the unique and moral character of the concrete situation is to transfer the weight and burden of morality to intelligence.[7]

Dewey used the language of situationism and was profoundly suspicious of ethical absolutes. He did not, however, attempt to call his position a Christian ethics. Nor did he put it under the patronage of Augustine.

One special feature of contemporary situationism should be noted before we turn to the moral teaching of St. Augustine. Distinctive of this new school is the use of sensational examples, mostly chosen from the field of sexual problems, to illustrate the theory of situation ethics. Possibly some of the popular appeal of this type of ethics is due to this characteristic. Something of this sensationalism may go back to the prison writings of Dietrich Bonhoeffer, the Lutheran theologian who was executed in 1945 for alleged involvement in a plot to assassinate Adolf Hitler.[8] He has lent prestige to the situationist movement by the circumstances of his death and by his obvious sincerity. Bonhoeffer continually argues that what is all-important morally is a good intention. Any act (tyrannicide is his usual example) may be justified by the immediate situation. What Bonhoeffer has that is lacking in some other Christian situationists is the intimation that God may guide the troubled soul in its personal decision by a special communication.

John Robinson, Anglican Bishop of Woolwich, is one of the most prominent British advocates of situation ethics.[9] He appears to be somewhat fascinated by the dual problems of sexuality and warfare. He regards "the Christian ethic as a radical 'ethic of the situation,' with nothing prescribed — except love."[10] Nothing is intrinsically evil, says Bishop Robinson, with the possible exception of the lack of love. Joseph Fletcher shares this preoccupation with the weaknesses of the flesh. In both his *Commonweal* article and his book, Fletcher dwells on problems of promiscuity, fornication and adultery. He is well aware of this emphasis: "Actually, the 'new morality' is a wide-ranging ethical theory of far more varied bearing than sex, but that is what it is focussed upon in the street debates. So be it."[11] This is a very Christian fixation, he argues, because there are biblical examples of good women who used sex in an approvable way for good ends. He discusses the case of Judith. Only the "ethical dishonesty of legalism" has obscured this point in the early Judaeo-Christian tradition.[12] More interesting to

Fletcher are the examples of women who engage in seduction in order to entrap men spying on the women's country. There is also the extraordinary case of the German woman in a Russian prison camp who could be released if found pregnant. She arranged for a guard to impregnate her, was duly freed, and returned to take care of her family. In both cases, Fletcher feels quite sure that the women were justified by the concrete requirements of the situation.[13]

No one familiar with medieval moral theology will think that sexual examples are either very new or very startling, of course. Indeed, it is amusing to read in an anonymous Greek commentary on Aristotle's *Nicomachean Ethics*, from the late classical age, the following anticipation of one of Fletcher's cases. "To copulate with the wife of another is evil but, if it be done to overthrow a tyrant, it is not an evil. For evil rests only in the intention."[14]

With the foregoing in mind, we may now turn to St. Augustine. Is it intellectually honest to assert that ethical situationism may be traced back to him? There is, of course, no question that Augustine did write: *Dilige, et fac quod vis.* The problem really is: what did he mean when he said, "Love and do what you will?" Let us look at the context in Latin:

> Videte quid commendamus, quia non discernuntur facta hominum nisi de radice caritatis. Nam multa fieri possunt quae speciem habent bonam et non procedunt de radice caritatis. Habent enim et spinae flores: quaedam vero videntur aspera, videntur truculenta, sed fiunt ad disciplinam dictante caritate. Semel ergo breve praeceptum tibi praecipitur, *Dilige, et quod vis fac*: sive taceas, dilectione taceas; sive clames, dilectione clames; sive emendes, dilectione emendes; sive parcas, dilectione parcas: radix sit intus dilectionis, non potest de ista radice nisi bonum existere.[15]

Augustine has been preaching about the two precepts of the New Law: to love God and to love one's neighbor. He does not suggest that having a good motive (the love of God is the only motive under discussion in the whole passage) permits one to act in discord with divine or natural law. What he does say is that a person imbued with real charity will willingly fulfill the law in all things.

This is evident throughout the treatise on St. John's Epistle. Augustine later examines the meaning of the precept to love one's neighbor. He is extremely critical of the man who says that he loves God but hates his neighbor. This man is like the person who says: "I love the emperor but I hate his laws!" Augustine makes his meaning quite clear by adding: "You say that you love Christ: then keep his commandment and love your neighbor."[16] As Fletcher admits, this is not antinomianism.[17] Augustine is not substituting love for law. It is not situationism, either, for Augustine always stressed obedience to the law of God in its entirety. Probably no great Christian writer has been more insistent than St. Augustine on the eternity, immutability and absolute character of the supreme law.[18] In his most famous work we read about: the true, inner justice which does not base its judgments on custom, but on the supremely right law of the omnipotent God, by which moral patterns of various places and times are determined according to those places and times, since it is the same everywhere and always, not differing in different places and at different times.[19]

Continuing this text, Augustine explains that what varies in the field of morality is the *application* of moral law to different cases in diverse sets of circumstances. He admits what is right for one man at one time in a certain place may be wrong for the same man under different conditions. What is good for one man may be bad for another under much the same circumstances. "But," Augustine asks, "is justice variable and mutable? Rather, the times over which it rules do not follow the same courses, for they are temporal."[20]

What the situationist ethician fails to understand is the difference between the domain of personal conscience, on the one hand, and universal laws on the other.[21] There is no school of "legalistic" ethics which maintains that man's individual moral actions are predetermined to be right or wrong by the automatic functioning of some rule of morality. Such teaching would be nonsense. It is one thing to reason on the level of universal rules or precepts, quite another thing to make a personal, moral decision.[22] Augustine speaks of people who have been confused when they hear of unusual cases in the Old Testament, where the Prophets or other characters were permitted to do extraordinary things.

> When men, ignorant of any other manner of living, happen to read about these deeds, unless they are deterred by an authority, they consider them sins. They cannot understand that their own entire mode of living, in connection with marriage, banqueting, dress, and the other necessities and refinements of human life, seems sinful to people of other nations and other times. Aroused by this diversity of innumerable customs, some souls, drowsy so to speak, who were neither settled in the sound sleep of folly nor able to waken fully to the light of wisdom, have thought that justice did not exist of itself, but that each nation regarded as right that which was its own custom . . . They have not understood (not to multiply instances) that the maxim, 'Do not do to another what you do not wish to have done to you,' cannot be varied in any way by any national diversity of customs. When this rule is applied to the love of God, all vices die; when it is applied to the love of our neighbor, all crimes vanish.[23]

It is a tremendous misunderstanding of St. Augustine to interpret him as an ethical relativist. There is no such suggestion in the standard expositions of his moral teaching.[24] In fact, Augustine's whole treatise, *On the Spirit and the Law*, seems to have been written to establish the contrary. It is the work of reason to know the law and to declare its obligations in general terms; it is the function of the heart to accept the law with love and to carry out its commands.[25] Augustine sees no antithesis between what is required by law and by love.

> Not that the law is itself evil but because the commandment has its good in the manifesting of the letter rather than in the helping of the spirit; and if this commandment is kept from the fear of punishment and not from the love of justice, it is kept in a slavish way and not freely, and thus it is not kept. For no fruit is good which does not stem from the root of charity. If, then, that faith which works through love be present, there is a beginning of that joy in the law of God according to the inner man; and this joy does not pertain to the letter but is a gift of the spirit.[26]

This attempt of situationists to divorce the motivation of charity from the rule of law would not be very important if it were but an isolated and passing phenomenon. Unfortunately, such is not the case. There is a strong movement within Catholic thought in our day toward a Catholic situationism. This is part of a general reaction against older traditions. Professor Fletcher cites in his support, for Catholic readers, a book by Louis Monden which discusses situationism and makes a rather favorable judgment on it.[27] If Father Monden means that Catholic morality pays attention to the concrete circumstances of proposed actions, then we may agree that the actual situation should be emphasized in every moral decision. But situation ethics implies much more than this approach to the prudential judgment. This new morality is part of a general attack on intellect, the life of reason, the order of nature, and the reality of specific natures.[28]

Fletcher knows that a difference in metaphysics makes a difference in ethics. He contrasts the old, legalist ethic with the new, love ethic. The former is supported by the "legalists or absolutizers" who are realists in their view of natures and intrinsecists in their approach to good and bad action. The latter position is held by situationists who are relativists and nominalists in their notion of natures and extrinsecalists in their judgment of right and wrong. "The intrinsic idea of moral quality is Thomist, the extrinsic idea is Occamist," according to Fletcher.[29]

We are not here concerned with the accuracy of this judgment on Thomism and Ockhamism. It is hoped that this short study has indicated where St. Augustine belongs. He is not an extrinsecalist on the question of the moral quality of human actions. Good and bad are not mere attributions by extrinsic denomination. Above all, it should be evident that St. Augustine is not a situationist ethician.

NOTES

1. *Situation Ethics. The New Morality*, Philadelphia 1966, p. 81. Joseph Fletcher is a professor of ethics at the Episcopal Theological Seminary, Cambridge, Massachusetts.

2. *Commonweal* 83, 14 (Jan. 14, 1966) 427-432; the article was followed, pp. 432-437, by a response written by Herbert McCabe.

3. *De conscientia Christiana in invenibus recte efformanda* (radio address by Pius XII, Vatican City, March 23, 1952); "Allocution to the World Federation of Catholic Young Women" (in French, April 18, 1952); both are published in *Periodica*, 41 (June-Sept. 1952) and in English in *Irish Ecclesiastical Record* 77, 1952, pp. 137-142.

4. Fuchs, Joseph: *Situationsethik in theologischer Sicht*, in *Scholastik* 27, 1952, pp. 161-183; Paquin, Jules: *La 'Nouvelle' Morale*, in *Relations* 1952, pp. 234-237; Poppi, Antonino: *La morale di Situazione. Presentazione e analisi delle sue fonti*, in *Miscellanea Franciscana* 57, 1957, pp. 3-63; von Hildebrand, Dietrich: *True Morality and Its Counterfeits* (New York 1955); published in German as, *Wahre Sittlichkeit und Situationsethik* (Düsseldorf 1957); McGlynn, J. V. and Toner, J. J.: *Existentialism and Situation Ethics*, in *Modern Ethical Theories* (Milwaukee 1963), pp. 93-114.

5. Grisebach, Eberhard: *Gegenwart: eine kritische Ethik* (Halle 1936). Cf. Rauche, G. A.: *The Philosophy of Actuality* (Fort Hare,

Cape 1964) a full-length analysis of Grisebach's thought. See also: Alcala, Manuel: *La ética de la situacion y Th. Steinbüchel* (Madrid 1963).

6. *Situation Ethics*, p. 55. The title of his seventh chapter is illuminating: "Love justifies its means," pp. 120-133.

7. *Reconstruction in Philosophy* (New York 1920), p. 162.

8. Two books are now available in English: Bonhoeffer's *Letters and Papers from Prison*, and his *Ethics* (finished and edited by his friend Pasto Bethge); (New York 1965).

9. See his two ethical works, *Christian Morals Today*, Philadelphia 1964; and *God, Sex, and War* (Philadelphia 1965).

10. Cf. Ved Mehta: *The New Theologian*, in *New Yorker*, November 13, 20 and 27, 1965.

11. *Love is the only measure*, p. 429.

12. *Ibid.* p. 431.

13. *Situation Ethics*, pp. 163-165.

14. *In Ethica Nicomachea*, Lib. II-V, ed. G. Heylbut in *Commentaria Graeca in Aristotelem*, XX (Berlin 1892), p. 142, lines 9-12; cf. Gauthier, R. A.: *La morale d'Aristote* (Paris 1958), p. 78.

15. *In Epistolam Ioannis ad Parthos*, 4, 7, 8 PL 35, 2033.

16. *Ibid.* 9, 11: "Quis est qui dicat, *Diligo imperatorem, sed odi leges eius?* In hoc intellegit imperator, si diligis eum, si observentur leges eius per provincias. Lex imperatoris quae est? *Mandatum novum do vobis, ut vos invicem diligatis.* Dicis ergo te diligere Christum: serva mandatum eius, et fratrem dilige."

17. *Situation Ethics*, p. 81.

18. Cf. Combés, Gustave: *La doctrine politique de saint Augustin* (Paris 1927), p. 129; Schubert, Alois: *Augustins Lex-Aeterna-Lehre* in *BGPM* 24, 2 (Münster 1924), pp. 3-20.

19. *Confessiones* III 7, 13 translation by Bourke (New York 1953), p. 61.

20. *Ibid.* "Numquid iustitia varia est et mutabilis? Sed tempora quibus praesidet non pariter eunt; tempora enim sunt."

21. Cf. Bourke: *Ethics in Crisis* (Milwaukee 1966), "Foreword."

22. See *De ordine* II 8, 25.

23. *De doctrina Christiana* III 14, 22, translation by J. J. Gavigan (New York 1947), pp. 134-135.

24. See, for example: Armas, Gregorio: *La Moral de San Agustin* (Madrid 1954); Mausbach, Joseph: *Die Ethik des hl.*

Augustinus (Freiburg i. Br. 1909-1929); Roland-Gosselin, B.: *St. Augustine's System of Morals*, in *St. Augustine: His Age, Life and Thought* (New York 1957), pp. 225-248; Koerner, F.: *Vom Sein und Sollen des Menschen. Die existentialontologischen Grundlagen der Ethik in augustinischer Sicht* (Paris 1963).

25. See especially, *De spiritu et littera* 28, 49.

26. *Ibid.* 14, 26. Note that both the "letter" and the "spirit" are aspects of the "law" and neither is contrasted with it.

27. *Sin, Liberty and Law* (New York 1965). From it Fletcher quotes: "we must clearly affirm with the great classical authors that Catholic morality is, in fact, a situation ethics," *Commonweal*, p. 437.

28. Cf. Kline, George L.: *European Philosophy Today* (Chicago 1965). In particular the two essays: Ferrater Mora, José: *The Philosophy of Xavier Zubiri*, pp. 15-28; and J. Gray Glenn, *The New Image of Man in Martin Heidegger's Philosophy*, pp. 31-58.

29. *Love is the only measure*, p. 429.

CHAPTER 10

Ethico-Legal Voluntarism

Controversy was a great stimulant to Saint Augustine. In the throes of polemic his mental adrenalin ran strong and flowed into new patterns of thought. He recognized his own ability to change his mind and gloried in his capacity for self-correction.[1] One instance of such a change is found in his explanation of the ultimate basis of moral law. The present brief study is designed to suggest how he moved from an early natural-law position to a legal voluntarism, in later life. Indeed, it could be argued that his thinking on this matter ran through four periods, as we shall see.

LEGAL VOLUNTARISM TODAY

Voluntarism is the key term in this investigation. Since it is used in a variety of ways, we shall first state how it is understood here. In general any theory which stresses volition over and above other psychic functions may be called voluntaristic. Some voluntarisms are metaphysical, making will the fundamental principle of reality; others are dynamic, making will the original force manifested in all events; still other voluntarisms are cognitive, reducing all knowing to willing. None of these three types is necessarily attributed to Augustine in this study. What we are examining is the view that the source and standard of moral good is the will of some legislator.[2] In the case of the older Augustine, this law-maker will be God. It should also be added that legal voluntarism always implies some downgrading of the role of intellect or reason in the origination of law.

This position of ethico-legal voluntarism is very prominent today. Protestant "Christian Ethics" is frankly voluntaristic. Many readers will have seen this exemplified in the situation ethics of Joseph Fletcher which is addressed to the general public. It also characterizes more scholarly treatises. Helmut Thielicke, the eminent Lutheran theologian, quotes with approval the famous dictum of Martin Luther on the harlotry of reason. Thielicke argues that dependence on reason is un-Christian.[3] As Carl Michalson sees the history of moral thinking there are two distinct traditions which merge in Kant. One is *rational*, represented in Christian works by Pelagius, Thomas Aquinas, Erasmus and the seventeenth-century Jesuits; the other is *voluntaristic*, "represented by Augustine, the voluntarists of the fourteenth century, the Reformers and the Jansenists." Michalson thinks that the "predestinarian categories of the Augustinian tradition clash with both the rationalistic and the moralistic categories of the Greek and Roman traditions."[4] Another writer on Christian ethics claims that "Augustine's *Confessions* and Emil Brunner's *Man in Revolt* are classic expressions of this voluntarism normative in Christian thought."[5] This is not a view peculiar to Lutheran theology. John Calvin was an equally thorough voluntarist in the domain of morality: "La volonté de Dieu est tellement la reigle supreme et souveraine de justice: que tout ce qu'il veult, il le fault tenir pour juste, d'autant qu'il le veult."[6]

Contemporary phenomenology and existential philosophy are also anti-rational and voluntaristic in their moral stances. As one popular work puts it: "the fact remains that Voluntarism has always been, in intention at least, an effort to go beyond the thought to the concrete existence of the thinker who is thinking that thought."[7] At least some commentators feel that St. Augustine was a pioneer advocate of existential voluntarism.[8]

Somewhat associated with this anti-rational voluntarism of Protestant ethics and some recent philosophers is the new religious position of certain Catholic writers. Leslie

Dewart, for instance, has claimed that traditional Christian thought of the Scholastic variety has been vitiated by the rationalism, naturalism and legalism of Greek philosophy. Whatever the merit or demerit of such charges (to my mind their merit is minimal) it is a fact that ethico-legal voluntarism is quite prominent in recent religious and philosophic thought — and that Augustine is frequently cited as an originator of this emphasis on will. The older standard expositions of Augustine's thought, particularly those done by Catholic scholars, give little indication of this voluntarism but this may be due to a certain neglect of the polemical treatises of the later period.

REASON AND LAW IN AUGUSTINE'S EARLY WORKS: A.D. 388-398

Some interpreters of Augustine are quick to stress the rational and natural-law features of his thought. As a principle or source of law, *ratio* is certainly emphasized in the works written between 388 and 398. In this decade, while still a young convert with a background in classical literature, Augustine was much impressed with the Platonic world of Forms. These ideal forms become the *rationes aeternae*, eternal principles in the mind of God, in accord with which all created things possess definite natures, all of men's certain judgments are verified, and all practical decisions and actions in the moral-religious area are to be guided.[9] Fused with this theory of the *rationes* is Cicero's Stoic conception of the law of nature.[10] Both the language and thought of Augustine's early works are influenced by texts from Cicero, such as this:

> Est quidem vera lex ratio naturae congruens, diffusa in omnes, constans, sempiterna, quae vocet ad officium iubendo, vetando a fraude deterreat . . . nec erit alia lex Romae alia Athenis, alia nunc posthac, sed et

omnes gentes et omni tempore una lex et sempiterna et
immutabilis continebit, unusque erit communis quasi
magister et imperator omnium deus: ille legis huius in-
ventor, disceptator, lator; cui qui non parebit, ipse se
fugiet ac naturam hominis aspernatus hoc ipso luet
maximas poenas, etiamsi caetera supplicia, quae
putantur, effugerit.[11]

Compare this Ciceronian description of natural law
with the following section from Augustine's dialogue *On Free
Choice* (this part was probably written as early as 388):

Quid? illa lex quae summa ratio nominatur, cui semper obtemperandum est, et per quam mali miseram,
boni beatam vitam merentur, per quam denique illam
quam temporalem vocandam diximus, recte fertur,
recteque mutatur, potestne cupiam intelligenti non incommutabilis aeternaque videri? An potest aliquando
injustum esse ut mali miseri, boni autem beati sint; aut
ut modestus et gravis populus ipse sibi magistratus
creet, dissolutus vero et nequam ista licentia careat?
Evodius: Video hanc aeternam esse atque incommutabilem legem.
Augustinus: Simul etiam te videre arbitror in illa tem-
porali nihil esse justum atque legitimum, quod non ex
hac aeterna sibi homines derivarint.[12]

At much the same time (probably in the early 390's)
Augustine explained in his *Eighty-three Different Questions* that
all things are made and governed by God according to a rational plan. The reasons (*rationes*) for all things are contained
in the divine mind and are the eternal and immutable standards from which all laws are derived.[13] Writing in 394,
Augustine further related this rational approach to a famous
text of St. Paul (Rom. 2:14-16), to which he gives a natural-
law interpretation.

When will such people grasp that there is no soul,
however perverse, but with some trace of a reasoning

faculty [*quae tamen ullo modo ratiocinari potest*], that has
not God speaking to its conscience? For who was it that
wrote the law of nature into the hearts of men, if not
God? It was this law concerning which the Apostle
says: *For when the Gentiles, who have not the Law, do by
nature those things that are of the Law, these having not the
Law are a law to themselves, who show the work of the Law
written in their hearts, their conscience bearing them witness and
their thoughts between themselves accusing or also defending one
another, in the day when God shall judge the secrets of men.*
Wherefore, if concerning each single rational soul,
even when blinded by passion, whatever is true in its
reasoning as it thinks and reasons, must not be attributed to itself, but to the light of truth itself by which
it is enlightened, only dimly, perhaps — according to its
capacity — so as to perceive a modicum of truth in its
process of reasoning . . .[14]

In later years, this text of St. Paul will be given other
explanations by Augustine but in this first period he clearly
takes it as teaching that God legislates as a rational being,
writing the law on the hearts of men, illuminating their
reasoning powers as to the truth of eternal law. The whole
interpretation is expressed in a cognitive framework, stressing the rational nature of man.[15] St. Paul is saying that God
enables all men to know, by reasoning, what they must do
to love well. There is no suggestion of legal voluntarism in
these works that Augustine wrote before A.D. 400.

A PERIOD OF TRANSITION: A. D. 398-410

Frequently cited as the Augustinian definition of eternal law is a sentence from a work written in 400, where he
says: "Eternal law, then, is the divine reason or will of God,
commanding the preservation of natural order, and pro-
hibiting its disturbance."[16] The passage goes on to stress the

importance of reason in man but it hesitates as to whether God's reason or will is the source of divine commands. Then, in one of Augustine's sermons on the Psalms (thought to date about 403) the will of God is bluntly identified with God's law.[17] Similarly, a *Sermon*, probably preached in 410,[18] states that justice is that which God wills.[19] It would seem that Augustine's growing familiarity with Scripture and the earlier Fathers may have now influenced his language, so that he speaks more frequently of the will of God.

However, the key work in what looks like a transitional period in Augustine's thinking about law is the *Confessions* (398-403). This work is obviously open to diverse emphases by various interpreters. Some readers see it as stressing the rational character of eternal law, while others hail it as a classic presentation of divine voluntarism. St. Paul's law "written in the hearts of men" is still held to be available to all men and "even iniquity does not erase it."[20] But the human justice of those who judge "by man's tribunal" (1 Cor. 4:3) is regarded as much inferior to "the supremely right law of the omnipotent God, by which moral patterns of various places and times are determined according to those places and times, since it is the same everywhere and always, not differing in different places and at different times."[21] God's omnipotence as a ruler and legislator is now stressed, as is usual in voluntaristic writings:

> But, when God commands something opposed to a custom or compact of any people, though it has never been done there, it is to be done; if it is neglected, it is to be reinstated; and if it has not been established, it is to be established. For, if the ruler of a state is permitted to command something, in the state which he rules, which had never been commanded before . . . how much more are we to obey unhesitatingly the God who is the Ruler of all His creatures, in those things which He commands! Just as among the powers of human society the greater power is placed above the

less in the matter of obedience, so is God placed above all.[22]

Divine reason is now de-emphasized and divine power imposes absolute commands on mankind. This is not to say that the *Confessions* suggest that God is irrational, of course, for "everything which begins to be, or ceases to be, begins and ceases to be at that very time at which it is known in the Eternal Reason that it should begin or cease . . ."[23]

The *Confessions* also offer us the famous sentence: "Grant what Thou dost command and command what Thou wilt."[24] What this formula really means has been much disputed but it does seem to anticipate the move toward legal voluntarism in the later period. About twenty-five years later in the treatise *On Grace and Free Choice*, Augustine suggest his own explanation:

> Why does He command, if He himself will grant it? Why does He grant it, if man will do it, unless in the sense that He grants what He commands, when He helps man to do what He commands? For there is always a free will in us but it is not always good. Indeed it is freed from justice when it is subservient to sin, in which case it is evil; or else it is freed from sin when it serves justice, and then it is good. However, the grace of God is always good and through it man comes to be of good will, even though he was previously of bad will. Through this grace it also develops that good will itself, which has already come into being, is increased and comes to be so great that it can fulfill the divine commands which it wills, whenever it does will in a really perfect manner.[25]

At the same time (A.D. 401-414) Augustine was writing *De Genesi ad litteram*[26] in which the whole theory of *rationes*, both eternal and seminal, is much developed. There is no doubt, then, that Augustine continued in this period to think of God as a rational creator who has made and governs a universe of a reasonable character.

VOLUNTARISTIC REACTION TO PELAGIANISM:
A. D. 411-418

Quite possibly the first two periods in Augustine's thinking about law are not as clearly distinct as is suggested in the foregoing. If one prefers to think of the years before 411 as a time in which Augustine was not directly concerned with the doctrine of divine grace but was impressed with the reasonableness of God's regulation of mankind, then there can be no objection to taking the years 388-410 as his natural-law period. It was a time in which the divine will was mentioned as the source of eternal law but not to the exclusion of the reason and wisdom of God.

What turned Augustine's attention to divine volition and the need for grace was his discovery of the views of Pelagius, in the year 411. From this time onward, his legal thinking becomes increasingly voluntaristic.[27] It was in 412 that he wrote the treatise *On the Spirit and the Letter*, as a refutation of what Augustine then knew of Pelagianism. In the *Retractations* he recalls that his friend Marcellinus had drawn his attention to the problem of whether any man could live without sin in this life. Augustine understood that Pelagius was teaching that man does not need divine grace in order to live a good life.[28] Whether this was Pelagius' actual teaching is not our concern here.[29] The point is that Augustine, in this third period, formed his own notion of what "Pelagianism" means — and he reacted strongly to it.[30] Thus Augustine becomes less confident of the rationality of man and the capacity for good in human nature, and he grows more inclined to say that man can do nothing that is really good without the special help of God's grace. Moreover, since he seems to identify Pelagius' position with natural-law thinking, Augustine now shifts to the view that God's will is the omnipotent and unqualified source of all just laws. In other words, during the years 411 to 414, Augustine becomes a legal voluntarist.[31]

We now find him offering a new interpretation of the

key text of St. Paul (Rom. 2:14).[32] Where earlier he had suggested that the eternal law may be partly written in the
hearts of *all* men (and so, all may have the moral guidance
of natural law), Augustine now limits this participation to
those who have accepted the Christian faith.

> If therefore the Apostle, when he mentioned that the
> Gentiles do by nature the things contained in the law,
> and have the work of the law written in their hearts, he
> intended those to be understood who believed in Christ
> [*illos intelligi voluit qui credunt in Christum*] . . . so that
> belonging to the new testament means having the law
> of God not written on tables but on the heart — that is,
> embracing the righteousness of the law with innermost
> affection, where faith works by love. 'Because it is by
> faith that God justifies the Gentiles' [*quia ex fide justificat
> gentes Deus*].[33]

So, it is by grace granted by God's completely free will that
men are enabled to live good lives and achieve eternal happiness. As Augustine now expresses it, "a man is justified
freely by His grace without the works of the Law."[34] The
power and will of God are now stressed in contrast to
Pelagius' emphasis on reason and nature.

Similar volitional emphasis is found in 413, when
Augustine used the famous imperative: "Love, and do what
you will!"[35] He was not abandoning the concept of eternal
law: it still regulates all things.[36] But he is growing more em-
phatic on the importance of the love of God and neighbor,
rather than the use of reason.

A letter of this period (A.D. 411-415) marks the real
break with natural-law thinking.[37] In it, he again speaks of
the law written in the hearts of men and gives the golden rule
as its main expression: "do not do to another what you would
not wish to suffer yourself." But he now quotes a new text
of St. Paul (Rom. 4:15): "for where there is no law, neither
is there transgression." Then he proceeds to develop the
theory that both the law of men's hearts and the Mosaic Law

are of little account, if not fulfilled through faith in Christ and acceptance of the precepts of love. Not law but the grace of God enables men to avoid sins.[38] At the same time, we find him writing in the tenth book of the *City of God* that "the will of God is the intelligible and immutable law."[39]

Probably in 417-418 Augustine wrote the well known passage in the treatise *On the Trinity*, where he speaks of man's seeing the rules (*regulae*) of moral judgment.[40] Man does not discover these standards in his own mutable nature, nor in some endowment (*habitus*) of his mind, for the rules are identical with justice and human minds are not just. Rather, man finds these rules written "in that book of light which is called Truth, from which every just law is copied."[41] This is a clear statement of that moral extrinsecism which is always associated with legal voluntarism. Augustine is now teaching that the first principles of justice are not present naturally in the constitution of man, nor that they are innate in man as *a priori* forms of moral judgment.[42] These rules must be found *outside man's nature*, for he does not possess them himself (*quod ipse non habet*). They are imprinted from without, from God, and their transfer is accomplished without loss to God—just as a signet ring impresses wax with its seal, without losing the seal. There is no longer any suggestion, in the older Augustine, that the moral law is naturally available for man's rational cognition.

The foregoing is not simply the conclusion of the present writer—nor is it merely the opinion of many Protestant interpreters of Augustine who might be influenced by the anti-rationalism of some of the original Reformers. A Catholic scholar such as Guido Fasso sees this development starting with *De spiritu et littera:*

> Saint Augustine, then, abandoned the position of natural law and rationality inherited from Greek and Ciceronian philosophy . . . and he repudiated this position to take refuge in voluntarism and in the ethics of grace.[43]

This is not to say that there is no mention of the *rationes aeternae* and the immutability of human nature in the later works: the point is that the emphasis shifts to the will of God as the supreme standard of morality and legality.

THE IRRESISTIBLE WILL OF GOD: A. D. 418-430

It is not absolutely necessary to the main contention of this study to deal with what happened in the last decade of Augustine's thought: the point is already clear that the polemic against Pelagius led to a new view of law. However, it may indirectly support the thesis of a change to voluntarism, if we show how Augustine treated God's will after 418. The fact is that he now came to teach that whatever good man does is worked entirely by God within man's will-action. Man cannot resist the divine impulse to the good; evil acts are done by man's own willing, with the permission of the divine will. Thus, in 423-424 he wrote: "Nothing therefore happens unless the Omnipotent wills it to happen: He either permits it to happen, or He brings it about Himself."[44]

The treatise on *Grace and Free Choice* (A.D. 427) states this anti-Pelagian thesis most bluntly: "The Omnipotent works within the hearts of men, even the very movement of their will, so that He does through them that which He wills to be done through them."[45] And in the same year but in another treatise, Augustine is explaining that God's will is irresistible:

> Accordingly, there is no doubt that human wills cannot resist the will of God [*humanas voluntates non posse resistere*], 'who hath done whatsoever he pleased in heaven and on earth,' [Ps. 134:6] and who has even 'done the things that are to come' [Isa. 45:11 Sept.] Nor can the human will prevent Him from doing what He wills, seeing that even with the wills of men He does what He wills, when He wills to do it.[46]

Commenting on this and similar late texts, Guy de Broglie notes that the teaching on the irresistible divine will is not found as early as the *De spiritu et littera* (A.D. 412), where God seems to guide free wills indirectly, through congruent graces.

> But [adds de Broglie] from 418 onward, Augustine insists more and more on this empire which is 'interior, hidden, marvelous and ineffable,' and which God exercises with full right on created wills (*De gratia Christi* 24.25, PL 44.373), this power that is '*occultissima et efficacissima*,' through which He works our very volitions within us (*Contra duas epistolas Pelagianorum* 1.20.38, PL 44.569).[47]

Thus the role of law and the significance of legal voluntarism become unclear in the last writings of Augustine. For, if man cannot resist the divine impulse toward good action, when it is granted him, then law (in the affirmative sense, at least) becomes superfluous. Possibly Augustine reacted so strongly to the naturalism and rationalism of Julian of Eclanum that he eventually identified eternal law with grace.

In these late years Julian was attacking Augustine and claiming that the Bishop of Hippo had never really advanced beyond Manicheism. The *Opus imperfectum contra Julianum* (A.D. 429) has a good deal to say about the difference between divine and human justice. Julian had insisted on the reasonableness and justice of God—hence he argued against the inheritance of original sin, saying that it is not just for children to suffer for the sins of their fathers.[48] To this Augustine replies: "*Aliter ergo iudicat Deus, aliter homini praecipit ut iudicet: cum Deus homine sine ulla dubitatione sit iustior.*" So, God has his own unique justice and it is quite different from the other justice which He provides as a basis for human judgment.

A recent study concludes from this that the older Augustine denies that man can know anything about divine law or the will of God. As Refoulé sees this development:

> Nous ne sommes pas en mesure, assure même
> Augustine de déterminer à priori, par voie rationelle,
> ce qui est juste ou injuste quand il s'agit du vouloir
> divin car la justice de Dieu est si transcendante qu'elle
> est sans commune mesure avec la justice humaine.
> Augustin va jusqu'à soutenir que ce qui serait injuste
> pour l'homme ne l'est pas nécessairement pour Dieu,
> affirmation qui, prise à la lettre, reviendrait à nier tout
> analogie entre Dieu et la créature.[49]

This would mean that there is no understandable relation
between man's nature and God's eternal justice. Scholars
such as F.-J. Thonnard admit the seriousness of Refoulé's
charge but argue that Augustine did not mean to deny the
analogy between man and God.[50] In my judgment, Refoulé
has not distorted the general sense of these later works.
Toward the end of his life, Augustine felt that men, using
their natural abilities, could know little or nothing about the
transcendent justice of God. This, of course, is in keeping
with the claim that Augustine's legal voluntarism grew more
definite and less rational, as he advanced in years.

SIGNIFICANCE OF AUGUSTINE'S SHIFT
TO VOLUNTARISM

Quite properly one might ask why it is important to
determine whether Augustine ever taught that eternal law
originates in God's will. Is not the divine will identical with
the divine mind, and with God's very substance?[51] To this
question one would have to reply that Augustine always
maintained that man comes to know the invisible things of
God through prior knowledge of the things that God has
made.[52] The whole program of the fifteen books *On the Trinity* is to work through various triadic analyses of human
functions, particularly psychic activities, in order to offer
some partial suggestions as to what is characteristic of each

of the three divine Persons. It is the third Person, the Holy Spirit, that is characterized as Love — and love is identified with will.[53] Of course, Augustine always thought of the Holy Spirit as having to do especially with the providential governance and regulation of creation — and thus, the Holy Spirit has a good deal to do with eternal law.

The point, then, is not to suggest that Augustine thought that one "part" of God is the ultimate origin of all law. Rather, we are concerned with how men on earth may view the function of a supreme lawmaker. It is in terms of the limitations of human thinking that the distinction between a voluntaristic and an intellectualistic theory of law would have to be made. Surely God himself is not concerned about whether eternal law is an expression of His cognition or His volition! It makes quite a lot of difference to men, however, because legal voluntarism usually develops into moral relativism and an intellectualist approach to law is frequently associated with a rigid absolutism.

Granting all of this, the point remains that some people think of law as the fiat of some legislative will, while others say that no law has any validity unless it stems from an understanding of what is required by the order of reality. Two philosophical views are usually associated with legal voluntarism in the history of post-Augustinian Christian thought: one is nominalism and the other is an obsession with the omnipotence of God. Let us test our thesis by examining each in reference to Augustine.

It would be very difficult to demonstrate that St. Augustine was a nominalist. For one thing, the problem of universals does not appear in Latin writings until the century following Augustine, when Boethius introduces it. Augustine was not really interested in determining what *genera* and *species* are; he will use these words but not in the technically logical sense. Convinced that God knew all about the different kinds of things that can or do exist, he thought that there is a divine Idea for each and every individual in the whole of creation. Augustine's divine exemplarism, then, makes nonsense of the problem of universals. Both extreme realists and nominalists in the later Middle Ages can appeal to his patronage. However, there is one important difference between Augustine and later nominalists: he strongly supported the distinction of "natures" in all created things. Thus, for Augustine, each thing grows according to its kind, "a bean does not grow from a grain of wheat, or wheat from a bean, or a man from a beast, or a beast from a man."[54] Each existing thing is one definite being (*unum aliquid*) and has a definite bodily nature.[55] This is hardly the position of a nominalist. Hence, Augustine's acceptance of natures for all things probably separates his voluntarism from the better known theory of William Ockham.[56]

On the other hand, we have seen that Augustine's response to Pelagius, Caelestius and Julian consisted in an increasing stress on the almighty power of God. Particularly in the writings from the last decade of his life, we find as much emphasis on divine omnipotence as in any fourteenth-century voluntarist. Toward the end he seems to be saying that God can do anything—even what is logically contradictory.[57] This refusal to acknowledge any limits, even logical, to God's power is something that the older Augustine may have in common with the later tradition of voluntarism. Indeed, there can be little doubt that Luther was much indebted to the anti-Pelagian works of Augustine.

One of the most direct statements of Augustine on the will of God as regulator of human action is found in a sermon on Psalm 93, preached well after his first encounter with Pelagianism (possibly in 414). A passage from it may be a fitting conclusion for our study:

> Don't try to twist the will of God to your will; rather, correct your own in terms of God's will. For the will of God is certainly a rule (*regula*): now think, do you twist the rule that serves as a standard for your own correction? Indeed, this rule endures without corruption: it is an immutable rule. As long as this rule is unbroken,

you have something to which you may turn and correct
your iniquity, you have a means of correcting what is
twisted in you. What is it that men will? It's of little importance, because they have each his own twisted will:
in their hearts they wish to make God's will twisted, so
that God may do what they will, when they themselves
ought to be doing what God wills.[58]

In view of the obvious sincerity of such a preacher, one may
well conclude that he understood a good deal about man's
relation to God.

NOTES

1. *Epistola* 148.7 (PL 33.588): "quoniam si illi [the reference
is to *De libero arbitrio*] quod iam in multorum manus exierunt, corrigi non possunt, ego certe quoniam adhuc vivo, possum."

2. See Charles Curran, 'Law and Conscience in the Christian context,' in *Law for Liberty* (ed. J. E. Biechler, Baltimore 1967)
158-160: "In the voluntaristic viewpoint, something is good precisely because it is commanded." (p. 159).

3. *Theological Ethics: Volume 2, Politics* (Philadelphia 1969)
508. Later (575) Thielicke speaks of the teaching of Reformed Or-
thodoxy that the will of God cannot be in self-contradiction, and
adds: "In contrast, it is of the heart of the Lutheran view that God
does contradict himself, that he sets his grace in opposition to his
judgment and his love in opposition to his holiness; indeed, the
gospel itself can be traced to this fundamental contradiction within
God himself."

4. 'Christian Faith and Existential Freedom,' in *Faith and
Freedom. Essays in Contemporary Theology* (ed. C. B. Ketcham and J.
F. Day, New York 1969) 99-100.

5. Waldo Beach, 'Freedom and Authority in Protestant
Ethics,' *ibid.* 56, note 4.

6. *Institution chrétienne* (ed. Lefranc-Chatelain-Pannier, Paris
1911) 478.

7. William Barrett, *Irrational Man. A Study in Existential
Philosophy* (New York 1962) 101; on p. 95 Barrett remarks: "The

existentialism of St. Augustine lies in his power as a religious psychologist."

8. "The mode of thinking called 'existential' which has come into prominence in recent decades is both old and new. The excitement about its 'newness' . . . has largely operated to conceal its intellectual connection with classical voluntarism. This voluntarism, whose source seems more largely biblical than Greek and whose earliest and most articulate spokesman was St. Augustine, may be briefly characterized as a view which asserts the primacy of will over intellect." C. B. Ketcham and J. F. Day, 'Introduction,' *Faith and Freedom* 8. (Simply to keep the record straight, it is possible that St. Cyprian was a much earlier Christian voluntarist; see *De singularitate clericorum* (PL 4.847-8) which is attributed to Cyprian.)

9. *De diversis quaestionibus LXXXIII* (A.D. 388-396) in which q. 46 is the key text on the Christianizing of Plato's world of Ideas; it simply reinforces the Platonism of the earlier *Contra Academicos* and *De ordine*.

10. Thus A.-H. Chroust points to Augustine's placing of the Platonic Ideas in the mind of God and to his adoption of Stoic 'cosmic reason' as the main contributions of Augustine's legal thought. See 'St. Augustine's Philosophical Theory of Law.' *Notre Dame Lawyer* 25 (1950) 287; this article is much the same as 'The Philosophy of Law of St. Augustine,' *The Philosophical Review 53* (1944) 195-202.

11. *De re publica* 3.22.33; cf. *De legibus* 1.6.

12. *De libero arbitrio* 1.6.15 (PL 32.1229).

13. *De div. quaest.* q. 46.2 (PL 40.30); for another comparison of eternal and human laws, see q. 27 (PL 40.18)

14. *De sermone Domini in monte* 2.9.32; the English is from *The Lord's Sermon on the Mount* trans. J. J. Jepson (ACW 5, 120-121).

15. Cf. Guido Fasso, *La legge della ragione* (Bologna 1964) 44: "*nel De sermone Domini in monte* . . .é chiaro che ess [parole dell'Apostolo] sono interpretate in senso giusnaturalistico, e cioé riferite a tutti gli uomini in quanto tali, nei cui cuori la legge é scritta in virtú della loro stessa natura umana, esplicitamente identificata con la ragione, e per i quali essa é strumento di conoscenza della veritá."

16. "Lex vero aeterna est ratio divina vel voluntas Dei, or-

dinem naturalem conservari iubens, perturbari vetans." *Contra Faustum Manichaeum* 22.27 (PL 42.418).

17. *Enarrationes in Psalmos* 36.3 (PL 36.357): "Voluntas Dei ipsa est lex Dei."

18. See F. Moriones, *Enchiridion Theologicum Sancti Augustini* (Madrid 1961) 710, for list of dates for this and other *Sermons*.

19. *Sermo* 124.3 (PL 38.700): "quod Deus vellet, ipsa iustitia est."

20. *Confessiones* 2.4.9; compare 1.18.29.

21. *Conf.* 3.7.13.

22. *Conf.* 3.8.15 (trans. Bourke, FOC 21, New York 1953) 64.

23. *Conf.* 11.8.10.

24. *Conf.* 10.29.40: "Da quod jubes et jube quod vis"; cf. 10.37.60.

25. *De gratia et libero arbitrio* 15.31; this treatise is from A.D. 426-7 and may reflect a different view from the *Confessions* of A.D. 400.

26. Gustave Bardy, 'Notes Complémentaires,' to *Retractationes* (Paris 1950) 571, indicates that *De Genesi ad litteram* may even have been started as early as 393.

27. On this change in Augustine's thought, I owe a good deal to the research of Guido Fasso. In the book previously cited (*La legge della regione* 29-46) he shows rather clearly how the controversy with Pelagius and Caelestius moved Augustine to reject natural-law jurisprudence. In another book (*Storia della filosofia del diritto* [Bologna 1966] Fasso restates his thesis (I, 195-201) and concludes: "La controversia con Pelagio gli fa [Agostino] assumere una posizione radicalmente voluntaristica."

28. *Retract.* 2.37 (ed. Bardy 517); cf. *De spiritu et littera*1.1 (PL 44.201).

29. Recent more complete editions of the works of Pelagius and his associates have given a basis for studies by G. de Plinval, R. F. Evans and others (see J. Morris, 'Pelagian literature,' *Journal Theol. Studies* n.s. 16 [1965] 26-60) to suggest that Augustine did not fully understand what Pelagius was teaching.

30. "Pelagianism as we know it . . . had come into existence; but in the mind of Augustine, not of Pelagius." Peter Brown, *Augustine of Hippo* (Berkeley and Los Angeles 1967) 345.

31. Cf. Fasso, *Storia* I.199; Peter Brown, *op. cit.* 353, sees the year 414 as "the end of a period of Augustine's intellectual life."

32. *De spiritu et littera* 26.43 — 27.48.

33. *De spiritu et litt.* 26.46; the English by P. Holmes is from *Basic Writings of St. Augustine* (New York 1948) I.497.

34. *De spiritu et litt.* 26.45: "cum dicat gratis iustificari hominem per fidem sine operibus legis" (echoing Rom. 3:24-29).

35. "Dilige et quod vis fac." *In Epistolam Ioannis ad Parthos* 4.7.8 (PL 35.2033); on this, see my article 'St. Augustine and Situationism,' *Augustinus* 11 (1967) 117-123.

36. *In Epist. Ioannis ad Parthos* 4.9.11.

37. *Epistola* 157: *De Pelagianismo* (CSEL 44.449-488).

38. *Ibid.* 3:15: "Quae tamen nisi mala postea consuetudine roboretur, facilius vincitur, non tamen nisi gratia Dei. Lege autem alia praevaricata, quae est in usu rationis animae rationalis in aetate hominis iam ratione utentis, praevaricatores fiunt omnes peccatores terrae." Cf. H. A. Deane, *The Political and Social Ideas of St. Augustine* (New York 1963) 280, for helpful comment.

39. "De illa quippe superna civitate, ubi Dei voluntas intelligibilis et incommutabilis lex est . . ." *De civitate Dei* 10.7.

40. Bardy, *op. cit.,* 580 puts the last books *De Trinitate* after 416.

41. "Quibus ea tandem regulis iudicant nisi in quibus uident quemadmodum quisque uiuere debeat etiamsi nec ipsi eodem modo uiuant? Vbi eas uident? Neque enim in sua natura, cum procul dubio mente ista uideantur, eorumque mentes constet esse mutabiles, has uero regulas immutabiles uideat quisquis in eis hoc uidere potuerit; nec in habitu suae mentis cum illae regulae sint iustitiae, mentes uero eorum esse constet iniustas. Vbinam sunt istae regulae scriptae, ubi quid sit iustum et iniustus agnoscit, ubi cernit habendum esse quod ipse non habet? Vbi ergo scriptae sunt, nisi in libro lucis illius quae veritas dicitur unde omnis lex iusta describitur et in cor hominis qui operatur iustitiam non migrando sed tamquam imprimendo transfertur, sicut imago ex anulo et in ceram transit et anulum non relinquit?" *De Trinitate* 14.15.21 (ed. W. J. Mountain, *Corpus Christianorum L.A.*) 450-451.

42. "Nec in habitu suae mentis . . ." Note that Augustine had written in *De div. quaest.* q. 31: "Iustitia est habitus animi com-

muni utilitae conservata, suam cuique tribuans dignitatem." (This was, of course, Cicero on natural justice.)

43. "Sant' Agostino dunque, partito dalle posizioni giusnaturalistiche e razionalistiche ereditate dalla filosofia greca e ciceroniana . . . e le ripudia, rifugiandosi nel volontarismo e nell' etica della grazia." *La legge* 46.

44. *Enchiridion* 24.95; the English is from L. A. Arand (trans.) *Faith, Hope and Charity* Westminster, Md. 1947) 89.

45. "Agit enim Omnipotens in cordibus hominum etiam motum voluntatis eorum, ut per eos agat quod per eos agere ipse voluerit." *De gratia et libero arbitrio* 21.42 (PL 44.908).

46. *De correptione et gratia* 14.45 (PL 44.943-4); the English is by J. C. Murray (FOC 4, New York 1947) 299; Latin parenthesis added by Bourke.

47. 'Pour une meilleure intelligence du *De correptione et gratia,*' *Augustinus Magister* (Paris 1955) III, 332, note 1.

48. Julian's *Libri VIII ad Florum* appear, section by section, in Augustine's *Opus imperfectum* (PL 45.1049-1608); see 3.12 for Julian's argument and Augustine's answer.

49. F. Refoulé, 'Misère des enfants et péché originel d'après S. Augustin,' *Revue Thomiste* 71 (1963) 356. (Because this article has been much criticized, I am keeping the quotation in the original French, so as not to change its meaning.)

50. F.-J. Thonnard, 'Justice de Dieu et justice humaine selon saint Augustin,' *Augustinus: Strenas Augustinianas P. Victorino Capanaga* (Madrid 1967) I.395, where he admits that Refoulé's study is well supported by numerous texts in the *Opus imperfectum.*

51. "Will you men say that those things are false which the Truth tells me . . . namely, that His substance is changed in no way through periods of time and that His will is not something outside His substance?" *Conf.* 12.15.18.

52. "Oportet igitur ut creatorem *per ea quae facta sunt intellecta* conspicientes trinitatem intellegamus cuius in creatura quomodo dignum est apparet *vestigium." De Trin.* 6.10.12 (ed. Mountain, L.242).

53. *De Trin.* 12.17 and 12.20.

54. *De Genesi ad litteram* 9.17.32; cf. Bourke, *Augustine's View of Reality* (Villanova 1964) 76-79.

55. "Haec igitur omnia quae arte divina facta sunt et

unitatem quandam in se ostendunt et speciem et ordinem. Quidquid enim horum est et unum aliquid est sicut sunt naturae corporum . . ." *De Trin.* 6.10.12 (ed Mountain 242).

56. Cf. Francis Oakley, 'Medieval Theories of Natural
Law: William of Ockham and the Voluntarist Tradition,' *Natural
Law Forum* 6 (1961) 65-83.

57. "Qui non ob aliud vocatur omnipotens, nisi quoniam
quidquid vult potest." *De civ. Dei* 21.7.1 (PL 41.719). See *Enchirid.*
24.95 (PL 40.275) where the omnipotence of God's will is illustrated by His ability to save one child and to condemn another
child to eternal perdition, "when the cases of both were identically
the same."

58. *Enarr. in Ps.* 93.18; Moriones (*op. cit.* 720) dates this in
414.

IV
Socio-Political Issues

CHAPTER 11

Augustine's Political Philosophy

"Ideas of worldly rule by the Church were already prevalent in the fourth century. St. Augustine, a citizen of Hippo in North Africa, who wrote between 354 and 430, gave expression to the developing political ideas of the church in his book *The City of God*. *The City of God* leads the mind very directly toward the possibility of making the world into a theological and organized Kingdom of Heaven. The city, as Augustine puts it, is 'a spiritual society of the predestined faithful,' but the step from that to a political application was not a very wide one. The Church was to be the ruler of the world over all nations, the divinely led ruling power over a great league of terrestrial states."[1]

It is the purpose of this chapter to show that these words of Mr. Wells are quite incorrect and inaccurate. St. Augustine did not intend to endorse any particular form of Government.[2]

His main political thesis is concerned with the subservience of earthly politics to the life of heaven. Were man a mere animal he could be satisfied, as beasts are, with the peace and order and harmony of this life. But, because of his rational soul, man subordinates all such things to his desire for eternal peace in heaven. This does not mean that man must entirely ignore earthly rule. On the contrary, the love of man's neighbor, the desire to live a harmonious, well-regulated earthly life, is always a concomitant, but an inferior one, of the desire for heaven.[3]

Throughout the early philosophical dialogues St. Augustine searches as diligently for a satisfactory answer to the question, 'What is the happy life?' as he does for truth. It is in the treatise on *Free Will* that he seems to find this answer for the first time. He realizes too, that this is the end of his search for truth. *God* is the happy life of the soul.[4] This view is reiterated later. As the life of the body is the soul, so the happy life of man is God. Even such people may have a temporal harmony of government but they can never enjoy the true felicity of eternal peace.[5]

Social life on this earth is good for the man of wisdom — but it is much disturbed. There are so many things which try the patience even of the good man. Quoting Terence, St. Augustine says: "I am married; this is one misery. Children are born to me; they are additional cares." Human life is full of slights, suspicions, quarrels, war and other evils.[6]

This does not mean that St. Augustine is pessimistic in his regard for earthly things. Rather should one say, he is clearly conscious of the proper, but inferior, position of mundane matters in the hierarchy of being. After speaking dolefully of the miseries of life, he makes a 'volte face' and enumerates in glowing words the contemporary delights of industry.

What wonderful and stupendous advances have been made by human industry in the making of clothes and buildings, what improvements in agriculture and in navigation! What skill is shown in the designing and making of vases and statues and pictures! What incredibly marvelous presentations are seen and heard in our theatres! What incredibly marvelous presentations are seen and heard in our theatres! What ingenious devices have been contrived for the capture, killing or taming of wild animals! And what poisons, weapons and warlike machinery have been invented to oppose other men, and again what remedies and medical aids are used to ensure bodily health or to repair it. What various condiments and appetizers are found! What a varied multitude of signs, such as words and letters, are used to convey thought! For the delight of the mind, what rhetorical flourishes and what a quantity of different songs there are.[7]

This is not the language of a recluse who knows nothing of the goods of this life. It is the speech of a man who has known all such things and found them wanting. He has come to realize that of all goods, be they spiritual or bodily, there is none to compare with virtue.[8] Present happiness can only consist in the strong hope of future happiness with God in heaven. A man who entertains such a sure hope is superior to all earthly ills and is even more happy than Adam was in his state of perfection in Paradise because, even while there, Adam was uncertain of his fate.[9]

Mr. Wells, in suggesting that St. Augustine proposed an earthly program for the Catholic Church in the field of politics, is quite wrong. Man's chief concern is his salvation not his earthly journey. The purpose of the Church is even less connected with earthly matters than that of the individual. It is for this reason that there is no complete theory of politics in the thought of St. Augustine. But there are in his writings the germs, what one might call the logical 'seminal reasons,' of a political system. Frequently he follows the lead of Plato or of Cicero. But always does he remember that he is a Christian. Though Plato's thought is important, to him Christ's teaching is supreme.[10]

In the thought of the ancients one finds, nearly always, a dualism of the *idea* of a city state and the actual *realization* of this idea. One is acutely conscious of this distinction when the *Laws* of Plato are read in conjunction with the *Republic*. One cannot but feel that the *Republic* is a beautiful ideal which is hopeless of attainment and that the numerically-exact state described in the *Laws* is less beautiful but more practicable.[11]

St. Augustine has also a dualism in his political thought but it is not the same. He distinguishes not the ideal and the actually existent but the earthly and the heavenly. There is no basis for comparison between these two sets of terms. The earthly city is not that which is a realization of the ideal state nor is the ideal city to be identified with the heavenly city.[12]

Nor is the Church to be represented by the heavenly city and the Civil State by the earthly city. It is true that much of the dispute between Church and State in the Middle Ages was waged with materials taken from the *City of God*. It is true that this work of Augustine's, along with the Holy Scriptures, furnished the mediaeval Church with a doctrine of society.[13] It is true that St. Augustine suggested the economic and industrial program of the Middle Ages.[14] It is true that Charlemagne found much of his inspiration in the *City of God*.[15] But even in writing of the ideal Christian Emperor, St. Augustine stresses the other-worldly motive. He ends a long discussion of the happiness and glory of the emperor with these words — "Such Christian emperors, we say, are happy in the present time by *hope*, and are destined to be so in the enjoyment of the reality itself, when that which we wait for shall have arrived."[16]

But in spite of the enormous influence of Augustinism in the development of mediaeval society and in spite of the fact that certain members of the mediaeval Church did become ambitious and desirous of temporal power — it is true that St. Augustine never preached in favor of the Church entering into earthly politics. His whole attitude in the Donatist controversy is indicative of this stand. As Figgis has so ably written, one finds in the *City of God*, the "final repudiation of the old views, as much Jewish as Pagan, that temporal felicity follows the service of the true God — alike for the individual and for the nation."[17]

Perhaps the most fundamental axiom underlying the political thought of St. Augustine is that all nations desire peace. Just as every man wishes to be happy so all bodies politic desire peace. A society will even go to the extremity of war in order to secure peace with glory. That peace is

always the end in view is shown by the numerous occasions
upon which states have admitted making war to gain peace
but never does one find a state making peace in order that
it may eventually be at war. Considering even a group of
robbers, a certain internal peace is always found in their
organization or they will not long remain banded together as
a successful gang. Even a man of unusual strength and dis-
agreeableness of nature, who is accustomed to being a bully,
maintains peaceful relations with those whom he cannot
bully and with those whose good opinion he wishes to keep.
The most beastlike and savage of men must maintain a certain peace with their own bodies or else they will soon de-
stroy themselves.[18]

The timeless insight of these views of St. Augustine on
peace and war is amply illustrated in the mob slogans of the
last World War. It was the Great War which was to end war.
It was the struggle to save democracy. It resulted in peace
of very doubtful longevity.

Peace, then, is that for which all nations strive—but
what is it in itself? Going on with the analysis in the nineteenth book of the *City of God*, one finds that the 'peace of all
things is the tranquillity of order.' In the body, there is a pro-
portional arrangement of parts. In the irrational soul, there
is a harmony of the appetites; in the rational soul, an agreement of knowledge and action. In the individual, there is the
orderly relation of body and soul. Between man and God,
peace lies in the faithful adherence to the eternal law. Between men, peace is a well-ordered concord. Likewise there
is domestic and civil peace. Finally, and at its best, peace is
found by men in the heavenly city as the perfectly ordered
and harmonious enjoyment of God, and of one another in
God.[19]

Peace may be divided into three parts—that of the Unjust, that of the Just, in this life, and that of the Just with
God.[20]

The first type of peace should not be lightly esteemed—

though, because it is that of the wicked, it is not lasting. But
it is temporal peace and both the good and the bad may enjoy it together.[21]

The peace found among the just people in this life is
not easy to understand. They now enjoy God by faith —
hereafter they will enjoy Him by sight. This earthly peace
of the good is often rather the 'solace of our misery' than any
positive happiness. When the final and perfect stage of peace
comes, then man is with God. "Our nature shall enjoy a
sound immortality and incorruption, and shall have no
more vices, and as we shall experience no resistance either
from ourselves or from others, it will not be necessary that
reason should rule vices which no longer exist, but God shall
rule the man, and the soul shall rule the body, with a
sweetness and facility suitable to the felicity of a life which
is done with bondage. And this condition shall be eternal,
and we shall be assured of its eternity; and thus the peace of
this blessedness and the blessedness of this peace shall be the
supreme good."[22]

The proper 'milieu' of man is society. Human nature is
essentially sociable and men are united by bonds of kinship.
In all ordinary circumstances a man should live with his
fellow man.[23] The life of the wise man both on earth and in
heaven is social.[24]

Each individual man is considered by St. Augustine to
be the unit of society.[25] The family is also a very fundamental element in social life. The home should be the beginning
of the city. Civic peace depends directly upon domestic
peace. The father of a family should see that his household
lives in conformity with the civic regulations.[26]

As Figgis in his commentary on the *City of God* notes,
it is more correct to translate the word 'civitas' by 'society'
than by state or city. 'Res publica' is the word used for state
or commonwealth.[27] But, whatever the term used, it remains clear that St. Augustine has a great deal of respect for
civic authority.[28] Justice he did not consider a necessary concomitant of a commonwealth such as the Roman one. How-

ever the true state whose founder and ruler is Christ will always have justice.[29] Scarcely any one would interpret this to mean that Christ had actually founded an earthly society which would compete with other republics.

In several places St. Augustine insists that a ruler receives his authority from God. Both good and bad kings receive whatever power they have by the providence of God.[30] Not chance or fate or the actions of the stars but the power of God is the source of worldly authority.[31] All men are naturally equal. Some, because of their pride, strive for power and glory. This urge to dominate others is a vice.[32]

Personal property also depends on the Divine right. Earthly goods are given to man to be used. If he uses them properly then they can be said to belong to him. If he puts them to bad use, or abuses them, then they are not his possessions. Private property is not wrong—it is not a bad thing to have such goods. It is wrong to prefer property to superior things such as truth, justice, wisdom and eternal happiness.[33]

A nation, a society, or a people is an assembly of reasonable beings bound together by a common interest or love. The higher the object of love—the more superior is the nation.[34] The teleological definition of a nation is the reason for St. Augustine's theory of the two cities. Probably the most general analysis of the ends of societies is that which he made. Some societies desire and cherish *good* things—other societies pursue *bad* things. The social purpose of a nation is either good or bad. If it be bad, then it is the end of a society of reprobates—if good, then it is the goal of a society of saints. This bipartite division had been previously made in the *Rules of Tyconius*.[35] There one finds a description of two cities, one of the devil and the other of God. This work is mentioned and summarized by St. Augustine in his work on *Christian Doctrine*.[36] The evil city can be called Babylon and its citizens are all those who are wicked. The good city may be called Jerusalem and all the saints make up its membership.[37]

The earthly City is maintained by a concord of a civic obedience. Its members seek an earthly peace and this is attained best by the agreement of men's wills with regard to the things which are helpful in this life. On earth the members of both cities are mingled together. Even the citizens of the heavenly society must obey the civic laws in order that harmony may result. In religion, however, the two cities cannot have common laws. On this all-important point the saints must be civic dissenters.[38]

Frequently there is an imperfect form of peace enjoyed in the City of the earth. This is gained usually as the result of war. It is not an enduring form of happiness.[39]

All those who belong to the City of this earth and are satisfied with the 'pax terrena' shall get their ultimate reward in hell. They shall inherit eternal misery, their soul shall die a second death and the bodies of these people will remain in everlasting pains.[40]

Those who belong to the Heavenly City are guided, while on this earth, by faith. They *use* the earthly peace which they may find but it is not an ultimate end for them.[41] These celestial citizens also live in hope. The true blessings of the soul are only to be enjoyed in eternity. The hopeful anticipation of such everlasting felicity is the blessing which the saints enjoy here below.[42] In heaven, charity alone is necessary.[43] The City of God merely means the social life of the Blessed. Their happiness is symbolically expressed by the word 'Jerusalem' — vision of peace.

This centering of one's attention upon the world to come — this contempt for temporal happiness — this walking in faith and hope toward the eternal life of charity — this, was the spark which St. Augustine left to light the flame of mediaeval religious zeal. The mark of other-worldliness is strong upon the mediaeval man. It has left the modern world. More than any other writer, St. Augustine gives the clue to this spirit. It is the solution to much that is otherwise incomprehensible in mediaeval politics.

NOTES

1. H. G. Wells, *The Outline of History* (Reprint January 1930, Star Edition, N.Y.), pp. 525-526.

2. "Saint Augustine n'a jamais préconisé l'adoption d'une forme determinée de gouvernement civil." E. Gilson, *Introduction à l'étude de Saint Augustin* (Paris: Vrin, 1931), p. 231.

3. *De Civitate Dei*, XIX, 14; *Patrologia Latina* t. 41, col. 642.

4. "Sicut enim tota vita corporis est anima, sic beata vita animae *Deus* est." *De Libero Arbitrio*, II, 16, P.L. 32, col. 1264.

5. *De Civ. Dei*, XIX, 26, col. 656.

6. *De Civ. Dei*, XIX, 5, col. 632.

7. *De Civ. Dei*, XXII, 24, col. 790.

8. *De Civ. Dei*, XIX, 3, col. 626.

9. *De Civ. Dei*, XI, 12, col. 328.

10. Augustine "works consciously on Plato's lines and formulates from the political philosophy of that master and of Cicero a system in which the leading dogmas of the Christian faith assume a controlling part." W. A. Dunning, *A History of Political Theories, Ancient and Modern*, p. 157.

11. Cf. F. Thilly, *History of Philosophy* (New York: Holt, 1931), p. 73.

12. Cf. *The Encyclopedia of the Social Sciences*, vol. II, p. 314.

13. Cf. "Holy Writ and the expositions thereof, Patristic Lore and more especially the De Civitas Dei of St. Augustine, these furnished the medieval Doctrine of society with its specifically Christian traits." Otto Gierke, *Political Theories of the Middle Ages* (transl. Maitland), p. 2.

14. T. Sommerlad, *Das Wirtschaftsprogramm der Kirche des Mittel Alters*, pp. 212-220.

15. J.N. Figgis, *The Political Aspects of St. Augustine's City of God*, p. 82.

16. *De Civ. Dei*, V, 24, col. 171.

17. *Op. Cit.*, p. 9.

18. *De Civ. Dei*, XIX, 12, col. 637-638-639.

19. *De Civ. Dei*, XIX, 13, col. 640-641. Cf. Justice as harmony of parts in Plato: *Republic* IV, 433.

20. *The Encyclopedia of the Social Sciences*, Vol. 2, p. 314.

21. *De Civ. Dei*, XIX, 26, col. 656.

22. *De Civ. Dei*, XIX, 27, col. 657.

23. "Quoniam unusquisque homo humani generis pars est, et sociale quiddam est humana natura, magnumque habet et naturale bonum, vim quoque amicitiae:" *De Bono Conjugali*, I.

24. *De Civ. Dei*, XIX, 5, col. 631.

25. *De Civ. Dei*, IV, 3, col. 114.

26. *De Civ. Dei*, XIX, 16, col. 644-645.

27. Cf. Figgis, *op. cit.*, p. 51. see *Civ. Dei*, XV, 1, col. 437.

28. On civic duty — see *De Moribus Ecclesiae Catholicae*, I, 30 t. 34.

29. *De Civ. Dei*, II, 21, col. 68-69.

30. "Etiam talibus tamen dominandi potestas non datur nisi summi Dei providentia, quando res humanas judicat talibus dominis dignas." *De Civ. Dei*, V, 19, col. 166.

31. "Prorsus divina providentia regna constituuntur humana." *De Civ. Dei*, V, 1, col. 141.

32. "Cum vero etiam eis qui naturaliter pares sunt, hoc est, hominibus, dominari appetat, intolerabilis animi superbia est." *De Doctrina Christiana*, I, 23, t. 34, col. 27.

33. *Epist.* CLIII, 6, t. 33, col 653-4; *Epist.* XCIII, XI, t. 33, col 343; Tractatus VI in *Joan. Evang.*, 25, t. 35, col. 1425; Sermo L, c. 2, t. 39, col. 1841. Cf. A. J. Carlyle, *History of Medieval Political Theory in the West* (2nd to 9th Cent.), pp. 136-140. J.N. Figgis, *op. cit.*, p. 54.

34. "Populus est coetus multitudinis rationalis, rerum quas diligit concordi communione sociatus." *De Civ. Dei*, XIX, 24, col. 655.

35. F. C. Burkitt, *The Book of Rules of Tyconius* (Cambridge, 1894).

36. *De Doctrina Christiana*, B. III, t. 34, col. 66-90.

37. Enarr. in Psalm. 86, 6: t. 37, col. 1106.

38. *De Civ. Dei*, XIX, 16 and 17, col. 644-5-6.

39. *De Civ. Dei*, XV, 21, col. 466.

40. " . . . hoc est duas societates hominum: quarum est una quae praedestinata est in aeternum regnare cum Deo; altera, aeternum supplicium subire cum diabolo." *De Civ. Dei*, XV, 1, col. 457. See also: *Civ. Dei*, XIX, 28, col. 658.

41. *De Civ. Dei*, XIX, 17, col. 657.

42. *De Civ. Dei*, XIX, 20, col. 648.

43. *Soliloq.* I, 7, XIV. t. 32, col. 875.

CHAPTER 12

Tolerance and Religious Controversy

Augustine's views on tolerance have been the subject of discussion for centuries. Two recent publications illustrate contrasting approaches to this problem.

A new book by Peter Brown[1] explains very clearly how this Oxford historian came to write his previously published and highly regarded biography of St. Augustine.[2] Brown's articles and reviews of works on a wide variety of themes in late Roman and early Christian history are now collected in a useful volume. These studies all date from the 1960-1970 decade and all point up Brown's growing realization that Augustine is central to most important historical developments in his time. Nearly all of these studies preceded the Augustine biography and they led, with a curious historical determinism, to the writing of his study of Augustine's life. So, to the reader already familiar with Brown's work, these articles and reviews may come as something of an anticlimax. Eight are book reviews and nine are articles of substantial length. Footnotes have been updated in this collection in order to record new publications that have appeared since the articles were first printed.

Brown has arranged this gathering of his studies under three categories: I, *Religion and Society*; II, *Rome*; and III, *Africa*. In point of fact, all are directly or indirectly connected with Augustine — not so much as a thinker but rather as an active ecclesiastical leader. Indeed, there are times when one wonders how much attention Brown has paid to the philosophical and theological content of Augustine's writings.

Perhaps Brown's finest contribution lies in his updating of our information on five different religious movements which competed with, and challenged, Augustine's version of Christianity. These were Neopaganism, Judaism, Pelagianism, Donatism and Manichaeism. On the history of all five present-day scholarship is much better informed than that of any previous century. That is not to say that nothing more remains to be done.

As a religion, paganism was certainly deteriorating in Augustine's time. Before the twentieth century it was usual for scholars to write about the paganism of the late Roman Empire as a rural phenomenon, peculiar to the inland towns and farm areas, remote from the culture of the great metropolitan centers. However, it has always been known that there still flourished in Rome, Milan, and other cities influential pagan families and public figures. With many of these people, Augustine had cordial, or at least interesting, relations. At various times pagan scholars, teachers and government officials sought his views on philosophical and religious problems. To these inquiries he responded with courtesy. Augustine's contacts with political and military personages were sometimes complicated, of course, by their lack of understanding of what he felt to be the mission of a Christian bishop.

The major impact of Neopaganism on Augustine, however, was in the thought area. This influence centered in his interest in the ideas of pagan writers of a much earlier time. What Augustine owed to Virgil, Cicero, Varro, Plato and Plotinus has been thoroughly studied. But there was a new pagan theology, still cultivated in these late Roman centuries, and its influence on Augustine is largely ignored by Brown. From the Plotinism of Porphyry the ensuing centuries inherited a sort of rehabilitated paganism, couched in mystical and philosophical language but still concerned with daemons, multi-functional gods and multifarious acts of propitiation. Something of this comes out in Brown's essay on sorcery but the theoretical pretensions of later paganism play little part in his studies.

Then, as now, Judaism was the religion of a floating minority. Jews were persecuted by people belonging to all other religious cults. It has long been recognized, for instance, that the followers of Mani were somewhat antisemitic. More work is to be done on the status of Jews and Jewish thought in these early Christian centuries. Brown's frequent references to W.H.C. Frend's appraisals of Judaism and Christianity show how important this problem is to the historian. Yet the matter of Augustine's own attitude toward Judaism is scarcely broached by Brown. Some modern Jewish scholars see Augustine as an antisemite. Culturally and geographically he had more affinities with the ancestors of the Arabs than with the Jews. His knowledge of Hebrew was apparently minimal and his etymological discussions of Hebrew words were frequently misleading. On rare occasions, in a few sermons, Augustine did criticize the behavior of some Jews. On the other side of the ledger is Augustine's great love for the Old Testament. A man who writes eight lengthy explanations of the Book of Genesis and who devotes his longest writing to a commentary on the Psalms is not contemptuous of Judaism. He rebuked the Manichees for their rejection of the Old Testament. It is time for some competent and unbiased scholar to do an objective investigation of Augustine and Jewish culture.

In its study of Pelagianism, recent scholarship has shifted from the emphasis on heresy to more positive studies of what this movement meant in history. We now know a good deal about Pelagius and his associates. Some of this increase in knowledge is due to the discovery of new sources but most of it stems from a more accurate and objective interpretation of what has always been available. The two studies in Brown's book ("Pelagius and His Supporters" and "The Patrons of Pelagius" pp. 183-226) are reprinted from the *Journal of Theological Studies*. They are fully documented and provide easy access to recent literature on the subject.

Indeed, on the basic question of the relation of the works of nature and of grace, recent studies of Pelagius bring him rather close to the moderate position of St. Thomas Aquinas. Possibly, as Gerald Bonner has remarked,[3] this interpretive development requires some restraint. What now seems obvious, however, is that Pelagianism was much more than the personal thought of Pelagius. It embraced a plurality of views on the problems of original sin and infant baptism.[4] Peter Brown is fully aware of the complex character of Pelagian teachings.

Much the same thing can be said about the study of Donatism: present-day writings make it a complicated matter. There is a great difference, for instance, between the views of Paul Monceaux and the more recent findings of W. H. C. Frend. In reviewing a book critical of Frend,[5] Peter Brown stresses the importance of studying the actual facts of Donatist procedures in evangelization. In fact, where Gerald Bonner distinguishes three theological issues in the Donatist controversy (1. the nature of the Church, 2. the sacraments and their validity, and 3. coercion of schismatic and heretical Christians[6]) Brown concentrates on the third only and seems to neglect the first two. It is just as well to say frankly that, even after the lapse of fifteen centuries, the Donatist movement is still viewed with some favor by representatives of various national reforms in Christianity and with some disfavor by Catholics who stress the continuity and unity of their religious traditions. Perhaps it is not possible for a scholar with definite religious convictions to be wholly impartial in interpreting the meaning of a schism.

Manichaeism is the last of these religious movements to be discussed here: it figures in many of Brown's studies. Both Pelagianism and Donatism reacted to the religion of Mani. Until the twentieth century historians were mostly dependent on Christian polemical writings (chiefly those of

Augustine and Evodius) for details about Mani and the teachings of his followers. It was difficult to determine whether Manichaeism was primarily a heretical movement with its roots in Christianity — or really an offshoot from Iranian Zoroastrianism. Significant non-Christian sources of information have come to light in this century, both from the far East and from Egypt.[7] One school of writers on Manichaeism still views it as a proto-Protestant revolt against traditional Christianity.[8] Another interpretive tradition sees the religion of Mani as an outgrowth from Zoroastrianism and as only tangentially related to Christianity.[9] Early Greek and Latin treatises on heresy frequently listed the Manichees as Christian heretics. Some modern studies stress the diversity of teachings within Manichaeism and associate it with several older religions. In this category are articles by H. J. Grondijs[10] that are criticized by Brown as bringing this syncretic interpretation to the point of absurdity.[11] Brown's main article on this question ("The Diffusion of Manichaeism in the Roman Empire"[12]) is a masterly survey of the matter. He strongly defends the claim that Manichaeism was essentially a form of "crypto-Christianity." In spite of my respect for Brown's far-reaching scholarship in this area, I remain unconvinced. I continue to think that the non-Christian background of this religion of Mani was far more important than the Christian influence on Manichaeism. It would be difficult to document this conviction, however.

Turning from Brown's accounts of these special religious traditions and their historical context to his over-all approach to this period of history, I find that he is the victim of three distinctive prejudices. These are: (1) a tendency to overstress the political aspects of Augustine's thought and career; (2) an anti-monastic bias; and (3) an extreme reaction to what Brown calls the "pornography" of religious coercion. May I comment briefly on each of these points.

Both the *Introduction* ("Religion and Society in the Age of Saint Augustine") and the first study in Part I (a chapter on Augustine from *Trends in Political Thought*, a book edited by Beryl Smalley[13]) illustrate the first bias. Thus we read:[14] "The central problem of Augustine's thought is one which we all have to face: to what extent is it possible to treat man as having a measure of rational control over his political environment?" This is an important human question but I do not agree that it is central in Augustine's thought. Of course, we must keep in mind that this excerpt comes from an essay on Augustine's political views — but, even so, it strikes me as a distortion. Brown cites the psychological introspections of *Confessions*, Book X, and the Augustinian conclusion that man is nothing apart from God, as foundations for the political conviction that citizens should be passively obedient to their rulers!

My reaction to this odd argument is twofold. In the first place, Augustine's political philosophy was as much the product of his cultural milieu as it was of his philosophico-religious speculations. The *Pax Romana* which one encounters throughout the *City of God* was not a theoretical invention of Augustine's. In his day, a bishop was a semi-political figure (at least on the municipal level), consulted by all sorts of people on many socio-political problems. Nevertheless, as Othmar Perler has abundantly demonstrated,[15] Augustine was a man broadened by travel, a representative of a minority group in the Roman Empire, and certainly not a chauvinist. Second, and more important, the political order was not the focal point of Augustine's thinking. He was forced by circumstances to act and write about political matters, at times. But any reader of the *Soliloquies* will recall that there were two things that he wished to know about, God and his soul.[16] Neither is politicized by Augustine. True, he sees all social order and peace coming from God as the supreme source of order. This does not mean that political problems are of primary importance to Augustine. He was a complex character, an other-worldly man[17] who was moved by his historical context to write in the *City of God* and elsewhere about many matters that were not of primary concern to him. If he became, inadvertently, one of the sources of the dream of a Holy Roman Empire, this much later development in political "Augustinianism" would, as I see it, have amazed St. Augustine.

In several later essays in Brown's collection there appears the suggestion that Augustine sought out influential political personages, like Marcellinus and Volusianus, with a view to securing their friendship and favor. Thus Brown speaks of Volusianus as an upper-class pagan official, "courteously besieged by Christian bishops."[18] At another point there is the suggestion that Marcellinus, a Catholic, was subject to pressure from the bishops on the Catholic side at the Conference of Carthage (A.D. 411) which found the Donatists disruptive of the unity of Christendom.[19] Now this sort of charge seems to me to be unfair. Augustine's social position, as a bishop and leading participant in many Church councils in Africa, forced him into public view. He naturally encountered various Roman officials. He was a friendly man and several of these personages did become his friends. I do not think that the relationship went beyond that. Quite possibly other bishops cultivated important people to gain their support: we really know very little about that.

In particular, the fragmentary accounts of the Conference of Carthage suggest that both Marcellinus and Augustine did everything that they could to be fair to the Donatist representatives. The findings of this Conference were simply a factual account by Marcellinus of the divisions within the Christian Church in North Africa. He gathered evidence but did not judge the Donatists.

A second unfortunate prejudice that appears in Brown's studies is an antipathy to monasticism. He views the early monastic establishments as centers of ascetic eccentricity.[20] Indeed, the tendency of some zealous Christians to leave the "world" and live in their own communities is

regarded as anti-social and even a contributing factor to the
decline of Rome![21] What is more, Brown seems to regard the
monastery as a means of withdrawing from Christian obligations to the poor. At one point he comments on "ascetic
bishops, withdrawn from the world," who were "left no time
for the humble business of loving their neighbours."[22] All
that one can say to this is that there is little evidence of
neglect of the poor in Augustine's writings or in his life activities. The few details given in Possidius' contemporary
biography point toward the opposite. The monasteries spon-
sored by Augustine cherished poverty for their residents, including Bishop Augustine, and offered hospitality to visitors
and strangers, irrespective of their economic status.[23] In any
case, Brown shows no great understanding of, or sympathy
for, the kind of religious community life that was so highly
prized by Augustine. His monasticism was no negative withdrawal from human interests and obligations. In good part,
Augustine's growing desire to establish religious communities originated in the Platonic dream of a group of like-
minded scholars living together and sharing in those dialogues of the spirit that were to lead to a very high level of
religious thinking. Augustine's attempts at withdrawal were
more efforts to avoid the wealthy than to evade his duties to
the poor. Possidius wrote that it was a much greater privi-
lege to live and converse with Augustine in his monastery at
Hippo than to read all his great theological works.[24] The
monastery, for Augustine, provided a positive and enriched
form of human living.

Finally, Brown overstresses, I think, what he calls the
"pornography of religious coercion." This is no one-time ex-
pletive: the theme is reiterated a dozen times in these
studies.[25] One whole essay is devoted to this notion of violent
intolerance.[26] My reaction is to protest the emphasis on this
subject. There was some intolerance and even persecution of
dissident sects in the Church of these centuries. I doubt,
however, that religious coercion was a distinctive feature of

the history of this period. Brown has the grace to admit that Augustine showed "moral tolerance" to schismatics within the Christian Church.[27] The implication is that he was tough-minded in regard to those outside the Church. I see little evidence for this view.

Emilien Lamirande's 1974 Saint Augustine Lecture[28] provides another important, though brief, review of the difficult problem of Augustine's attitude toward religious tolerance. It is well known, of course, that his views on this subject changed from an early benevolence toward those whom he considered unorthodox to a more severe later stance. The ramifications of this evolution extend to many other issues: to personal and social freedom, the autonomy of moral conscience, the nature of authority, the relation of the Bishop of Rome to Church Councils, the Church-State problem — and so on.

Emilien Lamirande has published several French works on ecclesiology, with special reference to the Church in Augustine's time. He is eminently qualified to judge the impact of St. Augustine on the topic of religious tolerance. In general his book gives an up-to-date, well informed, judicious survey. To get to the heart of Lamirande's study the reader must be prepared to overlook a style that is more French than English and some printing errors that should have been caught by the editors.[29] In spite of such superficial defects, the Lecture has a permanent reference value for libraries and individual scholars.

While other sects are involved, Donatism is the focal point of Lamirande's inquiry, as it should be, for it was this schismatic movement within the Christian Church in Africa which occasioned the shift in Augustine's stance on religious freedom. Almost a hundred years before Augustine's episcopacy there was a dispute in Carthage as to who was really the bishop. One prelate was charged with handing over the Sacred writings to pagan persecutors; he was deposed and replaced by another Christian bishop, whose successor was a Bishop Donatus. By the end of the fourth century, Christendom in North Africa was divided into two almost equally large groups, the adherents of Donatus and the Catholics who remained in communion with the Christians outside Africa. At the investigation of Donatism presided over by Count Marcellinus, A.D. 411, over five hundred bishops appeared as representatives on both sides of the dispute. In the early years of Augustine's episcopacy the Donatists had a large cathedral at Hippo and they outnumbered the regular Catholics there. We know that the Donatist owners of the bakeovens in Hippo were instructed at one point to bake no bread for Catholic households.[30]

Naturally, in one lecture it was impossible for Lamirande to dwell upon the history of Donatism. He rather supposes that the basic facts of the schism are known and that the unresolved question is the extent of the change of mind that Augustine experienced by A.D. 405, or earlier, in regard to the treatment of the Donatists. This brevity in Lamirande's work is somewhat unfortunate because several recent studies of Donatism have tended to regard it as a laudable effort to free African Christianity from external domination by outside authorities, both civil and ecclesiastical. In other words, writers such as W. H. C. Frend and Peter Brown have pictured the Donatists as members of a national Christian Church, persecuted by supporters of the Pax Romana who were encouraged in this persecution by Augustine. A noteworthy exception to this trend in recent scholarship is Gerald Bonner who offers a moderate view of the claims of Donatists and Catholics.[31] It would appear to be time, now, for a fair reassessment of the history of the Donatist troubles in the light of scattered twentieth-century research on the subject. Possibly Lamirande will have the opportunity to write this more complete study in the future.

Questions remain, for instance, as to the person (Donatus) who gave his name to this schism. Writings by Donatists are generally non-extant and it is hard to get the facts from Catholic controversial works, such as those of

Augustine and Optatus. For a long time scholars maintained that there were two involved bishops named Donatus but Gustave Bardy (in 1950) argued that this was nonsense and that there was but one.[32] In point of fact, there were three men named Donatus who were involved. The original Donatus of Casa Nigera became bishop in Carthage, possibly in 313, and he was the man who gave his name to the already existing schism. As Bardy observed (*loc. cit.*), Augustine seems to say that there were two bishops of Carthage named Donatus, for he erroneously distinguished Donatus of Carthage from Donatus of Casa Nigera.[33] Now, there *was* another Donatist bishop whose see was at Bagai; this second Bishop Donatus encouraged the violence of the Circumcelliones and was himself killed in the year 347.[34] Donatus of Bagai was never bishop of Carthage but he was a leader in the schism before mid-century. A third Donatus involved was an African proconsul in office at the beginning of the fifth century. It was to this Donatus that Augustine wrote, A.D. 408, asking that the death penalty be not used against the Donatists.[35] In the case of this third Donatus, then, we have a Roman official who was an anti-Donatist. As in other instances in the story of Augustine, plural holders of the same name are the source of historical confusion. The *Index Generalis* in the Maurist edition of Augustine's writings (tome XII, 710) lists fourteen uses of the name Donatus in the *Opera Omnia*; just how many different persons are indicated is a problem for the historian. (There was even a Donatist bishop named Augustinus![36])

In the light of present interest in women's rights, another intriguing problem in the history of Donatism is the extent to which the schism stemmed from feminism. The whole story of the activities of Lucilla, a Spanish woman resident in Carthage in the early days of Donatism, has yet to be written. She is mentioned, unfavorably, in several of Augustine's letters and anti-Donatist polemics, in Optatus' history of the Donatist schism, and in the *Proceedings* presided over by the Consul Zenophilus. Lucilla is described as a very wealthy and troublesome woman who had great influence in Carthage at the start of the fourth century.[37] Apparently Caecilianus, deacon in Carthage, had imposed a penance on Lucilla which offended her. When Caecilianus was consecrated Bishop of Carthage, she bribed a number of bishops to replace him with another man, Majorinus, who in turn was succeeded by Bishop Donatus.[38]

Whatever the historical facts were concerning the intervention by the Lady Lucilla in the affairs of the cathedral at Carthage, it is clear from Augustine's anti-Donatist works that he considered her the prime instigator of the split in the African Church. It was a period in which women played a prominent part in Christian activities, even at times in Church politics. The affair of Lucilla may be one of the reasons why Augustine always remained suspicious of female "theologians." Of course there were Christian women, such as Therasia the wife of Bishop Paulinus of Nola, for whom Augustine had the highest esteem.

Still another feature of Augustine's reaction to Donatism, passed over lightly by Lamirande, is the question of doctrinal differences between the two divisions of the African Church. Many historians hold that the Donatists were quite orthodox on all major articles of belief—and Augustine usually admits this. There was, of course, the matter of rebaptism, because the Donatists challenged the validity of a sacrament conferred by an unworthy minister. Lamirande quotes (p. 10) the Edict of February 12, A.D. 405 (from the *Codex Theodosianus*) to show that rebaptism was forbidden eventually by state law. This difference concerning baptism was important[39] but it may not be the only doctrinal aberration in Donatism.

More significant doctrinally is the claim made by Augustine in a sermon dated A.D. 416[40] that some Donatists believed that Christ was not equal with God the Father. Augustine admitted that many Donatists have the same belief as Catholics, concerning the equality of the Persons in the Trinity, but he adds: "There are other Donatists, however, who while professing that He [Christ] is of the same substance as the Father, deny that He is equal with the Father."[41] Other anti-Donatist *Sermons* suggest vaguely that some Donatists held erroneous views regarding Christ but it is in the treatise *On Heresies* (written in 429) that Augustine identifies the Donatist who denied the equality of Persons in the Trinity. He was, Augustine says, Majorinus, the first bishop in the schismatic movement in Carthage. Moreover, Augustine now admits that it is hard to find other Donatists who shared this error of Majorinus.[42] It would seem, then, that Augustine tried to be scrupulously fair in making charges of doctrinal error against the Donatists. The differences between Catholics and Donatists centered on three issues: 1) whether the Church was for all men or only for an elite group; 2) whether a sacrament is valid if the minister is unworthy; and 3) whether Church and State must be kept entirely separate.[43]

The question of Augustine's toleration of Christian heretics other than Donatists is given little place in this book of Lamirande's. This is probably due to the fact that movements such as Pelagianism and Arianism elicited much less political disturbance than Donatism. In their case the matters at issue were doctrinal differences, rather than disputes about divisions of authority in Church and State. One cannot say this concerning Augustine's attitude toward non-Christian religions. Here there were problems involving tolerance. Many Jewish scholars feel that he was unfair in his comments on members of their faith. One must admit that Augustine shared some of the prejudices that distinguish some present-day Arabs; yet he had a profound respect for the Jewish Scriptures and Prophets. Perhaps we need an up-to-date study of this aspect of Augustine's thought. Much the same comment applies to his stand on paganism. Here too, his attitude seems to have been mixed. He varied from outright condemnation of the obscenities of some forms of pagan worship to obvious admiration for the simple virtues of the early Roman pagans. This tension is observed throughout the *City of God*.

Another problem only slightly broached by Lamirande is that of Augustine's alleged "imperialism." Like St. Paul he was proud of being a citizen of the Roman Empire. Support for civil authority is characteristic of clerical officials in the first centuries of Christianity. St. Clement of Rome (one of the first bishops to assert the primacy of the Roman episcopacy) shares the view of St. Peter (who may have ordained Clement) that it is part of the duty of the Christian to respect and promote good order in the body politic. This includes praying for, and cooperating with, state authorities.[44] Though perhaps surprising, since many early Christians were migrants and minority peoples, this loyalty to the *Pax Romana* laid the foundation for similar attitudes in the age of Augustine. Of course some of his prominent Christian friends, such as Ambrose and Evodius, had been government officials before their consecration as bishops. Moreover, Augustine had studied for a career in public service and his parents shared that ambition for him. His friendships with many imperial functionaries are well known. So he remained a strong supporter of state authority and rarely complained about interference from political officialdom. This is a fact of his toleration for other authorities which deserves further investigation.

As far as Lamirande's central thesis is concerned, one can make no adverse criticism. He gives a balanced appraisal of Augustine's change from an attitude of sweet reasonableness toward the Donatists to a realization that force was necessary to resist their violence. Speaking of Augustine's shift, Gerald Bonner says: "it did not, as we have tried to show, represent the total reversal of his opinions as many critics have claimed . . . When all allowance has been made, it is difficult to see how any state could have tolerated Donatism in the form in which it expressed itself, or that the Church is to be condemned for welcoming the action of the state."[45] With this estimate Lamirande is in full agreement. His lecture is a significant contribution to the literature of the Church-State problem in early Christian times.

NOTES

1. *Religion and Society in the age of Saint Augustine* (London: Faber and Faber, 1972. Pp. 352. Pounds 3.25.)

2. *Augustine of Hippo: a Biography* (Berkeley and Los Angeles: University of California Press, 1967).

3. *St. Augustine of Hippo. Life and Controversies* (Philadelphia 1963) p. 316: "It is possible that the pendulum has swung too far and that the heresiarch [Pelagius] now enjoys a more favourable reputation than he deserves . . . "

4. G. Bonner, "Rufinus of Syria and African Pelagianism," *Augustinian Studies* 1 (1970) 31-47, brings out this pluralism.

5. Emin Tengstrom, *Donatisten und Katholiken: soziale, wirtschaftliche und politische Aspekten einer nordafrikanischen Kirchenspaltung* (Göteborg 1964). The review is reprinted from the *Journal of Roman Studies* 55 (1965) 281-283, on pages 335-338 of *Religion and Society*.

6. Bonner, *St. Augustine of Hippo* p. 278.

7. For the research on Manichaeism in the four centuries preceding the twentieth, see the survey articles: Julien Ries, "Introduction aux études Manichéennes: Quatre siècles de recherches," *Ephemerides Theologicae Lovanienses* 33 (1957) 453-482; 35 (1959) 362-409. Brown calls this study the "best account"; see *Religion and Society* p. 96, note 2.

8. Isaac de Beausobre initiated this "Reformation" view in the eighteenth century with his *Histoire critique de Manichée et du Manichéisme* 2 vols. (Amsterdam 1734-1739). Ries, *art. cit.* vol. 33, p. 470, calls this the first serious study of the Manichaean sources. An Amsterdam dissertation by L.J.R. Ort, *Mani: a Religio-Historical Description of His Personality* (Leiden 1967) pp. 1-4, shows the continuing influence of Beausobre. In the same school is: F.C. Burkitt, *The Religion of the Manichees* (Cambridge 1925) which remains a standard work for English readers.

9. A good example is George Widengren, *Mani and Manichaeism*, translated by Charles Kessler (London 1965).

10. "Le diversità delle sette manichee," *Studi bizantini e neoellenici* IX (1957) 176-187; and "Analyse du manichéisme numidien au ive siècle," *Augustinus Magister* III (1955) 391-410.

11. *Religion and Society* p. 108, note 3.

12. *Ibid.* pp. 94-118.

13. *Ibid.* pp. 9-45.

14. *Ibid.* p. 48.

15. *Les Voyages de saint Augustin* (Paris 1969).

16. *Soliloquia* I.2.7: "A. Deum et animam scire cupio. R. Nihilne plus? A. Nihil omnino." Compare *De ordine* II.18.47: "To philosophy pertains a twofold question: the first treats of the soul; the second, of God. The first makes us know ourselves; the second, our origin." (Translated by R.P. Russell, O.S.A., *Writings of Saint Augustine*, New York 1948, p. 324.)

17. On this other-worldly emphasis, see my article: "The Political Philosophy of St. Augustine," *Proceedings American Catholic Philosophical Association* VII (1931) 45-55.

18. *Religion and Society* p. 206.

19. *Ibid.* pp. 321-322.

20. "Ascetic eccentricity was clamped in the monasteries." (*Ibid.* p. 115.) And later: "The ascetic fringe knows its place, in the monasteries." (p. 118.)

21. See p. 148, where Brown is reporting on E. A. Thompson's similar criticism.

22. *Religion and Society* p. 334. At issue here are the views of Hans-Joachim Diesner — but Brown states his agreement and even endeavors to trace this problem of disinterest in the poor to "inner tensions within the system of Christian ethics."

23. Cf. Perler, "L'Hospitalité chrétienne," in *Les Voyages de saint Augustin* pp. 106-115.

24. Possidii, *Vita sancti Augustini* cap. 31; cf. Bourke, *Augustine's Quest of Wisdom* (Milwaukee 1945) p. 302.

25. "Religious coercion belongs to the pornography of Late Roman history." (*Religion and Society* p. 14.) Later, "it was the new intolerance of the 'respectable' Catholicism of the later fourth century which kept the barbarian kingdoms 'barbaric' . . . " (p. 54.) Again, "in the treatment of Manichaeism we have a clear index of

the fusing of Roman prejudice with Christian doctrinal intolerance." (p. 106). And we are even told (p. 152) of the "intolerance that went hand in hand with religious creativity . . ."

26. "Religious Coercion in the Later Roman Empire: the Case of North Africa," originally in *History* 48 (1963) 283-305; reprinted in *Religion and Society* pp. 301-331.

27. "Augustine, for all his harsh emphasis on the necessity of baptism for those outside the Church, appears, paradoxically, by contrast to Pelagius, as the great exponent of moral tolerance inside it." *Ibid.* p. 205.

28. Emilien Lamirande, *Church, State and Toleration. An Intriguing Change of Mind in Augustine* (Villanova University Press, 1975. Pp. 78).

29. While there are infelicities in English expression throughout, the more important errors are items like "reappraisal" for "reprisal" (p. 9) and "heartedly" for "heartily" (p. 17).

30. Augustine cites this as an incident still remembered by members of his congregation: "Nonne apud Hipponem, ubi ego sum, non desunt qui meminerint Faustinum vestrum [i.e. a Donatist] regni sui tempore praecipisse, quoniam catholicorum ibi paucitas erat, ut nullus eis panem coqueret . . . " *Contra litteras Petiliani* II.81.184.

31. *St. Augustine of Hippo. Life and Controversies* (Philadelphia: Westminster Press, 1963). See especially chapters 6 and 7.

32. *Les Révisions* (Œuvres de s. Augustin XII, Paris 1950) "Introduction" pp. 116-117: "Les premiers historiens du schisme donatiste, en particulier saint Optat de Milève, ne connaissent qu'un seul personnage du nom de Donat."

33. *Retractationes* 1.21.3: "Item quod dixi 'Donatum,' cujus epistolam refellebam, [Augustine is reviewing his own book, *Contra Epistolam Donati Haeretici*] 'rogasse ut imperator inter ipsum et Caecilianum transmarinos episcopos iudices daret,' non ipsum, sed alium Donatum, eiusdem tamen schismatis, hoc fecisse probabilius invenitur."

34. For a brief survey of this event, with references to Optatus Milevitanus, *De Schismate Donatistarum,* see Bonner, *op. cit.* pp. 242-243.

35. Augustini, *Epistola Donato proconsuli Africae* 100.1: "diligimus inimicos nostros et oramus pro eis . . . corrigi eos cupimus,

non necari . . . " The importance of this letter lies in its evidence that even three years before the famous meeting in Carthage (A.D. 411) Augustine rejected the use of capital punishment in such cases.

36. See *Contra Epistolam Parmeniani* 1.12.19: "quemdam Augustinum episcopum eorum."

37. *Epist.* 43.6.17: "pecuniosissima mulier quadam Lucilla . . ." *Contra Epist. Parmeniani* 1.3.5: "Lucilla pecuniosissima tunc et factiosissima femina . . ." *Contra Cresconium Donatistam* 111.28.32: "Lucilla tunc praepotens et pecuniosissima femina . . ." The *Gesta apud Zenophilum* are quoted, *ibid.* 111.29.33, as calling Lucilla "clarissima femina."

38. *Contra Cresconium* 111.28.32: "Lucilla tunc praepotens et pecuniosissima femina odiis accensa furialibus vehementer instaret, ut contra Caecilianum veluti damnatum alter ordinaretur episcopus." *The Gesta apud Zenophilum (ibid.* 29.33) say that Lucilla paid forty "pence" (*quadragentis follibus*) to bring about the removal of Caecilianus and the installation of Majorinus — and that this originated the Donatist schism (*ut fieret Majorinus episcopus, et inde factum est schisma*).

39. Bonner, *op. cit.* p. 30, concludes that "the theological position of the Donatists was the logical development of one aspect of St. Cyprian's doctrine of the unity of the Church, and the invalidity of the sacraments administered outside her."

40. For the date of *Sermo* 183 (PL 38, col. 993-995) see Franciscus Moriones, *Enchiridion Theologicum S. Augustini* (Madrid: B A C, 1961) p. 711.

41. *Sermo* 183.9: "Donatistae plurimi hoc confitentur de Filio quod nos, quod aequalis sit Patri Filius, ejusdemque substantiae: alii vero eorum, ejusdem quidem substantiae confitentur, sed aequalem negant." The English is from Quincy Howe, Jr. (trans.) *Selected Sermons of St. Augustine* (New York: Holt, Rinehart and Winston, 1966, p. 78).

42. *Liber de Haeresibus* LXIX: "Extant scripta ejus [Majorinus] ubi apparet eum non catholicam de Trinitate habuisse sententiam, sed quamvis ejusdem substantiae, minorem tamen Patre Filium, et minorem filio putasse Spiritum-sanctum."

43. These are treated at length in G.G. Willis, *St. Augustine and the Donatist Controversy* (London: S P C K, 1950) pp. 93-168.

44. See chapter 60 of St. Clement of Rome, *Epistle to the Cor-*

inthians, trans. J.A. Kleist (ACW 1, Washington 1946) for such a prayer in the first century.

45. Bonner, *op. cit.* p. 307.

CHAPTER 13

The City of God and History

"Prime Minister H. F. Verwoerd, of South Africa, was shot by David Pratt on April 9th, 1960." On the surface, this statement of recent historical fact seems easy to understand. The event occurred; the wounded man is now recovered; there is nothing more to it. It may be recorded as one of the unambiguous "facts" of twentieth-century history.

However, it is not that simple. The mere fact that a man was shot is not a memorable event in world history. Probably hundreds of men, throughout the world, are shot every month. In most cases, these acts of violence are not of historic significance. What made the shooting of the Prime Minister of South Africa important was the context. The surrounding conditions were charged with meanings which students of history in the twenty-first century may understand only with difficulty.

There is the political context: this wounded man is a key official in the government of his country. As a consequence, the shooting was an attempted assassination. There is the social and cultural context: this man is an outspoken advocate of *Apartheid*, in a country where differences of color loom large. There is the context of past but pertinent events: this man is of Dutch extraction, his assailant has an English background; we recall the Boer War. There is the context of analogous events: this incident brings to mind the assassination of an obscure archduke at Sarajevo, and the consequent holocaust of World War I. Even partially to understand such a fact of history can be a tremendously complicated matter.[1]

There are some historians who would see this fact in a

still broader framework. If St. Augustine were living today, he would be vitally interested. It is quite possible that this great Christian was of Berber extraction and that he was as dark as the average Moroccan of our day. One of his first thoughts would be that this shooting shows the hand of divine Providence in human affairs. Augustine was completely theocentric in his thinking.[2] He was ever aware that nothing happens in this world that escapes God's knowledge and divine permission. His contextual framework for the interpretation of the events of history is the City of God.

To understand what the City of God meant to Augustine it is advisable to start with his general view of all reality.[3] It is a picture on three levels. At the top is God, wholly immutable, superior to all the vicissitudes of space and time. With God are the *rationes aeternae*, the eternal principles of all that is permanent in being, truth and goodness. At the bottom of the picture are all bodies, including human ones. They are mutable both in space and in time. Of themselves, bodies and bodily events are so variable and unsteady that they cannot be the objects of true knowledge. There are principles of change in living bodies (the *rationes seminales*, but these seminal reasons are not bodies. On the middle level are finite spirits (human souls and angels) which are immutable in regard to space but quite mutable in time.[4]

Now, in Augustinism man is much more clearly identified with his soul than with his body. Indeed, in an early work, Augustine speaks of man as "a soul using a body."[5] So, men are situated between the immutable and the mutable. Men have only to look up in order to contemplate the eternal truths. Likewise, they have only to glance downward to lose all notion of what is of permanent value. It is from this context that we derive the famous concepts of *conversion* and *aversion*: the soul is free to turn its gaze toward or away from its Creator. This is not merely a question of knowledge; it also makes possible two kinds of love. In a famous passage, Augustine suggests the connection between this dualism and two sorts of societies:

These are the two loves: the first is holy, the second foul; the first is social, the second selfish; the first consults the common welfare for the sake of a celestial society, the second grasps at a selfish control of social affairs for the sake of arrogant domination; the first is submissive to God, the second tries to rival God; the first is quiet, the second restless; the first is peaceful, the second trouble-making; the first prefers truth to the praises of those who are in error, the second is greedy for praise however it may be obtained; the first is friendly, the second envious; the first desires for its neighbor what it wishes for itself, the second desires to subjugate its neighbor; the first rules its neighbor for the good of its neighbor, the second for its own advantage; and [these two loves] make a distinction among the angels, first belongs to the good angels, the second to the bad angels; and they also separate the two "cities" founded among the race of men, under the wonderful and ineffable Providence of God, administering and ordering all things that have been created; the first city is that of the just, the second is that of the wicked. And though they are now, during the course of time, intermingled, they shall be divided at the last judgment; the first, being joined by the good angels under its King, shall attain eternal life; the second in union with the bad angels under its king, shall be sent into eternal fire. Perhaps, we shall treat, God willing, of these two cities more fully in another place.[6]

This text offers a key to the understanding of the City of God. It is a society of persons under God as their Head, united in a common bond of love and cooperation, transcending differences of time, race, nationality and institutions. We need not hesitate over the source of this conception of a divine City. It is doubtless true that the point had been developed previously by the Donatist scholar, Tychonius.[7] There is a much more obvious and ultimate source than this. The City of God and the earthly City are contrasted in many verses of the Psalms.[8] Jerusalem is the heavenly City and Babylon is the earthly one.[9] In that remarkable series of sermon notes on the Psalms which we know as the *Enarrationes*, Augustine summarized his views on the two Cities:

> All who have a taste for earthly things, all who prefer earthly felicity to God, all who seek their own things and not those of Jesus Christ, belong to that one City which is metaphorically called Babylon and has the Devil for its king. But all who have a taste for the things that are above, who meditate upon heavenly things, who live in this world with care lest they offend God, who are wary of sinning, who are not ashamed to confess that they are sinners, humble, meek, holy, just, pious and good—all these belong to one City that has Christ as King . . .
>
> It delights me to speak a little more to you about this sweet City of God. For the most glorious things have been said of thee, O City of God (Ps. 86:3). And if I forget thee, O Jerusalem, let my right hand be forgotten (136:5). For, but one homeland is sweet, and truly but one homeland, the only homeland; apart from it, whatever occurs to us is but a pilgrimage . . .
>
> And these two Cities are intermixed during the present; they are to be separated in the end. They are in mutual conflict: one on the side of iniquity, the other on the side of justice; one on the side of vanity, the other on the side of verity. At times, this temporal mixture causes some who belong to the Babylonian City to take charge of matters that belong to Jerusalem; and again, some who belong to Jerusalem are made to administer things that belong to Babylon . . .
>
> You know that the citizens of the evil City administer some of the affairs of the good City. Let us see, now, whether the citizens of the good City administer

some of the affairs of the bad City. Every earthly state (*res publica*) will certainly perish sometime, for its rule is to pass away when that Kingdom comes for which we pray: "Thy Kingdom come"; and of which it has been foretold, "His Kingdom will be without end." So, the earthly state has our citizens administering its affairs. Indeed, how many of the faithful, how many good men, are magistrates, judges, leaders, public officials and kings, in their cities? All these are just and good, having nothing in their hearts but the most glorious things that are said of thee, O City of God.[10]

It is these same themes that are treated in extended form in the great treatise, *On the City of God*, from Book XI to XXII.[11] The Scriptural origin of this treatment of the two Cities may even be traced back to Genesis. They are prefigured in the separation of heaven from earth, of light from darkness, of the waters from the dry land, and so on.[12] However, we must not understand such statements mechanically or in a deterministic fashion; those who belong to the heavenly City do so by their own free will, and the citizens of Babylon are such by virtue of their own voluntary commitment.

AUGUSTINE AND PHILOSOPHY OF HISTORY

Now, in what sense does Augustine's concept of the City of God offer a basis for a Christian philosophy of history? Let us first of all dispose of the terminological problem presented by the word, *philosophy*. Etienne Gilson has argued forcefully that what we find in Augustine is not a philosophy but a theology of history.[13] It is quite true that we do not discover in Augustine a purely rational and naturalistic interpretation of human affairs. If this is what we mean by philosophy of history, Gilson is correct, as usual. However, Augustine did not use the term, *philosophia*, in this exclusive sense. Writing against the Pelagians, he says: "the philosophy of the non-believers (*Gentium*) is not more worthy than our Christian one, which is the one true philosophy, provided that the pursuit or love of wisdom is what is meant by this word."[14] It becomes obvious, then, that in Augustine's usage he has a philosophy of history but he would not distinguish it from a theology.

Of course, he has long been accepted, in Catholic and non-Catholic scholarship alike, as one of the founders of philosophy of history. Indeed, many modern works simply take it as accepted that he is most typical of Christian thinking in this area.[15] Perhaps it has almost been forgotten that Pope Leo XIII wrote a famous *Letter on Historical Studies*, in 1883, in which he told Cardinal Nina: "The great doctor of the Church, Augustine, was the leader of all in thinking out this philosophical art of history, and he brought it to perfection."[16] One enthusiastic writer has even suggested that a complete theory of history is found in the *City of God*.[17]

There is, then, in St. Augustine a Christian view of history and whether we call it philosophy or theology is of small consequence. Some who think on human history, today, see nothing but a string of unconnected and meaningless events.[18] Augustine, on the contrary, finds Providence manifested in all temporal events. It is not that he derives a theory of morality or value *from* history.[19] Instead, what the City of God conception means is that one must look to the eternal to find the meaning of the temporal.

Implicit in the Augustinian view of history are certain essential beliefs of Christianity: there is but one God; all men are creatures of God and have Adam as a single ancestor; all things and events come under the care of divine Providence; mankind has fallen from a more favorable original condition and is now subject to suffering and other evils; mankind has been redeemed through the Incarnation; and there is an ultimate end, a final happiness, with God in a future life in eternity, which men are free to work for and

to attain.[20] Seen from the vantage point of this Christian setting, the events of temporal history become actions in the
drama of redemption and salvation.

If we recall the prevailing pagan notion of human life
and destiny, still widely current in Augustine's time, we can
better appreciate the appeal of the City of God ideal. The
dominating ancient view was that man lived like a puppet
bound to the wheel of fate. Time was thought to be circular
and repetitious. This is the cyclic theory of history which M.
Eliade has so thoroughly studied.[21] It meant that mankind
and the individual person were doomed to a perpetual recur-
rence of the same joys, sorrows and trials. No real progress
was possible. Man was on a huge merry-go-round from
which escape was utterly impossible. Toynbee has said of
this cyclicism:

> We can hardly escape the conclusion that we are
> the perpetual victims of an everlasting cosmic prac-
> tical joke, which condemns us to endure our suffer-
> ings and to overcome our difficulties and to purify our-
> selves of our sins — only to know in advance that the
> automatic and inevitable lapse of a certain meaningless
> measure of Time cannot fail to stultify all our human
> exertions.[22]

Now, Augustine's way of looking at human history
broke this wheel of fate. He showed that its view of time and
human destiny was wrong, that there is hope for release
from the cares of this world, that human life is not a rat-race
on an enclosed treadmill but a short journey to a promised
land. He straightened out the movement of time, made
man's temporal progress linear and real. Speaking of the
problem of how temporal events occur, Augustine says:

> The philosophers of this world thought that there
> was no possibility or proper way of solving this prob-
> lem, unless they postulated temporal cycles, whereby
> the same things are always renewed and repeated in the
> order of nature; and so they claimed that these cycles

of future and past ages are to occur successively and without ending.[23]

In his criticism of this necessitarianism, Augustine is blunt. "Far be it from us," he says, "to believe such things. Christ died but once for our sins. Now that He is risen from the dead, He will die no more . . . and after the resurrection, we shall be with the Lord always."[24] Notice how this refutation relies solely on the great fact of Christ's death, not on science or on rationalized argument. This fact, thoroughly attested in sacred and secular documents, freed men's minds from the burden of determinism and fate. It gave mankind a positive goal beyond time and temporal history. Christ died but once for our sins.

More than this, Augustine's philosophy of history charted a program for world peace. This plan has nothing to do with a federation of nations, with international pacts and leagues of nations. Nor was it a charter for a Holy Roman Empire: the City of God is not a political institution.[25] Augustine is not a patron of the identification of Church and State. Charlemagne's ill-fated Empire was much more the creature of the Byzantine notion of an all-embracing Christian society (as exemplified in Eusebius of Caesarea[26]) than of the *City of God*.

It is quite evident that what Augustine called for was a reform of the hearts of individual men, rather than of political institutions. For a better world society, we simply need better men. We see this in his famous analysis of peace:

> The peace, then, of the body lies in the ordered equilibrium of all its parts, the peace of the irrational soul, in the balanced adjustment of its appetites, the peace of the reasoning soul, in the harmonious correspondence of conduct and conviction; the peace of body and soul taken together, in the well-ordered life and health of the living whole. Peace between a mortal man and his Maker consists in ordered obedience, guided by faith, under God's eternal law; peace be-

tween man and man consists in regulated friendship.
The peace of a home lies in the ordered harmony of
authority and obedience among the members of a family living together. The peace of the political community is an ordered harmony of authority and obedience
among citizens. The peace of the heavenly City lies in
a perfectly ordered and harmonious communion of
those who find their joy in God, and in one another in
God. Peace, in its final sense, is the tranquillity of
order in all things.[27]

THOMAS AQUINAS AND THE CITY OF GOD

It is interesting to see what happened to this ideal of the
City of God, in the writings of St. Thomas Aquinas. The
first thing that strikes the reader is that the expression, "City
of God," is apparently never used by Aquinas.[28] Of course,
St. Thomas does discuss the *regnum Dei*, as this term is used
by St. Paul.[29] What he says is simply an expansion of the
Pauline text:

The Kingdom of God consists principally in interior
acts but, as a consequence, all those things without
which interior acts would be impossible also belong to
the Kingdom of God. Thus, if the Kingdom of God is
interior justice and peace and spiritual joy, then all the
exterior acts that are incompatible with justice, peace
and spiritual joy are also incompatible with the Kingdom of God; and so, in the Gospel they should be pro-
hibited in the Kingdom.[30]

Clearly, St. Thomas is not developing any special notion of human history in such a commentary. Indeed, he has
a much less sophisticated approach to history than Augustine. History is a mere chronicle of events, for Aquinas.[31]

Apart from the question of words, it may even be
doubted that St. Thomas ever thought in terms of a society

such as the Augustinian City of God. In some sense, Augustine's heavenly society requires to be contrasted with its opposite, the earthly City.[32] But St. Thomas appears to think of *all* men as constituting a universal community under God, by virtue of the community of human nature. In several places, he hints that, because all men have by *nature* the same ultimate end, beatitude, and because this beatitude is only attainable in that highest common good which is God, therefore all men are actually or potentially members of one vast human society, with God as Ruler. This universalism is difficult to pinpoint in the text of St. Thomas but here is one way in which he suggests it:

> Just as men who are associates in a state agree on this point, that they are subjects of one prince, by whose laws they are governed, so too do all men, to the extent that they naturally tend toward beatitude, have a certain general agreement in relation to God, as to the highest Prince of all, the Source of beatitude, the Legislator of the whole of justice . . . In the aforementioned community, in which all men agree as to the end that is beatitude, each man is considered as a part, while the common good of the whole is God Himself, in Whom the beatitude of all men lies.[33]

It is to be noted in this text, taken from a highly personal work of Aquinas, that all men are placed in this same universal society. We may well wonder whether St. Thomas could view social history as Augustine did, whether Thomism is open to that initial bifurcation of mankind which characterized the Augustinian social view. There is a short text in St. Thomas' *Exposition of the Sentences* which throws additional light on his position. There, he speaks of a divine community (*communicatio divina*) of all men in the one body of the Church. He adds that this membership is either actual or potential, and that it is a friendship in charity which extends to all, even to enemies.[34]

One can hardly avoid the conclusion that Thomas

Aquinas places much less stress than Augustine on the contrast between men of good will and those who turn away from God. Sometimes we may wonder whether Aquinas was sufficiently aware of the pluralistic character of actual human societies. In his *Sermon on the Creed*, preached in Naples near the end of his life, he confidently asserted:

> It is well known, in fact, that the whole world used to worship idols and to persecute Christ's faith. To this, even the histories written by pagans give testimony. Today, however, all are converted to Christ — the wise, the nobles, the rich, the powerful and the great — all are converted to the preaching of those who are simple and poor, of those few men who preach Christ.[35]

In view of such a statement, it seems probable that, if Aquinas said little or nothing about the City of God, he had still less to say about the earthly City. Rather, he regarded mankind on the natural level as ordered and unified in a common tendency toward happiness, and on the supernatural level as unified within the all-embracing arms of divine charity. He is not unaware that there are many men who are individually evil but he does not view them as members of an evil society. Possibly this is why St. Thomas offers us no developed philosophy of history. One may, of course, take some of the characteristic Thomistic views of human life and society and elaborate a modern scholastic theory of history. This has been done by Jacques Maritain, Martin D'Arcy, and others.[36] Such works are the personal products of present-day thinkers rather than interpretations of Thomas Aquinas.[37]

THE CITY OF GOD AND HISTORY TODAY

With certain notable exceptions, of whom Christopher Dawson is an outstanding example,[38] Christian historians have failed to make full use of the Augustinian concept of the

City of God. To some extent, this failure is understandable.
It is very easy to pervert Augustinism. One may concentrate
too much on Augustine's sweeping assertions concerning
God's foreknowledge and end with something very much
like Calvinistic predestination. One may exaggerate the
depths to which men have fallen as a result of the sin of
Adam — and thus achieve a neo-Jansenism. One might overstress his assertions that man, his actions and his world,
are nothing without God — and thus repeat the errors of
Ontologism.

Ironically enough, Augustine has anticipated the judgment of contemporary positivism on human history. *Of itself*,
the course of human events has no ultimate meaning for
Augustine. What he would add (and there is no doubt that
this is authentically Christian) is that we must not try to
understand human affairs and institutions, *by themselves*.
There are no absolutes for those who abandon an Absolute
God. Ultimate values disappear, if we deliberately turn
away from the Ultimate Being. This seems to me to be the
foundation stone of a Christian philosophy of history.

Human events become significant when we view them
in the light of divine Providence.[39] God becomes the focal
point of an ultimate explanation of the human societies
through time. This explanation admits of various interpretations, even within Augustinism. To some interpreters, the
high point of history is the incarnation. When God became
man, humanity reached its peak. All later human events are
anti-climatic.[40] A second way of interpreting the Christian
view of history is the eschatological. This shifts the emphasis
to the End of Time and sees humanity as in process toward
a not yet attained but ultimate condition of mankind.[41] Such
a view would see in temporal history a continuing and increasing fulfillment of the Redemption. It is not foreign to
Augustine's thought, as any reader of the last four books of
the *City of God* will realize.

To stress the role of divine Providence in history is not
a narrow "Catholic" position. In his introduction to the fa-

mous *Lectures on the Philosophy of History*, the Protestant Hegel
said: "our earnest endeavor must be directed to the recognition of the ways of Providence, the means it uses, and the
historical phenomena in which it manifests itself."[42] It would
be difficult to state the plan of a Christian view of history
more succinctly. Of course, Hegel proceeds to describe the
ways of God, in accord with his own dialectic, but the point
is that Hegel did not exclude some sort of providential explanation of history.

Another very informative recognition of the other-
worldly context of history is to be found in the late mediaeval
treatise by the Mohammedan, Ibn Khaldûn. He began his
work with a terse statement of the need for history as a part
of philosophy:

> The inner meaning of history, on the other hand, in-
> volves speculation and an attempt to get at the truth,
> subtle explanation of the causes and origins of existing
> things, and deep knowledge of the how and why of
> events. [History] therefore, is firmly rooted in philoso-
> phy. It deserves to be accounted a branch of philosophy.[43]

But Ibn Khaldûn is a theist. Within a few pages, he
adds: "God is the guide to that which is correct."[44] His understanding of the work of divine Providence is not identical
with a Christian one, yet there are fundamental similarities.

This brings us to a final point. A Christian view of
history places political institutions in a position of secondary
value; these things are not ends in themselves but means to
a good human life on earth. This does not mean that the
Christian historian should hold earthly peace and societal
order in contempt. The relation between the City of God
and the Church is not without ambiguity. Sometimes Augustine seems to suggest that they are identical; sometimes he
radically distinguishes them. If we take the Church as a visible institution on earth, then the City of God is much more
than that. But if we understand the Church in the broadest
sense, as embracing all men of good will, from all the ages,

past, present and future, we more nearly approach the limits of the heavenly City. What stands out in Augustine's account of the progress of the City of God through history is his insistence that the good and evil men are never separated in this world, or in time. Only at the Last Judgment will this final separation be effected.[45] There is no question that Augustine never expected to see complete peace in this world. I do not think, however, that he was opposed to efforts to establish good political order throughout the world.[46]

The citizens of God should be noteworthy for their tolerance and charity toward all. We cannot pass a final judgment now: there are good and bad men in every period, race, community and nation. The City of God makes room for all, on the basis of their personal qualities of mind and heart. In this spirit, we may close with Augustine's words:

> So long, then, as the heavenly City is wayfaring on earth, she invites citizens from all nations and all tongues, and unites them into a single pilgrim band. She takes no issue with that diversity of customs, laws, and traditions whereby human peace is sought and maintained. Instead of nullifying or tearing down, she preserves and appropriates whatever in the diversities of divers races is aimed at one and the same objective of human peace, provided only that they do not stand in the way of faith and worship of the one supreme and true God.[47]

NOTES

1. See Etienne Gilson's discussion of the statement, "Charlemagne was crowned emperor in 800," ("Doctrinal History and Its Interpretation," *Speculum*, XXIV [1949] 483-492) for a more thorough demonstration of this point.

2. J. Grabowski, *The All-Present God. A Study in St. Augustine* (St. Louis: Herder, 1954).

3. B. Cooke, "The Mutability-Immutability Principle in St. Augustine's Metaphysics," *The Modern Schoolman*, XXIII (1946), 175-193; XXIV (1946), 37-49.

4. *Epist.* 18, 2: "Est natura per locos et tempora mutabilis, ut corpus. Et est natura per locos nullo modo, sed tantum per tempora etiam ipsa mutabilis, ut anima. Et est natura quae nec per locos, nec per tempora mutari potest, hoc Deus est." Cf. *De Genesi ad litteram*, VIII, 20, 39.

5. *De moribus ecclesiae*, I, 27, 52: "Homo igitur, ut homini apparet, anima rationalis est mortali atque terreno utens corpore." See Gilson, *Introduction à l'etude de s. Augustin*, 3e éd. (Paris: Vrin, 1949), p. 58.

6. *De Genesi ad litteram*, XI, 15, 20; as translated in Bourke, *Augustine's Quest of Wisdom* (Milwaukee: Bruce, 1945), p. 249.

7. Cf. H. Scholz, *Glaube und Unglaube in der Weltgeschichte* (Leipzig, 1911), p. 78.

8. Ps. 47:1: "Great is the Lord, and exceedingly to be praised in the City of our God . . ." Ps. 86:3: "Glorious things are said of thee: O City of God." Ps. 47:5: "For behold the kings of the earth assembled themselves . . ." Ps. 48:2-3: "Hear these things all ye nations: give ear, all ye inhabitants of the world. All you that are earthborn, and you sons of men . . ."

9. See all of Psalm 136.

10. *Enarr. in Ps.*, 61, 6-8.

11. A quick summary is offered in *Augustine's Quest of Wisdom*, pp. 263-284.

12. See Genesis 1:1-4, 9-17, etc.

13. See his *Introduction* to the *City of God* (New York: Fathers of the Church, 1949), vol. 1; in the Image Book condensation, pp. 30-31.

14. *Contra Fulianum Pelagianum*, IV, 14, 72: "Obsecro te, non est honestior philosophia gentium quam nostra Christiana, quae una est vera philosophia, quando quidem studium vel amor sapientiae significatur hoc nomine." Cf. *De beata vita*, 4.

15. "St. Augustine in the City of God advanced the first complete philosophy of history in which the past, the present, and the future are combined in one drama, a drama of sin and redemption." J.E. Boodin, "Philosophy of History," in *Twentieth Century Philosophy* (New York: Philosophical Library, 1943), p. 97. See also: Hans Meyerhoff, *The Philosophy of History in Our Time* (New

York: Doubleday Anchor Books, 1959), pp. 1-7; Roger Shinn, "Augustinian and Cyclical Views of History," *Anglican Theological Review*, 31 (1949), 133-141.

16. "Artem ipsam historiae philosophicam magnus Ecclesiae doctor Augustinus princeps omnium excogitavit, perfecit." *Lett. al Card. Nina*, Agosto 1883; cited in C. Butti, *La mente di S. Agostino nella Citta di Dio* (Firenze: Libreria Editrice Fiorentina, 1930), pp. 84-85.

17. "In questo concetto sintetico è tutta la teorica della filosofia della storia. La teorica originale e meravigliosa della *Citta di Dio*." Butti, *op. cit.*, p. 84.

18. Karl Popper takes this positivist position in *The Open Society and Its Enemies* (Princeton: Princeton U. Press 1950), pp. 449-458.

19. Morris Cohen mistakenly considered that this was the aim of Augustine. See *Reason and Nature* (New York and Chicago: Free Press, 1931), p. 377.

20. Cf. Butti, *op. cit.*, pp. 77-78.

21. Mircea Eliade, *The Myth of the Eternal Return*, translated by W.R. Trask (New York: Pantheon Books, 1954).

22. Arnold Toynbee, *A Study of History*, 4, 30; see the further comment on this passage, in Shinn, *art. cit.*, p. 141.

23. "Hanc autem se philosophi mundi hujus non aliter putaverunt posse vel debere dissolvere, nisi ut circuitus temporum inducerent, quibus eadem semper fuisse renovata atque repetita in rerum natura, atque ita deinceps fore sine cessatione asseverarent volumina venientium praetereuntiumque saeculorum." *De civitate Dei*, XII, 13.

24. "Absit, inquam, ut nos ista credamus. Semel enim Christus mortuus est pro peccatis nostris: resurgens autem a mortuis jam non moritur, et mors ei ultra non dominabitur: et nos post resurrectionem semper cum Domino erimus." *Ibid.*

25. On this, I agree with F.E. Cranz, *De civitate Dei*, 15, 2, and Augustine's Idea of the Christian Society," *Speculum*, 25 (1952), 215-225; see my article, "The Political Philosophy of St. Augustine," *Proc. Amer. Cath. Philos. Assoc.*, VII (1931), 45-55.

26. Cf. Cranz, *art. cit.*, p. 220.

27. *City of God*, 19, 11; translation of G. Walsh (Image Book edition, p. 456) with some modifications by the present writer.

28. It is difficult to establish a negative of this kind, when

one is dealing with works as vast as the *Opera Omnia* of St. Thomas. Let me simply say that *civitas Dei* is not indexed in the standard concordances (L. Schütz, the Leonine *Indices*, and Peter of Bergamo's *Tabula Aurea*) nor have I ever seen the phrase, apart from citations of Augustine's treatise, in the *Opera Omnia.*

29. Rom. 14:17.

30. *Summa Theologiae*, 1-2, 108, 1, ad 1; cf. *Expositio Pauli Epist. ad Rom.*, 14, lectio 2.

31. "Nam historia est . . . cum simpliciter aliquid proponitur." *S. T.*, I, 1, 10, ad 2. (This statement occurs in a discussion of the historical sense of Scripture.)

32. I do not suggest anything of Manichean dualism in Augustine's contrast; it is simply a fact for Augustine that there are two kinds of men.

33. *De perfectione vitae spiritualis*, c. 13 (*Opuscula Omnia*, ed. P. Mandonnet, 4, 223-224)

34. "Quarta communicatio est divina, secundum quam omnes homines communicant in uno corpore Ecclesiae, vel actu vel potentia; et haec est amicitia caritatis quae habetur ad omnes, etiam ad inimicos." *In 3 Sententiarum*, 29, 6, resp.

35. *Expositio devotissima super Symbolum Apostolorum, ad init.* (*Opuscula Omnia,* ed. Mandonnet, 4, 351).

36. J. Maritain, *On the Philosophy of History*, ed. by J.W. Evans (New York: Scribners, 1957); "The Christian and History," *Jubilee*, 5 (1957), 37-40. M. D'Arcy, *The Sense of History: Secular and Sacred* (London: Faber and Faber, 1959); *The Meaning and Matter of History* (New York: Farrar, Strauss and Cudahy, 1959).

37. From quite another point of view, that of the scientific character of the discipline of history, see: B.J. Muller-Thym, "Of History as a Calculus Whose Term is Science," *The Modern Schoolman*, 19, 3 (March 1942), 41-47; 19, 4 (May 1942), 73-76.

38. Besides his well-known historical monographs, Dawson's two essays: "The Dying World," and "The City of God", in *A Monument to Saint Augustine* (New York: Sheed and Ward, 1930), are still worth careful reading.

39. Thus understood, history can have a special meaning for Thomas Aquinas; indeed, he has so treated the sphere of human actions and society, in the Third book of his *Summa contra Gentiles.*

40. For this Incarnationist view, see: P. Henry, "The Christian Philosophy of History," *Theological Studies,* 13 (1952), 419-432.

41. Nikolai Berdyaev, *Smisl Istorii* (Berlin: Obelisk, 1923); translated as *The Meaning of History*, by G. Heavey (New York: Scribners, 1956). Possibly there is some parallel in the evolutionism of Père Teilhard de Chardin; see C. Tresmontant, *P. Teilhard de Chardin, His Thought* (Baltimore: Helicon, 1959).

42. G.W.F. Hegel, *The Philosophy of History*, translated by J. Sibree (New York: Willey Book Co., 1900), p. 14.

43. Ibn Khaldûn, *The Muqaddimah. An Introduction to History*, translated by F. Rosenthal (Bollingen Series, 43) (New York: Pantheon Books, 1958), vol. 1, p. 6.

44. *Ibid.*, p. 26.

45. *City of God*, 18, 54.

46. How else explain his admiration for the *Pax Romana?* See *City of God*, 18, 22.

47. *City of God*, 19, 17; translated by G. Walsh et al., Image ed., p. 465.

CHAPTER 14

Augustine in the Twentieth Century

Our age has often been criticized for its atheism, materialism, antisupernaturalism, and the general super-ficiality of its literature, yet one of our favorite authors today is a God-loving, spiritual-minded, other-worldly writer from fifteen centuries back. That many modern people still want to read St. Augustine of Hippo is strikingly attested by the publication of the *Basic Writings of St. Augustine.*[1]

Included in the *Basic Writings* are the *Confessions, City of God, On the Trinity*, together with twelve shorter works by St. Augustine. With the exception of two small treatises done by Prof. G. G. Leckie, all stem from nineteenth-century versions made by British scholars and republished in America in "A Select Library of the Nicene and Post-Nicene Fathers of the Christian Church." Eight of these American volumes were devoted to Augustine. For several decades, if one wished to read St. Augustine in English, these were practically the only available translations.

Catholic readers can have no cause for complaint, then, that all these translations in the Random House printing have been selected from non-Catholic sources. Until rather recently, there have been very few translations of Augustine done by English-speaking Catholics. Of course, both the *City of God* and the *Confessions* appear in the archaic English of the seventeenth century, and these Catholic versions have been reprinted with some revision and, in the case of the *City of God*, some mutilation. Sir Tobie Matthew (who sounds like something out of Shakespeare but was really the son of the Archbishop of York, a convert to Catholicism after what is alleged to have been a wild youth, and even-

206

tually a Catholic priest) put the *Confessions* into stately, but none too reliable, English in 1620. Another Catholic scholar, thought by some to be J. Healey, had translated the *City of God* ten years before (London, 1610). There are now two English versions of the work *On the Trinity*. One by Stephen McKenna (FOC 45, 1963) and the other by John Burnaby (LCC 8, 1955). No English version of the equally important *De Genesi ad litteram* has ever been published. The blunt truth is that Catholic scholars have shirked their obvious duty to make the great writings of the most influential Father of the Church available to English readers.

One of the first exceptions to this dreary outlook was F. J. Sheed's translation of the *Confessions*.[2] There is little question that the Sheed translation is superior to that of Pilkington, which is used in the *Basic Writings*. In fact, Dr. Pusey's century-old version (which is but a revision of the seventeenth-century Anglican work by William Watts) is not a bad piece of work. Neither the revision of Sir Tobie Matthew by Dom Roger Hudleston (London, 1923) nor of Watts by W. H. D. Rouse (Loeb Classical Library, 1942) surpasses it.

During the past two years, very positive steps have been taken under Catholic auspices to remedy this situation in Augustine studies. Two new translation series have begun to appear in the United States, both of which will eventually include nearly all the representative works of St. Augustine. One of these series is called "The Fathers of the Church." It is published in New York, under the general editorial direction of Dr. Ludwig Schopp. Its Board of Editors includes four men from the Catholic University of America (Rev. Wilfrid Parsons, S.J., and Drs. R. J. Deferrari, Stephan Kuttner and M. R. P. McGuire), two from Fordham University (Fathers R. Arbesmann, O.S.A., and G. G. Walsh, S.J.), together with Father R. P. Russell, O.S.A., of Villanova, Dr. B. M. Peebles, formerly of St. John's College, and Father Anselm Strittmatter, O.S.B., of St. Anselm's Priory, Washington. Of the seventy-two volumes pro-

jected in "The Fathers of the Church," about twenty-two will
be devoted to St. Augustine.

Three Augustine volumes are already printed in this
series. The first (1948) contains the four Cassiciacum dialogues.[3] Two treatises on the soul, two religious *opuscula*,
and the work *On Music* make up the second volume.[4] Volume IV includes four important theological works, one of
which is the famous *Enchiridion*.[5] Each translation is done by
an expert scholar; accuracy of meaning is matched by clarity
and attractiveness of English style. The introductions are
mostly brief but informative, with short bibliographies of the
most useful secondary works. Footnotes are intended to be
sufficient to enable the average intelligent reader to understand the text. In every case, the best available Latin edition
is made the basis of the translation and is plainly identified
in the introduction.

Of volumes scheduled for early appearance, several are
of interest to the student of St. Augustine. Dr. A. C. Pegis
is translating four of the most significant of the philosophic
and doctrinal treatises: *On Free Choice, The Teacher, On the
Nature of the Good,* and *The Soul and Its Origin.* Those who are
familiar with his essay, "The Mind of St. Augustine," in
Mediaeval Studies (VI, 1944, 1-61) know that he is very well
equipped to interpret these key works. Another volume will
contain Augustine's commentary on the *Sermon on the Mount,*
plus a group of selected sermons. This has been done by
Father Denis J. Kavanagh, O.S.A., whose work is already
known from his version of the *Answer to the Skeptics.*

Three translators have collaborated on the forthcoming
translation of the *City of God.* Begun by the late Demetrius
B. Zema, S.J., this work is now being carried on by Fathers
Gerald G. Walsh, S.J., and J. R. O'Donnell, C.S.B. It will
take up three volumes. An introduction of some length has
been written by Prof. E. Gilson and it will be included in the
first volume of the *City of God.* Augustine regarded this vast
treatise as his masterpiece and its appearance in a competent
English translation should be an event of primary impor-

tance in contemporary Catholic scholarship. Written to explain the revitalizing role of Christianity in a decaying pagan world, the *City of God* has a message which is as fresh and pertinent now as it ever was.

Also announced for early publication in "The Fathers of the Church" is the present writer's translation of the *Confessions*. While my doctrinal biography of the Bishop of Hippo[6] was being written, it became painfully evident that an accurate English translation of the *Confessions*, accompanied by adequate annotations, was a desideratum. Several critical editions of the Latin text have come out in the past few years. The best is that of M. Skutella (Leipzig, 1934) but also important are the texts by C. Vega (Madrid, 1930) and G. Capello (Turin, 1948). It is now possible to utilize their textual precisions and variants, and what is actually more important, their explanatory notes. Since the question has already been asked, Why another translation of the much-translated *Confessions*?, possibly the foregoing will be sufficient apology. It is quite true that a perfect translation of a work which is as personal in style and thought as the *Confessions* cannot be done. Yet the possibility of improving the English text must always be admitted. This volume is prefaced by an extensive general introduction to the study of St. Augustine, in which his life, works and thought are separately treated. It also includes a selected bibliography of one thousand studies, arranged topically according to the divisions of the *Introduction*. It is hoped that this will partly fill the need for a somewhat scholarly English introduction to Augustine studies.

Another group of Augustine translations under Catholic auspices is now appearing.[7] In this series, the volumes have fewer pages and the three now published contain but one treatise each. On the other hand, the notes in the "Ancient Christian Writers" are longer than those in the other series and seem to stress the theological implications of Augustine's writings.

A translation of *De Catechizandis Rudibus*, done by

Father J. P. Christopher in 1926, is revised and reprinted in this series.[8] It is a good translation and the notes are quite scholarly. *The Lord's Sermon on the Mount*,[9] translated by J. J. Jepson, S.S., is in Volume V; and a version of the *Enchiridion*, by L. A. Arand, S.S., appears in the third volume.[10] Those who wish to make a comparison of the two series of American translations may examine the translation of the *Enchiridion* in each. A criticism that has been made in regard to the "Ancient Christian Writers" series is that its notes make reference to many studies which are hard to get in American libraries. This does not seem to me to be a good criticism. One of the best ways of building up better Catholic libraries in this country is precisely by making clear references to, and evaluations of, the best European literature in one's field. No one wishes to be guilty of isolationism, or provincialism, in scholarship. It is possible to avoid these faults by broad but intelligently directed reading.

Most libraries can afford to buy both series mentioned. Their volumes are not expensive and not too many will be published in any one year. In comparing prices, it is well to note that the volumes of the "Fathers of the Church" run between four and five hundred pages, whereas those which are printed in "Ancient Christian Writers" average about one hundred and seventy-five pages. Catholic scholarship need not apologize for the quality of the work in either set.

But these series are not the only signs of an Augustinian revival in America. A new translation of *St. Augustine on Free Will* has appeared as Volume IV in the "University of Virginia Studies."[11] The translator, Carroll Mason Sparrow, died before publication of the book. The striking thing about the work is not so much its attractive (one might say, "courtly") English, but rather the background of the translator. Dr. Sparrow was a professor of physics at the University of Virginia, associate editor of the *Physical Review*, Fellow of the American Physical Society, and a member of several other scientific bodies. That he was an amateur (better, *amator*) in Augustinian scholarship is indicated by Dr.

Sparrow's failure to use the best Latin text of *De libero arbitrio*. However, his version is very readable; the best so far.

Father William G. Most, of Loras College, Dubuque, has just announced his forthcoming planographed edition of *A Digest of St. Augustine's City of God*. This is to be a text for college Latin classes. Judging from the ten-page *Introduction*, which shows that Father Most knows both his author and his audience, this should be a valuable addition to the classics curriculum of Catholic colleges. There is no reason why Catholic students should go through several years of Latin without ever discovering that one of the great masters of Latin prose, one of the most able teachers of ancient rhetoric, was also a Catholic and a Father of the Church. St. Augustine was certainly not neglected by Erasmus and his fellow humanists of the Renaissance. Why should he be overlooked in modern classes in Latin?

Parenthetically, what is very much needed now by American students of Church Latin, of patristics, of the history of early Christian thought and culture, is a first-rate *Patrology*. The standard works on patristics and Christian Latin literature are all in foreign languages, or in outdated translations of these works. Bardenhewer, Cayré, Norden, Monceaux, Altaner and De Labriolle, and the rest, do not fill the bill. Not one of them is adequate in regard to the listing of studies, translations and editions which have appeared in the English-speaking countries. Not one of them is properly indexed. An historical survey of Church literature — Greek, Latin and Oriental — from the beginnings up to the Renaissance, could be an invaluable contribution to American Catholic scholarship. It should include more than those writers who are formally recognized as Fathers of the Church. It should contain short but accurate biogaphies, exact dates and places of residence, full lists of writings with titles in the original languages, references to standard editions, translations and studies (particularly in English). In citing journal articles, the title of the study should be given, as well as the name of the periodical. Indexes should give the

full names of the patristic authors, the names of the authors
of secondary studies, the titles of reference works and collec-
tions, with understandable abbreviations. Short outlines of
doctrine should accompany each entry but should not crowd
out the factual information needed for further research.
Such a work could be done in one volume of six hundred
pages and, in case any publishers are listening, it would sell
like hot cakes.

What, in fine, does the contemporary revival of Augustine studies mean? It is not confined to America. Similar interest is found in France, Italy, Holland, Spain, Germany,
Switzerland and England today. In several of these countries
amazingly ambitious translation series and Augustine studies
are in process of publication. Letters of comment, both
favorable and unfavorable, have come to me from all these
countries, in connection with the appearance of *Augustine's
Quest of Wisdom*. People are craving for the insights and religious encouragement which St. Augustine offers. Apparently many who cannot study the systematic theologians of
the later Middle Ages and the Renaissance, find the works
of Augustine informative and attractive. There is no suggestion that a formal "school" of Augustinian theology is developing. Surprisingly, it is not the professional theologian who
swells the ranks of Augustine readers but the common man
from every walk of life. If there is to be a resurgence of
Christian culture in the modern world, the works of St.
Augustine may become one of the chief instruments in that
much-desired phenomenon. If we are to approach, even imperfectly, that "tranquility of order" which is peace, St.
Augustine may be the man to show us that all order comes
from but one Source.

NOTES

1. *Basic Writings Of Saint Augustine*. Edited with an Introduction and Notes by Whitney J. Oates (New York: Random House,
Inc., 1948). Two Volumes: Pp. xl, 847; 898.

2. *The Confessions of St. Augustine,* trans. F. J. Sheed (New York, 1943).

3. *The Fathers Of The Church.* A New Translation. Edited by Ludwig Schopp and a board of nine associates (New York: Cima Publishing Company, 1947 —). The first Augustine volume is the work of Dr. Ludwig Schopp and three scholars of the Augustinian order, Fathers D. J. Kavanagh, R. P. Russell, and T. F. Gilligan. Pp. 456.

4. The second of the Augustine volumes contains translations by Dr. Schopp, the Very Rev. Father John J. McMahon, Provincial of the Jesuits of the New York Province, Dr. R. C. Taliaferro, Dr. L. Meagher, Dr. R. J. Deferrari and M. F. McDonald. Pp. 489.

5. This volume contains *Christian Instruction*, by J. J. Gavigan, O.S.A., *Admonition and Grace*, by John Courtney Murray, S.J., *Christian Combat*, by Robert P. Russell, O.S.A., and *Enchiridion*, by Bernard M. Peebles. Pp. 494. The volume was reviewed in *Thought*, XXIII, No. 89 (June, 1948), 367f.

6. *Augustine's Quest of Wisdom* (Milwaukee, 1945); reviewed in *Thought*, XXI, No. 80 (March, 1946), 170ff.

7. *Ancient Christian Writers.* The Works of the Fathers in Translation. Edited by Johannes Quasten and J. C. Plumpe (Westminster, Md.: The Newman Press, 1946 —).

8. *Saint Augustine: The First Catechetical Instruction.* Translated and annotated by the Rev. Joseph P. Christopher, Ph.D. Ancient Christian Writers, No. 2. (Westminster, Md.: The Newman Bookshop, 1946). Pp. 171.

9. *Saint Augustine: The Lord's Sermon on the Mount.* Translated by the Rev J. Jepson. Ancient Christian Writers, No. 5. (Westminster, Md.: The Newman Press, 1948). Pp. 227.

10. *Saint Augustine: Faith, Hope and Charity.* Translated and annotated by the Very Rev. Louis A. Arand, S.S. Ancient Christian Writers, No. 3. (Westminster, Md.: The Newman Bookshop, 1947). Pp. 165.

11. *St. Augustine On Free Will.* Translated by Carroll Mason Sparrow. University of Virginia Studies, Vol. 4. (Richmond, Va.: The Dietz Press, 1947). Pp. xii, 149.

Name Index

Adam, K., 47 n.72
Adeodatus, 4, 5
Alaric, 6
Alfaric, 31, 42 n.12, 44 n.46
Allers, R., 45 n.54, 61 n.13, 90 n.43
Altaner, B., 48 n.89, 211
Alypius, 5, 19
Ambrose, St., 4, 71, 72, 76 n.26, 182
Anselm of Canterbury, St., 37, 105
    n.22
Anthony, St., 107
Aquinas, St. Thomas, 36, 61 n.11,
    84, 90 n.40, 90 n.41, 105
    n.29, 108, 122 n.10, 137, 172,
    197-198, 204 n.28, n.39
Arand, L. A. (S.S.), 210
Arbesmann, R., 41 n.11, 207
Arendt, H., 124 n.41,
Aristotle, 34, 38, 129
Armas, G., 47 n.75
Arquillière, H. X., 48 n.78
Athanasius, St., 24

Bardenhewer, O., 211
Bardy, G., 41 n.7, 43 n.28, 47 n.70,
    61 n.12, 88 n.20, 88 n.22, 89
    n.26, 89 n.37, 153 n.26, n.28,
    154 n.40, 179
Bardy, Canon, 31, 33, 84
Barrett, W., 151 n.7
Battenhouse, T. W., 44 n.38
Battifol, P., 30, 47 n.69
Beach, W., 151 n.5
Benedict XV, Pope, 29
Berdyaev, N., 205 n.41
Bertrand, L., 30
Blondel, M., 48 n.90

Boethius, 40, 149
Bonaventure, St., 84, 90 n.42
Bonhoeffer, D., 128
Bonner, G., 13 n.4, 15, 28 n.32, 68,
    76 n.19, 172, 178, 182, 183
    n.4, n.6, 185 n.34, 187 n.45
Boodin, J. E., 202 n.15
Bourke, V., 48 n.78, 62 n.2l, 103
    n.1, n.2, 105 n.21, 123 n.14,
    153 n.22, 155 n.46, n.54, 184
    n.24, 202 n.6, 212
Bovy, L., 46 n.67
Boyer, C., 39, 41 n.3, 41 n.7, 45
    n.52, n.60, 46 n.67, 47 n.73
Brechtken, J., 124 n.41
Brown, P., 13 n.2, 27 n.17, 153
    n.30, 154, n.31, 169-176, 178,
    183 n.7, 184 n.21, n.22.
Brucculerri, A., 48 n.77
Brunner, Emil, 137
Burkitt, F. C., 44 n.46, 168 n.35,
    183 n.8
Burnaby, J., 124 n.41, 207
Busch, B., 47 n.72
Buschman, Sr. R. M., 44 n.44
Bussell, F. W., 40
Butler, C., 48 n.79, 68
Butti, C., 203 n.16, n.20

Caecilianus, 186 n.38
Caelestius, 153 n.27
Callahan, J. F., 46 n.63
Calvin, John, 137
Capanaga, V., 46 n.67, 49 n.90, 62
    n.24, 155 n.50
Cappello, J., 90 n.44, 209
Carlyle, A. J., 168 n.33

215

Subject Index